Forensic Marketing

Optimizing results from marketing communication
The essential guide

Gavin Barrett

McGraw-Hill Book Company

London · New York · St Louis · San Francisco · Auckland
Bogotá · Caracas · Lisbon · Madrid · Mexico
Milan · Montreal · New Delhi · Panama · Paris · San Juan
São Paulo · Singapore · Sydney · Tokyo · Toronto

Published by
McGraw-Hill Book Company Europe
Shoppenhangers Road, Maidenhead, Berkshire, SL6 2QL, England
Telephone: 01628 23432
Fax: 01628 770224

British Library Cataloguing in Publication Data
Forensic Marketing: Professional's Guide to Optimizing
Results from Marketing Communication
I. Barrett, Gavin
658.8

ISBN 0-07-707900-0

Library of Congress Cataloging-in-Publication Data
Barrett, Gavin,
    Forensic marketing: the professional's guide to optimizing
results from marketing communication / Gavin Barrett.
        p.   cm.
    Includes bibliographical references and index.
    ISBN 0-07-707900-0
    1. Communication in marketing.   2. Marketing research.
3. Advertising.   4. Public relations.   I. Title.
HF5415.123.B37   1995
658.8–dc20   94-42550
                                                                           CIP

12345 BL 98765

Typeset by BookEns Limited, Royston, Herts
and printed and bound by Biddles Ltd, Guildford, Surrey.

Printed on permanent paper in compliance with ISO Standard 9706

Contents

Unless otherwise stated Gavin Barrett is the author of the chapter.

Series Foreword

The series title, Marketing for Professionals, was not chosen lightly, and it carries with it certain clear responsibilities for publisher, authors and series advisers alike.

First, the books must actually be intended and written for marketing practitioners. Most, if not all, will undoubtedly serve a valuable purpose for students of marketing. However, from the outset the primary objective of this series is to to help the professional hands-on marketer to do his or her job that little (but important) bit better.

In turn, this commitment has helped to establish some basic ground rules: no 'Janet-and-John' first steps for toddlers; no lessons in egg-sucking for grandmothers (who these days may have a Business Studies degree); and equally, no withdrawal into the more esoteric and abstruse realms of academe.

It follows that the subject matter of the books must be practical and of topical value to marketers operating—indeed, battling—in today's rapidly evolving and violently competitive business environment. Cases and case material must be relevant and valid for today; where authors deal with familiar marketing tools and techniques, these must be in terms which, again, update and adapt them, bringing them as close as possible to what, in the current idiom, we call the leading edge.

This has set demanding standards but, such is the calibre of authors contributing to the series, perfectly acceptable ones. The authors are either senior marketers or leading consultants and marketing academics with a strong practical background in management. Indeed, a number in both categories (and as the series extends, it is to be hoped, a growing proportion) are themselves members of The Marketing Society, with the prerequisite level of seniority and experience that implies.

McGraw-Hill Book Company Europe, as professional in its field as the target marketers are in theirs, has consulted The Marketing Society extensively in the search for suitable topics and authors, and in the evaluation and, if necessary, revision of proposals and manuscripts for new additions to the series.

The result is a well-presented and growing library of modern, thoughtful and extremely useful handbooks covering eventually all aspects of marketing. It is a library that every marketing professional will want to have on his or her bookshelf. It is also a series with which The Marketing Society is very pleased to be associated, and is equally happy to endorse.

Gordon Medcalf
Director General
The Marketing Society

THE MARKETING SOCIETY

The Marketing Society is the professional UK body for senior practising marketing people. It was founded in 1959 and currently has 2300 members.

The aim of the Society is to provide a forum for senior marketers through which the exchange of experience and opinion will advance marketing as the core of successful business growth. To this end it mounts a large and varied programme of events, and provides an increasing range of member services.

About the contributors

Wendy Aldiss

Wendy Aldiss has been involved with the use of the telephone as a sales and marketing tool since 1979. She is a telebusiness consultant, trading as Inbound Outbound, and since 1980 she has successfully championed telebusiness, from being a 'cold canvasser' through to her most recent position as managing director of TML; the telemarketing agency of EuroRSCG, Europe's largest marketing communications group. She was awarded the Institute of Director's Diploma in Company Direction in 1991. She was a founding committee member of AIMS (Association for Information Systems in Marketing and Sales) and of Women in Direct Marketing. Inbound Outbound was a founder member of the DMA (UK).

John Drewry

John Drewry is a copywriter and entrepreneur with experience below-the-line since the late sixties. He is chairman of John Drewry Associates Ltd, a marketing communications company. His specialism is sales and internal communications, which he has provided for many of the largest organizations in Europe including British Telecom, British Gas, Rank Xerox, Philips, Prudential Assurance, Pitney Bowes, Clerical Medical and the *Daily Telegraph*. In his non-commercial time he is chairman of an educational theatre charity in Kent.

Jim Hodgkins

Jim Hodgkins is an associate director at CCN Marketing, Europe's largest supplier of target marketing services. He is responsible for clients' applications of geodemographic data in their direct marketing campaigns and heads the list services division. He graduated in geography from Manchester University, where he was first involved in the analysis of census data. He has a diploma in direct marketing and speaks at conferences on the applications of geodemographic data.

Peter Hutton

Peter Hutton is a director of MORI and has been undertaking research since the mid-seventies. He is a graduate in social and political sciences from Cambridge University. His book, *Survey Research for Managers*, was published by Macmillan in 1988.

Jeffrey Lyes

Jeffrey Lyes is chairman of Good Relations, the public relations consultancy of Lowe Bell Communications Group. He has advised a wide range of companies and organizations—both private and public sector—with leading consultancies since the mid-seventies. A qualified journalist, he cut his teeth in public relations working for the police.

Wally Olins

Wally Olins is chairman and co-founder of Wolff Olins, one of the world's leading consultancies in corporate identity. He is visiting professor at Lancaster University, UK, and Copenhagen Business School and teaches at leading business schools throughout the world. He is author of a number of books on corporate identity and related matters. His latest book *Corporate Identity* is published by Thames & Hudson in the UK (1988) and Harvard Business School Press in the US (1989). There are also German, French, Spanish and Dutch language editions.

Stewart Pearson

Stewart Pearson is a leader and innovator in data-based marketing, in particular to add value to major brands. A statistician and economist, his career developed with *Reader's Digest*, O&M Direct and his agency Pearson–Paul–Haworth–Nolan (PPHN). He has launched a new business, ADAMAS Partners, to work with organizations to add value and deliver measurable gains, by creating new relationship marketing programmes.

Monica E. Seeley

Monica E. Seeley has been an international management

consultant since the late seventies. She specializes in helping organizations, and especially sales and marketing functions to use information technology to gain business benefits. Currently she is conducting an extensive longitudinal research study into why and how senior executives are using information technology to improve their personal effectiveness as executives.

Richard Webber

Richard Webber is the managing director of CCN Marketing, having joined CCN in 1986 from CACI Marketing Analysis Division where he was vice president and manager, European market analysis operations. He has been involved in the use of census statistics for targeting since 1982 and was one of the early pioneers in the development of the geodemographics industry in the UK. Since joining CCN he has been responsible for the development of CCN's target marketing services, more specifically MOSAIC, customer classification systems and database marketing.

Robin Wight

Robin Wight began his career in advertising in an unusual way. As an undergraduate at Cambridge, he set up Britain's first student advertising agency. His career went on from there: at the age of 23 he took over from Charles Saatchi as creative director of Richard Cope & Partners. In 1979 he helped start Wight–Collins–Rutherford–Scott (WCRS). In the mid-nineties WCRS is the European flagship of the EuroRSCG group, who are No 1 in Europe and seventh largest in the world. He has served as a marketing adviser to a minister for agriculture, stood as a Conservative candidate for Parliament, and is currently working closely with the Duke of Edinburgh's Award on their Charter for Business.

Robert M. Worcester

Robert M. Worcester is chairman of MORI (Market & Opinion Research International), which he set up in 1969. He is co-editor of several books including the *Consumer Market Research Handbook* (published in 1986 by McGraw-Hill). He has been an honorary visiting professor in the Graduate Centre for Journalism at City University, London, since 1989, and visiting professor of government at the London School of Economics and Political Science (LSE) since 1992.

Foreword

Raoul Pinnell,
Director of Marketing, National Westminster Bank

Many of us are constantly striving to gain a deeper understanding of the needs and motivations of today's customers. However, too often we either drown in the data, or end up with limited insights from which we can build differentiated propositions. And our struggle is in the context of an increasing rate in the pace of change. The urgency and responsibility of managers to create a 'future focus' for the businesses has never been more pressing. Does this mean that we have to learn to create a better blend between the analysis of statistical data, and instinctive and intuitive opinions, to create scenario predictions for tomorrow? And if so, how easy is this to do in the hurly-burly of active business life?

We are constantly on the receiving end of a wide variety of opinions and views from people with their own vested interests—unelected consumerists and activists who may not represent 'real opinion'; media sensationalism that dramatizes the problems of our society, but is incapable of offering any inspiring answers. How can we really serve rather than appease? How do we open up large organizations to the realization that we exist only because of, and for, customers?

How does one make sense of all this and get a deep understanding of:

1 what customers value?
2 using this knowledge as the foundation for all of our business actions?
3 going beyond the hype to make it happen?

In the mid-eighties I had the joy of being responsible for introducing a new product range called Findus Lean Cuisine. At the time it received all sorts of accolades from many quarters. My team and I were applauded and credited with a 'marketing breakthrough'. Some assumed that we had found some new 'magic marketing gold-dust'. What was the secret? Time and again I responded with my belief: 'The product tastes good. And I eat it at home'. The product used good ingredients, real food—in an imaginative way. And perhaps it was presented to meet the mood of the times. At that time marketers had got themselves into a mind-set of: 'the product ingredients don't matter—but the product packaging design does'. Somehow they could sleep at night with the notion 'customers are prepared to accept my product—but I certainly wouldn't eat it myself'. That type of cynical attitude never created new sustainable products that touch customers.

However, are personal views and intuition enough? No. We also need a focus on facts. We also need cold objectivity. And this is where I find the observations from academics can be powerful. They do view things from afar. They can see patterns from a different territory. They stop us from looking inwards and indulging in corporate chest-beating. But how do we connect the observations of academics, with the discipline of a focus on data and measuring our results, with our intuition? How do we translate the value of provocation in meaningful ways to those at the front of our businesses who touch customers?

Shopkeepers open their shops daily (or increasingly never close them). How do they learn to keep experimenting and evaluating how to entice more customers to come to their outlet, rather than a similar one down the road? How do we help marketers who listen to the market, who hear the issues, to engage the thousands of staff in large businesses and to deliver the changes to the products and services that customers want? I think we do it through listening and learning from real experience. And using what is relevant. Discarding what is not. Adding to our own store of learning. Filling the vacuum in direction by recognizing the power of our own leadership.

I love this book. I took it in bite-sized chunks—I read chapters on trains, planes, and on the underground. It gave me digestible pieces of—pauses for reflection.

I hope you get value from it too.

Acknowledgements

Besides my indebtedness to the authors of Chapters 4–12, there are many others to whom I am grateful for advice, ideas and encouragement offered during the book's development, in particular my colleagues at Sundridge Park, John Chadwick, Philip Foster, Peter Herriott, John Alderson, John Mills, Gordon Webster, John van Maurik, David Hickling and Peter Ranft. The support of Julia Riddlesdell and the team at McGraw-Hill, both in the UK and USA, has been splendid. Many of the ideas were born out of conversations and problem-solving sessions with clients in all corners of the globe: to them I offer thanks for their insights and challenges. Finally my thanks to Jenny Wessendorff for keeping me to the timetable and to my wife, Sue, for the support and forbearance that creating such a book demands.

Introduction: why FORENSIC?

The word Forensic has strong overtones of serious crime and its aftermath. For readers whose minds are already filled with images of green-clad boffins wielding blood-stained scalpels and dispassionately discussing the contents of the victim's stomach, let me reassure you and say that the only parallels between the forensic sciences, practised with consummate skill by police laboratories throughout the world, and the subject matter of this book can be found in the fundamental approach to discovering what happened in the past and why.

Some might argue that many crimes are committed in the name of marketing and it might, indeed, be a good idea to get some of the guilty parties in the dock for the general good. Certainly some aspects of marketing bear little scrutiny, notably the persistent levels of self-indulgence and assumptive behaviour.

FORENSIC is a mnemonic (see Fig. I.1) which is examined in detail in Chapter 3. At this initial stage it serves to concentrate the mind on the fundamentals of the marketer's life, which I shall argue should be based rather more on methodical, rational processes, even a scientific approach, than the intuitive art that it has so often come to mean. In the real world of forensic science the watchword is objective evidence leading to the truth—not in itself a bad nostrum for the marketer. Mnemonics, however, are no substitute for developing one's own path to a disciplined approach. While some readers will find the mnemonic checklist helpful as a work tool, for others it will serve better as a pointer towards the shaping of their attitude to marketing. Indeed I intend that the forensic theme be 90 per cent focused on aiding the reader's attitudinal shift and 10 per cent as a direct basis for subsequent marketing process control. It mainly serves the purpose of giving a start-point to the central issue of the book—that the marketing mind-set is ripe for a rethink.

FOCUS on facts
OBSERVATION
RESEARCH
EVALUATION
NEGATIVE indicators
STRATEGY compliance
INERTIAL barriers/factors
CHECK and re-check

Figure I.1 The FORENSIC model

Besides the centrality of the forensic approach to marketing, and, in particular, to the deployment of the communications tool-set, I shall explore the positional dilemmas for facing marketers: getting the professional approach sufficiently right to allow successful relationships with the internal corporate market (especially at senior levels), the supply-side with their diverse offerings and, of course, the market-place. This positional force-field is largely instrumental in leading marketers astray: satisfying one polarity is almost always at the expense of another.

What I hope the book will reveal is how to develop approaches to the various elements of marketing that will allow all professionals to have their cake and eat it. If it were not a politically discredited expression I should talk at length about the need for a back to basics approach, stripping away the barnacle-like accretions that marketing has acquired since the forties, and which obscure the obvious and evidently marketable proposition that it is the identification of mutual stakeholder advantage that is, or ought to be, at the heart of all business purpose.

Figure I.2 demonstrates the interaction between these stakeholders and the points where forensic approaches will make the difference between the ordinary solution and the exceptional. Securing ownership of this particular value-system is the overall purpose of Forensic Marketing.

I am indebted to the distinguished authors of Chapters 4–12. They are giants in their respective fields of marketing communications. Their given mandate was to champion their element of the communications mix without compromise to the others. In so doing they strip away many myths and legends and, in their place, make powerful and persuasive cases for why their particular approach is appropriate in specific circumstances. Without this expert advocacy of what are already complex ideas, I do not believe it would be

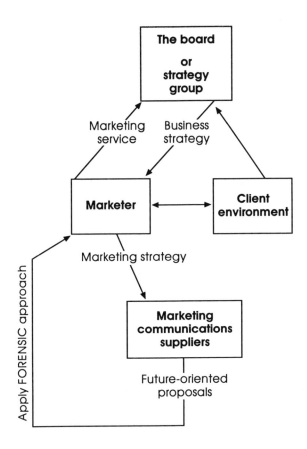

Figure I.2 Applying the FORENSIC model to the decision-making processes of the marketing function

possible to achieve the aim of the book—an objective understanding of choice for the marketing professional and the other key stakeholders in the discipline.

Gavin Barrett
Sundridge Park

1

The devil and the deep blue sea

This book is about choice and high-risk choice in particular. Marketing is primarily concerned with the management of choice. This would be challenging enough if it were simply a matter of customers having choice of use for disposable income, or commercial buyers for solutions to their needs, but it is not. The ways in which marketing professionals manage that choice are bewildering in their complexity, reflecting the range of demands placed upon the marketing function, from development of strategic markets to tactical opportunism in the 'fourth quarter fire fight'—when the race to achieve the sales budget becomes intense, and, not unusually, irrational.

Rosemary Stewart (1982) puts choice in context in her revealing study of what managers and professionals actually do. Her analysis demonstrates that all of us are faced with demands, constraints and choices. Demands are the largely non-negotiable component—targets, budgets, deadlines, decisions and actions. Constraints are the ever present factors of time, money and people, coupled with rules, protocols, standards of conformity and personal limitations in terms of attitudes, knowledge and skills to deal with the demands. Choices are about courses of action open to us in meeting the demands placed upon us. The less we know, the less choice we have. This is as true of the customer as it is of the manager.

Given that marketing professionals will want to satisfy as much market demand as can be secured profitably, they will need to be well informed about the choices available for the task. The constraints that they labour under vary enormously, but near the top of the list will be found budgets and risk aversion—typically quite closely related. In the following chapters we shall look at the demands, constraints and choices facing the marketing function and those whose roles require them to think marketing. In so doing we shall examine the various orientations of marketers, from ego-driven enthusiasts to the rigorously analytical, and see what the dilemmas really are. Then we shall review the orthodox thinking about marketing strategy, with the various theories competing for share of mind, and how political reality usually comes out on top.

The greater part of the book deals with what marketers can do with their disposable budget to achieve the aims of their strategy. Besides being the fun part of the role, it is the area of greatest choice and maximum confusion. Never in the realms of business have so few had so much to play with to such devastating effect— devastating to profitability as well as, more rarely, enduring success.

This kaleidoscope of choice, stimulant and risk is what the marketer must manage and manage consistently in full knowledge of what the choices really are, how they can be sorted and how the decisions made can be evaluated for their effectiveness. It is often argued that no one actually wants choice, they want confidence in their decision process. Forensic Marketing is aimed at those who want to grow their confident application of the communications tool-set. This is to an extent where even the rigour of forensic analysis of the scene of their 'crimes' will show the discerning mind of a professional at work, rather than the transient enthusiasm of the amateur.

The quart from the pint pot

There is, of course, never enough budget to do everything that we want. Even if there was at the start of the year, by the time the need for a final big push to finish the year in fine style is recognized by the whole management team, the cupboard is bare. We often feel that we are the victim of circumstances rather than the maker of them. Sales revenue below plan, general belt-tightening to reduce costs, product launch delays, service levels below standard and a rich palette of acts of God in the form of government waywardness, foreign exchange markets, unseasonable weather and the latest oriental 'flu, all conspire to sabotage the elegance of the marketing plan, written, of course, in sobriety as part of the annual budget-setting round.

Besides budgetary constraints, the marketer has to live with the variable nature of management policy—a very flexible friend or foe. Few marketers would deny the need for a consistent strategy for marketing in all its manifestations, whether brand development, service quality, product development, customer retention, distribution or profitability growth. The paradigm seldom allows this. Tactical expedience and management whim ensure that demand or enthusiasm for today's results will generally triumph over strategic reason. The very same arguments colour the column inches of debate on short-termism and lack of investment in manufacturing infrastructure that have dominated the media in the USA and UK since the early eighties.

The absence of consistent approaches to strategy formulation and implementation produces high levels of waste, missed opportunities and substitutional effect, rather than incremental gain. At its most flagrant, the tactical use of price-led sales promotion, while committed to building a durable value-for-money platform, amounts to criminal negligence of strategy in sectors where price has been shown to be creating a commodity market. A notable example of this relentless pursuit of the tactical option has been the personal computer (PC) market on a global scale: practitioners know that it is an unsustainable policy. Even those producers who have managed to take cost down ahead of price have reducing margin left for investment in brand values that will be needed when cost productivity can yield no more. They know it. We all know it. Yet this group hysteria continues: no one will get off the tumbrel as it races to the place of execution.

Expectations of what marketing can achieve may be unrealistic among management colleagues. What marketing does or ought to do is seldom clear to management teams, hence the belief in the white magic of the agency world. This implied belief in the total resilience of marketing strategy to any form of tactical distortion has been allowed to happen—allowed by marketers, perhaps none too clear about the issues themselves. What is it that stops marketing professionals from formulating and consistently delivering strategic marketing? The answer is something that we shall address in this book, but as a clue we might consider the siren call of the supply-side with its constant innovation of new and arguably improved techniques for reaching those parts of the market that other tools cannot. To resist these blandishments outside, and the insidious effect they may have on less well-informed management colleagues within, requires the self-control of a saint to resist, let alone critically evaluate.

If marketers are tested in the fire managing the internal market, they know the temptations of the devil when it comes to selecting their communications tool-set. This dilemma state is, we might argue, the result of generations of tolerance of intuitive approaches to the marketing role and a sustained failure to adopt a more rationalist, analytical, even forensic critical faculty. Faith, hope and charity are virtues—in the right place. In marketing? Surely not.

The trouble may be that marketers have a fondness for the intuitive over the reasoned since it supports the theory that marketing is an art not a science. It is a perfectly natural viewpoint, given that so much else in management is fuelled by an experimental approach. Where it falls down is in the field of learning from experience. Too often the intuitive marketer cannot articulate why a particular campaign is working or why not. If that cannot be done, how then can wisdom be found?

If the devil is the voice of ego-driven leaping in the dark, then the deep blue sea is the difficulty of rational analysis of experience.

What are the prizes beyond this awesome choice?

Marketers are all looking, as Nigel Piercy (1991) of Cardiff Business School argues in his important text, *Market-led strategic change*, for 'new practical tools for evaluating the marketing performance of their organizations and, as a result of that evaluation, for identifying how best to improve marketing performance'. He goes on to argue that 'the most common reasons why marketing fails in practice ... are to do with muddled and confused management decisions about strategic marketing issues and a lack of real commitment where it counts most to making marketing work'.

This just criticism of management commitment is echoed by Michael Porter (1985) in his authoritative *Competitive advantage*: 'the failure of many firms' strategies stems from an inability to translate a broad competitive strategy into the specific action steps required to gain competitive advantage' (page *xv*). We start to see that marketing may be caught on the horns of a dilemma that recognizes what ought to be done, but is unable to deliver because the specific actions are not valued in the management ethos. Paying lip-service to best practice in marketing is hardly a first in the pantheon of cultural tokenism. We might just as easily look at contemporary ideas of empowerment, collegiate behaviour, multiple careers, upward appraisal and women in management to find equal examples of yes meaning maybe and certainly not now.

We shall examine why this gap exists between what good

marketing is thought to be and what actually happens. Central to the debate is the view that marketing may be overprotected from the searching analysis commonly afforded to other forms of investment, and its partner in misery, the sales function. What, we must ask, are the things that marketing ought to be valued for and, by the same token, be measured upon?

We could start with a shortlist of goals for marketing that, if delivered, might change the ways in which it is evaluated and, therefore, esteemed. Marketing is not as authoritative in management debate as it might be. This list could alter that perception:

- Improvement in business results
- Measurable results
- Evidence of value for money from the supply-side
- Consistency of application within the strategic framework
- Management credibility
- Accommodation of ego-driven management decisions
- Learning from experience.

Briefly explored, each of these headings reveals surprising gaps between the vaunted claims and the reality.

Improvement in business results

General managers are targeted to achieve the two virtues of cost and revenue productivity, within a risk management framework. Cost productivity means eliminating the cost of what you cannot measure and leveraging the effectiveness of any cost that you can measure but cannot do without. It is not a concept for the sentimental. Revenue productivity is, at least in theory, another hard measure concept—sales by channel by product, return on sales, sales per employee, cash flow, stock turn and so on. In reality it is often larded with sentiment, myths and legends. But then it is the sales community's role to create optimism and belief that water can be pushed up hill, as long as it is left to them.

Both concepts are, in themselves, virtuous but commonly misapplied, especially in the marketing functional area. If the organization has no clear view as to what improvements in performance it could achieve, how then can it manage its affairs in such a way as those improvements are made? How many organizations know what marketing could do for them, let alone what they presently deliver? Not many.

Similarly, how many organizations know the cost productivity of the various tools of marketing and their impact on the performance of the business? Again, none too many. The oft-quoted saying of, variously, Lord Leverhulme, Henry Ford, and others, that 'I know that half my advertising works, but I only wish I knew which half', is too true to be funny. Why do we not know which half works?

The dilemma for marketers is that strategic marketing is validated only in hindsight, whereas decisions on marketing spend need to be made with foresight. Given the choice, most of us would be tempted to err on the side of caution and go for easy results rather than quality of strategy: after all we might not be around to collect the prize.

That temptation would be wrong. Sustainable growth comes from the courage to do more of those things that bring results than our competitors do. Whether those things are tactical or, better still, strategic investments, they need to be done in as well informed a way as is possible. This concept demands that the evidential link between action and reaction is positively established: that applies to marketing too.

It is often surprising to find how unclear managements are about the things they think they can improve; certainly they know about costs on the whole, but they can be remarkably unsure as to the proactive investment options available to them. In later chapters we shall look at some of the major choices available to the marketer and how they can be exercised through well-informed decisions.

Measurable results

Shortly after the privatization process of the water industry in the UK was completed, one company's finance director was minded to challenge the value of nearly £1 million expenditure on public relations (PR). 'Show me the return on this investment and you can have the budget'. Hands thrown up in horror, a search for the witches in *Macbeth* to conjure some dire fate for the hapless challenger, and a pessimistic view that while PR was obviously a good thing to have, its benefit could not be shown. On closer examination the PR department were able to identify some thirty commercial performance measures that were directly linked to their activity, the most notable being the impact on debtor days of a well-informed customer base who had a full understanding of what investment was being made in infrastructure, what was being done to beat sea pollution and why hose-pipe bans were the right policy.

The correlation between attitude surveys and debtor days improvement was absolute and credible to the finance director. The budget was confirmed.

The marketing professionals were, arguably, more surprised than their challenger. The received wisdom was that PR is not accountable, merely essential. It took three days of hard persuasion to shift the orientation from one of 'It cannot be done' to 'Do you think thirty ratios is rather pushing our luck?' A paradigm shift.

If it can be shown that spend on PR is directly related to business results then how much more advantage would come from demonstrating the business effectiveness of the full communications tool-set? If results are the most valued cultural symbol in business then it seems a wise investment of time to demonstrate the clear accountability of the function so that its authority is developed.

Evidence of value for money from the supply-side

A senior City of London lawyer remarked during the early recovery stage (mid 1993) from the UK recession that 'our clients are becoming too wise. If they go on learning at this rate about what we really can do, they will see our fees as exaggerated and avoidable. We are not worth what we used to be; the market will not stand it'. The result has been a sharp decline in real achieved fee rates by all branches of the legal profession.

It takes a sophisticated buyer to cope with a sophisticated solution. It is equally true that a sophisticated buyer will know when the solution is not. If the financial services markets in Europe and the USA continue to develop buyer sophistication at their present rate, the role of the intermediary is doomed. Already in the USA, most large corporate organizations can raise capital more cheaply than their bankers—partly a function of credit worthiness of course, but equally they know how to do it and what matters. The UK's most successful retail bank has become Marks and Spencer. The UK's most successful corporate banker for several of the last few years has been BP. The poacher has turned gamekeeper and knows when it is being sold less than full measure.

The question stands, how sophisticated are marketers in evaluating the value-for-money of their suppliers' offerings? The answer, like the curate's egg, is good in parts. We shall see, however, that for large proportions of the marketing spend, the accountability factor is low. Above-the-line advertising is commonly cited as unquantifiable in its benefits. Telemarketing is seen as very quantifiable. The evidence that this is important to clients comes from the USA where expenditure on the (quantifiable) techniques of telemarketing and selling exceeds press and TV advertising combined. The writing is on the wall—marketers must establish the accountable performance of each of the tools and techniques we deploy.

Consistency of application within the strategic framework

Joseph Stalin made the management mistake of believing that whatever went into his five-year plans would happen. It is written, therefore it is so. History mercifully makes a mockery of such dogma. The lesson ought to be well learned that a business strategy that is not dynamic, adaptable and consistently applied is likely to drive the business on to the rocks. Conformity with a single set of values and beliefs at a moment of history is a remarkably shaky basis for future development. Yet marketing strategy and its elder associate, business strategy, too often have a dogmatic tone, demanding slavish conformity rather than elasticity and consistency.

If conformity is blind, the absence of any strategic clarity is worse. We shall examine in the next chapter what marketers must demand of the business strategy, if only to establish where magnetic north is, then everyone in the organization can be issued with a compass.

Marketing has a major role in surveying the past, present and future within the strategy formulation process. It is the trustee of the learning from experience that will help the organization avoid the pitfalls of unproductive repetition of mistakes. It is the champion of the customer within the citadel and must identify their future needs and articulate them in terms of deliverable solutions.

If marketing has this important contribution to make, why then does it allow the customer to be marginalized during the implementation phase? Arguably the correlation between enhancing shareholder value and customer satisfaction is still sufficiently under-developed in the mind of general managers that the wisdom of vesting tactical authority for business strategy implementation in the marketing function, to ensure consistency, has not yet been established as widely as it ought. There are, of course, notable examples of marketing-led organizations such as Procter and Gamble, Nestlé, Coca Cola, Disney and Sainsbury, but even in an example like Virgin Atlantic the championship of customer satisfaction came at the cost of being able to satisfy shareholders and led to Richard Branson's decision to take the group private again.

Management credibility

How credible is the marketing function in your organization? If it is high what has led to it? If not, then why not?

Just as brand values have to be earned, so does confidence in marketing by general managers. Of the functional areas in business, marketing is the least trusted. Its accountability is so far under-developed that it might be argued that the most effective job marketing has done is to conceal the fact that it is an emperor with no clothes.

It is difficult to establish authority over the customer impacting parts of the business without high levels of internal credibility. This is certainly true if lip-service to customer satisfaction is to be converted into real levels of customer focus and delivery. The credibility that marketers must acquire consists of being able to demonstrate the value of what we do, not what we say. The forensic approach is about evidence, in hard fact terms, though the historical caution of 'anything you say will be written down and may be given in evidence' applies in full measure in some politically driven organizations.

The enthusiasm for Hammer and Champy's (1993) radical text on *Re-engineering the corporation* of many business leaders in the USA and UK suggests that a number are tired of the barnacle-like accretions of custom and practice that have grown up in organizations and have concluded that Michael Porter's (1985) 'Value-Chain' (pages 33–63) has become clogged with myths and legends about the value of this or that function. They are demanding that the fundamentals of business processes are assessed and the added value of each is demonstrable and evidential.

Marketers are not immune from the rigour of this re-engineering mind-set and have much to offer it. We all need to be sure that we know where we fit in the value-chain and where we provide real leverage to the key business processes. When that linkage is clear, marketing will have come of age.

Accommodation of ego-driven management decisions

Happily for most of us, management teams are still built of people, not expert computer systems. They have their human frailties just as marketers do. They come armed with prejudices, experiences, lacunae and fears not dissimilar to our own. They can feel as we do and identify with our hopes and aspirations. They can be persuaded of our viewpoint.

Equally they can be as deaf and as blind as our worst nightmares portray, pursuing competitive vendettas, chasing phantasmagorical opportunities, acquiring Star Wars technology to shoot turkeys, and selective in their mania from one day to the next.

That is what makes management interesting and challenging to the rationalist marketer who would rather some semblance of logic informed decisions than none at all. What seems to characterize poor management decisions overall is a high assumptiveness content—a belief in self-generated propaganda and self-image, rather than objective evaluation of the facts. We might ask why that is so. Not the least of the possibilities is that facts are hard to come by in terms of marketing and future direction.

Great entrepreneurs have not waited around for their marketing professionals to do an in-depth report and risk analysis. They have a powerful intuitive feel for opportunities that their experience has confirmed positively on enough occasions for it to become the established truth. How many entrepreneurs have got it right for a while and then lost it, because their vision of the right order of things has failed to encompass shifts in the market and competitive reactions to the original act of genius? Sir Clive Sinclair would not be the man he is had he not defied the wisdom of the age and sought to popularize the computer with his seminal ZX80 and derivatives. The magisterial success he attained in this field was not achieved with the ill-starred C5 electric car. Had he access to quality market intelligence or did he ignore it? Perhaps we shall never know, but the lesson for marketers is that powerful intuitive drive among business leaders is perfectly OK if it can be consolidated with quality market analysis.

Striking the right relationship with the ego factor in business is a challenge that is not going to go away. What may improve the balance between ego and rationality, or the art and science of management, is that the latter qualities come from a willingness to subject decisions to evaluation and learning. In many years of monitoring marketing and business successes I have not found too much evidence of this partnership of ideas. But it is coming and fast. Hence this book.

Learning from experience

The direct-marketing industry has come of age. It is now acceptable to talk of laser-precision marketing, regression analysis, Latin Squares, interactive campaigns and so on. Yet these are relatively recent phenomena on the wide stage of international marketing. Until the eighties the sophisticated tools of the direct-marketing world were administered in private by consenting adults in the *Reader's Digest* organization or *Time-Life*. What they knew, and the rest of us did not, was that the behaviour of markets could be modelled provided that there was a relentless search for behavioural data on as large a scale as possible. *Reader's Digest* is the epitome of how to accumulate data over decades and use it to refine a process engine capable of extraordinary feats of prediction.

Central to these core values is the willingness to learn from each and every experience. Today, the direct-marketing industry makes adequate use of testing, with no one solution being backed alone. Of course, the use of direct mail or telemarketing allows for high degrees of measurement and correlation, with single variables in the marketing mix being tested one at a time. That is quite proper to the particular channel of direct marketing.

However, we should continue to ask ourselves just how much we learn from other forms of marketing, and do so with high levels of objectivity, rather than the selective use of results to confirm a prejudice or belief? Generally, learning from experience is low where the organizational culture is intolerant of error. Imagine being challenged on why you are mounting any form of tests at all: 'Don't you know the right answer—what am I paying you for?' Blame cultures do not want risk. They are prone to driving looking in the rear-view mirror: the past is always so much more attractive. Consequently they do not want new discovery or the risk entailed in making it.

On the other hand, a tolerant forgiveness culture puts a high premium on learning from experience. Watching a rehearsal of the choir of King's College, Cambridge (arguably the greatest choir anywhere) I was struck by the occasional hand going up, whether from boy chorister or experienced lay clerks, while the performance continued uninterrupted. Only if the same hand at the same point in the music went up did the director of music stop and offer help. Each chorister was signalling the first time that he had made an error and knew it, and the second time, more rarely, that he could not overcome the difficulty. It is easy to see why it is the leading choir. A total forgiveness culture, self-aware, seeking the highest standards and demanding to learn from its experience. Would that were an easily transferable orientation.

Marketers should set out deliberately to test the frontiers of experience and to challenge the received wisdom. Only then will we know whether we actually hit the bull's eye or just the edge of the target.

The overwhelming case for a marketing strategy

This chapter has sought to offer more dilemmas than answers. The status quo is to be challenged. But a point comes when looking into the abyss induces vertigo and the inclination to go on and make the leap with one's hang-glider loses its attraction.

Yes, we are often between the devil and the deep blue sea and too often it is our fault. Marketing is not as credible as it ought to be; it is less valued in the councils of management than say the finance or operations functions. With few exceptions the marketing strategy represents an idealized view of the world rather than the harsh and manageable reality.

What is needed is a process that provides sufficient clarity of vision, with commercial integrity that the implementation of the marketing strategy is seen as management's highest priority. Marketers make their own luck and that of their business.

2

If you don't know where you are going, you will end up somewhere else

In Chapter 1 we considered the proposition that marketers would do well to increase their accountability and perceived credibility by providing more tangible evidence of the outputs of marketing activity, and in such ways as will establish the clear correlative link with accepted business performance indicators. This challenge applies equally to professional suppliers to the marketing function. As buyer sophistication grows so does the need to demonstrate significant added value. Mystique and technical jargon are poor substitutes for proof.

The well-informed marketer, learning from structured and imaginative experiences, is a mandatory orientation for all who aspire to formulate marketing strategy, let alone implement it. Without this analytical orientation, the lessons of the past will not be learned and a firm basis for new experimentation not established. Well-informed marketing is concerned to achieve sufficiency of risk in competitive terms, without the unnecessary risks of repeating old errors, one's own or someone else's. Sustainable competitive advantage comes from being more often right than wrong, in strategic and tactical terms, than competitors. It does not require marketers to be any more visionary than anyone else, rather they should be capable of asking the right questions.

The best strategies have at their core a relentless search for durable streams of customer needs unfettered by contemporary allegiances to products and markets. They put a high premium on consistent application of brand values that grow both in magnetic pull and market leadership. I use brand values here to denote the general perceptions of customers rather than a more specific definition.

In this chapter we shall review the processes of marketing strategy formulation and the key questions that need to be put. Here again, there are too many choices, too many models and matrices designed to take us in the right direction. The well-informed marketer will start with a set of fundamental tests and use further techniques only to refine the strategic statements.

Why bother with a marketing strategy at all?

Marketing strategy is the prime expression of the business strategy. It is the means whereby the objectives of the business, both long and short term, will be delivered. At the most prosaic level it is a means of ensuring that there will be any customers around to savour our solutions—creating our future markets as well as finding them. It is also concerned to ensure that our organization is well placed for the competitive fray, with the resources and focus to optimize the opportunities along the way. Above all, the marketing strategy exists to mark the boundaries, to provide a bench-mark fit for all new initiatives and to minimize internal polarization. If the latter is tolerated, there is only one certain winner, our competitors.

The Delphi technique (named after the Oracle of Delphi in classical Greek mythology) of future prediction suggests that if a number of people are asked to nominate three or four key factors likely to have a major influence on the business outlook, they will come up with a couple upon which they are all agreed, albeit independently arrived at. This aggregation of intuitive beliefs is important because it provides one basis for agreement on future direction, in the absence of more rational bases. These intuitive beliefs will, of course, reflect prejudices, desires, hopes and a need for some longer-term certainty, however spurious. It is this need to create our futures that makes the strategic process possible, since a purely rational application of logic to the future would be difficult and probably unrewarding. We might say of the future 'If we can dream it, we can do it!'

Most strategic commentators warn that the future is rushing towards us. It is not an option to maintain the status quo, guarding the gains of the past and, like the proverbial French peasant, keeping the gold under the mattress. Competitors have a powerful interest in taking our gains away and, if they are successful, it means that by definition we are in a worse condition. Strategy is there to give purpose, focus and direction to Darwinian competitive drive. We ignore the need for continuous proactive investment in our future at great peril. This was a lesson learned the hard way by IBM which,

Canute-like, sought to resist competitive onslaught with internal denial of even the possibility of their success. Complacency took a heavy toll in head-count terms and it is clear today that IBM has resolved never again to allow overwhelming self-belief to blind it to the harsh reality of global competition.

If, therefore, there is only the future to aim for, what should the strategist consider?

SWOT or something deeper?

Figure 2.1 shows a simplified approach to strategic planning, used by many organizations to start the process. Most of the stages of this model are already well understood and explored in depth elsewhere, so I shall here concentrate on those aspects that will, in the ultimate, have the greatest bearing on marketing and marketing communications.

A significant proportion of strategic reviews fall at the first fence by failing to establish the full gamut of stakeholder expectations. These stakeholders are the various publics that we shall meet again later in the field of PR: customers, shareholders, employees, suppliers, regulators, public, government, competitors, prospective customers and shareholders and generations as yet unborn. As Shakespeare's Cassius puts it in *Julius Caesar* (Act III, sc. i)

How many ages hence
Shall this our lofty scene be acted over
In states unborn and accents yet unknown!

It is with the eyes of future stakeholders, as well as those of the present, that we must evolve our strategy.

While some stakeholder expectations are reasonably predictable—shareholder need for sustainable economic value added, for example—others are more elusive—suppliers' and customers' to name but two. With the rising enthusiasm for supplier partnerships, sharing in joint strategic developments, their inclusion in the process seems less remarkable than once it did. Many organizations will not have the resources alone to meet competition head on; the alliance with key suppliers leverages their combined weight by an order of magnitude.

Customers as stakeholders have featured in the literature for some decades, but it is far from clear as to whether this is tokenism or not. I express serious doubt, if only because of the seemingly born-again

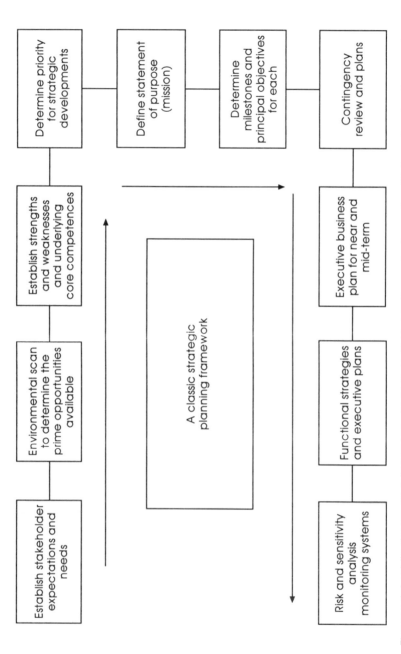

The model, while shown as a linear sequence is, in fact, continuously dynamic with loop-backs at every stage

Figure 2.1 A classic strategic planning framework

realization among some organizations that perhaps something ought to be done about customer retention, rather than replacement. In spite of well-attested evidence (McKenna, 1992) that it is far easier to sell to existing customers than to win new ones, the disposable customer remains a generic fact of life (or corporate death). Yet without customers the whole strategic intent is valueless.

The customer stakeholder in strategy formulation can provide vital inputs:

- Brand perceptions
- Buying motivations
- Competitive awareness
- Informed evaluation of products and services
- Possible needs
- The size of the credibility gap—ours versus the competition.

All of which helps to establish the start-line for change. Coupled with a rational analysis of customer behaviour over the previous strategic period, it becomes possible to see if customer perceptions today are at variance with recent practice and, if so, in which direction. While markets are often surprisingly conservative in the face of innovation, they seem to have an unerring sense of the possible, and hence should be heeded. Similarly, markets are capable of expressing valuable insights into future needs: the art is to help them articulate their intuitive feelings. We shall return to this theme when considering the role of research techniques.

The most demanding stakeholder grouping, whose views will dominate the strategic process, is corporate management itself: not unreasonably so, but a minefield for the unwary. If the management orientation is fixed upon survival rather than growth, then the past will seem more attractive than the future. They must be challenged: the past was an imperfect place, raddled with age and suffused with snares and delusions. The present may be uncomfortable and frustrating, as it is, by definition, reality. The only direction worth taking is forward, and forward with enterprise and commitment. The future holds the means to put right what is wrong today, to apply the lessons of past experiences and to build something of enduring value.

The word growth is misleading in that it implies volume. It does not need to. Rather, it should mean development in capability and enterprise. Key words like resilience, imagination, sufficiency of risk, competitiveness, responsiveness and effectiveness provide opportunities for growth. If the strategy formulation process is not geared to growth in these more specialist senses then it is unlikely to deliver the volumetric definition either.

Senior management will subscribe to this positive, dynamic orientation if they are equipped to see the future in terms that will feel credible and attractive. It is part of the marketing function to demonstrate that a future return for all stakeholders is attainable and realistic. Where marketing needs to put in extraordinary effort is in overcoming too much rationality during the first testing stage of strategy formulation. Marketing must drive up choice and viable options and then facilitate evaluation. Thinking beyond is the ability to imagine the future in terms of the future, uninhibited by present value systems. It is the real basis for bold strategy.

Sadly, the received wisdom of strategy formulation marginalizes this capacity to move out of the cocoon of today through the medium of the SWOT Analysis (see Fig. 2.2). If applied in the conventional way the process requires practitioners to define the business's present Strengths and Weaknesses before addressing its Opportunities and Threats (i.e. SWOT). This guarantees a view of the future firmly rooted in the present or past. While not a disaster for most businesses, this timid approach may well ensure that the business fails to see the major market opportunities of the future, simply because it rejects them on the grounds that it has not got the appropriate strengths. Why this reverse logic should be tolerated the length and breadth of the business community worldwide eludes me.

Arguably, the problem lies in the universal failure to see that the speed of change is accelerating at an unprecedented rate. I argue that today's apparent strengths may turn out to be a millstone about our necks in addressing the potential of the future. The alternative view that I put forward is to concentrate on potential *Opportunities* and their attendant *Threats* and then establish what *Strengths* would (OTSW) be needed to derive the full benefit. A straightforward (inhibiting Weaknesses) comparison between current and desired strengths would establish the first gap to be addressed by the strategy.

An alternative and hugely attractive view comes from two distinguished academics, Gary Hamel and C.K. Prahalad, in their series of articles for the *Harvard Business Review* in the early nineties. In the first, 'The core competences of the organization', Hamel and Prahalad (1991) argue that strategy formulation ought to concentrate on the durable strengths of the organization at a root system

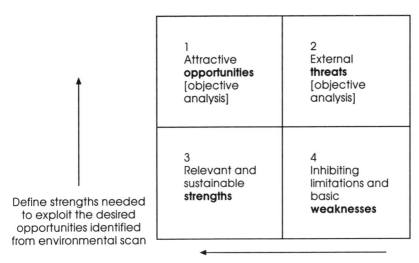

Figure 2.2 SWOT Analysis in the FORENSIC sequence

Figure 2.2 SWOT Analysis in the FORENSIC sequence

level, rather than the more typical SWOT Analysis. They propose that organizations drill down to find the genetic code that allows the core strengths or capabilities to become useful. In testing the capabilities of the organization Hamel and Prahalad apply three beguilingly easy tests that, in the aggregate, prove tantalizingly elusive.

The tests of core capability are as follows:

- They provide access to a wide variety of market applications.
- They bring real and significant benefit to customers in their perception.
- They are difficult or impossible to imitate.

Clearly, if all three conditions are satisfied the core competence is powerful indeed. Organizations, in considering their strategic purpose, could do worse than seek to identify their core competences. Once articulated, the core competences become the central focus for management. In applying our own analytical methodology, (work undertaken by Gavin Barrett and John Chadwick of PA Consulting Group's Sundridge Park Management Centre), to establish the Hamel and Prahalad competences of a wide variety of organizations, we have found them to be rare, often under-developed and unrecognized by management (see Table 2.1).

Table 2.1 A structured approach to core competence

Phase 1	Phase 2	Phase 3
Stakeholders' definition of desired future position—The vision statement: where we want to be	What unique assets have we got that underpin the core competences?	What is the role of each individual member of the organization in growing the core competence(s)?
SWOT Analysis (sequence: OTSW) Environmental scan Define durable opportunities and strengths needed for them	What factors make them unique? Can we replicate them? Where do they lie within the organization?	Establish that asset management and development is a priority within the normal operations of the organization
Isolate the capabilities that lie behind the durable strengths—What must we be able to do and what capabilities will we need?	Which functional areas of the organization can harness our core competences and can enrich them?	Include 'Your contribution to core competence' within the organization's appraisal systems
Apply three tests of core competence to the list of capabilities identified Determine the gap between capabilities and core competence status	Define why these core competences are needed and identify other processes that would benefit from developing them	Define training and development needs to support the capacity of individuals and teams to contribute to core competence management
List the core competences and develop a management commitment to manage them closely	What are we going to do specifically to maintain and enhance our core competences?	Reprise: where does each core competence fit within the organization's strategy?

Develop a priority list to convert latent
competences into core competences

What is, or should be, management's
role in sustaining and growing core
competences?

What is the communications plan to
ensure stakeholder ownership of our
core competences and their primacy in
our strategic plans?

An abbreviated schematic of the Sundridge Park methodology to help organizations establish and manage their core competences, based on Hamel and Prahalad's (1991) conceptual model. Once established, core competences become the prime focus of senior management and underpin the business and marketing strategies. When firmly established and deployed, core competences deliver massive competitive advantage

In this journey of discovery, however, many management teams have discovered to their horror that almost everything they do is imitable, often without much effort. Bankers have discovered that the only significant differentiator open to them is the transactional history of their customers. Having realized this, a number have observed that it is the interpretation of that transactional data that holds the key to core competence. Data that cannot be converted first into information and then, through structured marketing, into knowledge, are of very limited value.

In service organizations these core competences often centre upon data assets rather than business processes. Whereas manufacturing businesses have some chance to develop unique tools and techniques, possibly open to protection through patent law, the service providers are commonly in a trap of their own making, namely product and price imitation—a strategy that has little future.

Hamel and Prahalad (1990) cite numerous examples to confirm their thesis: Canon as a world-leader in low-level laser applications, Citibank for global trading technologies, and National Panasonic for the integration of computers and communication. Subsequently, for example, we believe that Reuters have core competence in information dissemination, *Reader's Digest* in list management, Prudential Assurance in distribution, Honda in internal combustion engine technology, Sony in miniaturization, and Sheraton Hotels in service delivery.

In a second article, 'Corporate imagination and expeditionary marketing', Hamel and Prahalad (1991) explore these notions, which build upon the earlier core competence model and show how organizations can stake out future territory by creatively exploiting their competences, often through fusion with other competences held by historic competitors. This concept of strategic alliance to achieve unassailable competitive distance ahead of the pack puts a high premium on both the management of core competences and the ability to integrate them imaginatively to create an even more potent cocktail of competitive advantage.

Key to this view of the world is the notion that we must give up thinking in terms of markets and products and, instead, think needs and solutions. They urge us to abjure the habit of viewing the future through eyes blinded by current products and technologies. Through knowing the needs that will dominate the demand-side, and how they may be met through solutions rooted in core competences, organizations are rendered capable of huge advances ahead of their competition.

The marketer needs to go further and see how the core competences of the organization, duly enriched with corporate imagination and lateral thought, can be made sufficiently visible to customers that they increasingly inform the brand values. Clearly if that corporate transformation can be achieved, the marketing strategy is written.

In the absence of core competences?

They are elusive, rare and well guarded by their owners. So what to do if you have no idea of your business's core competences? Besides the inverted SWOT Analysis reviewed above, there are numerous models to help define the optimum strategic direction and some are worth rehearsing in this introductory chapter, forming, as it does, the backdrop to the successful deployment of the communications tool-set.

Ansoff's Matrix (Ansoff, 1968) is one of the simplest and most approachable (see Fig. 2.3). The choices are simple: more of the same to someone else or something new to someone you know, with every combination in between? Given that it is rare for businesses to maximize their penetration of their home markets, it makes sense to sustain momentum in terms of market support. The

Market options open

P r o d u c t	Current range to current markets [penetration]	Current range to new markets [market expansion]
O p t i o n s	New range to current markets [development and retention]	New range to new markets [business diversification]

Figure 2.3 Ansoff's Matrix

well-informed marketer must quantify this heartland and the relative share held, as well as evaluating the trend of this share.

Then, the marketer will seek to establish if further markets can be found for the current product portfolio to release the potential for economies of scale and hence some price-based competitiveness. Winning these incremental markets requires judgement as to whether the yield justifies the investment, particularly if resources are limited. It may not make sense to divert precious budget into keeping an old product alive for pursuit of new markets, if that means that new product development is postponed to a point where it is no longer possible. Market extensions are often a fatal trap for the unwary and the inert, and should not be allowed to mask the harsh realities of market obsolescence. Innovate or die has a persuasive ring to it.

New product development (NPD) for existing or new markets has the attraction of forward momentum (see Fig. 2.4). The discipline involved, eloquently detailed in Malcolm McDonald's (1984) classic textbook *Marketing plans*, harnesses the full skills of marketers. That the hit rate for NPD is poor has much to do with assumptiveness—the triumph of enthusiasm and self-belief over rational evaluation of markets. The popular music industry represents a blatant example of hope springing eternal—perhaps a hundred singles released for only one to achieve any sort of hit parade success. That pop music is a fashion item and therefore subject to massive vagaries in market definition terms excuses some of this wasteful activity. The classical side of the business has less excuse, because the repertoire is more

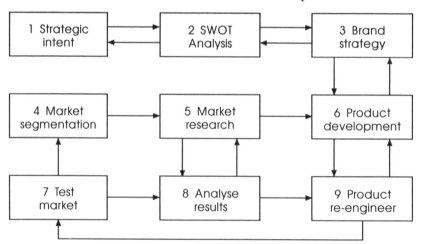

Figure 2.4 Continuous process of product development

clearly established. Why the industry sustains what is little more than an alchemical process loosely linking the enthusiasms of artists with the buying public, through a distribution chain concerned mainly with margin, stock turn and risk avoidance, is a wonder of the age.

NPD is concerned to push out the frontiers of experience and discover markets that can be exploited profitably. For this reason alone, NPD must be central to strategy. When coupled with a relentless drive to identify the fundamental characteristics of markets, that are likely to be sustained into the future, NPD is an ideal way to ensure that the organization remains responsive to markets, and imaginative in developing them. This is a central platform to relationship marketing covered in detail in Chapter 9.

If Ansoff asks apparently simple questions of market development, Michael Porter (1985) tests our ability to examine strategic development in the wider context of competition. His by now famous *Five Forces* model replicates the conditions under which businesses operate and causes us to evaluate the strength of each force on our competitive position (see Fig. 2.5). The well-informed marketer spends real time and effort in 360 degree scanning of the competitive environment—particularly considering where threats may emerge from and what strategic dilemmas must be resolved. As Hamel and Prahalad (1990) argue, organizations who spend all their time considering their immediate sources of competition are likely to miss the ones that will really cause them strategic worry. Porter (1985) rightly urges us to monitor the external forces on our market-place and avoid complacency in believing that we have our backyard under control.

British Telecom has come to recognize that cable operators, utilizing new infrastructure, advanced image compression technologies and access to programme material, will achieve a disproportionate share of consumer markets before BT can legally enter the fray with its own videos-by-phone service. During the late nineties the distribution of video images will be the most keenly fought-over battleground, encompassing the press media, television, cable operators and telecommunications companies (telecomms), as well as publishing and financial interests. Businesses not yet seen as players in this market have already taken strategic stakes in it, notably the French water and energy utilities, and the US telecomms sector.

The well-informed marketer must consider not only the specific threats to strategy from the existing competition, but also what

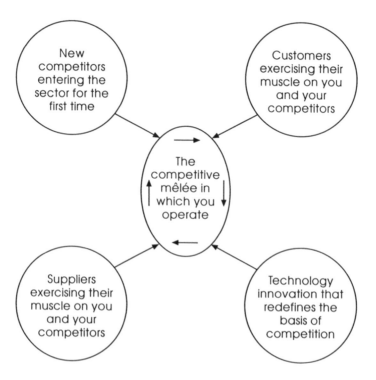

Strategy formulation must be dynamically responsive to this competitive force field in which your business operates–change is always being driven from one direction or another

Figure 2.5 Five Forces Model

innovations would permit access to the market by other non-current players. David Llewellyn (1989a, 1989b) has described the concept of asymmetric competition in which it becomes easy for one type of business to enter another sector while the incumbent businesses cannot reciprocate. He cites Marks and Spencer's move into consumer credit not being matched by the UK clearing banks selling shirts.

Generally, the strategy formulation exercise demands close attention to the whole commercial environment, often defined under the headings of political, sociological, economic and technological factors, usually on a global scale that are likely to represent challenge (or even opportunity) to the strategic intent of stakeholders. The well-informed marketer is fully acquainted with these factors and voracious in absorbing evidence of change in the operating environment, whether subtle or dramatic.

When to articulate the *mission* of the organization is a moot point, but as it is meant to be the statement of purpose to the chosen markets and other stakeholders, it seems reasonable to leave its definition until the future potential and core competences have been articulated and agreed. Why then do organizations rush headlong into mission writing, requiring some curiously flexible post-rationalization once the whole task is complete? It may well be that the distinction between mission and vision is not as clear as it might be. *Vision* is a private matter for internal consumption, defining for employees where the organization wants to be, drawing upon its core competences as well as its wildest dreams. The mission is for market consumption and is the aspiration behind the claimed brand values.

Subordinate to the mission we next come to the business objectives—the milestones on the endless road to nirvana—journey's end perhaps? For one Japanese organization (Sony Corporation) journey's end is at least 250 years hence (according to Sony's late chairman, Akio Morita in a television interview in the early eighties). None the less, the progress of the business needs to be modularized to give a sense of near-term focus for endeavour. Even when the goals are in the mid to long-term planning framework, the stages along the way are worth defining: these will include marketing criteria as well as financial.

I shall argue in later chapters that a lack of clear business objectives in the briefing to marketing suppliers is a serious mistake: if you cannot describe the next milestone or two, how can they help you get there? Where businesses need real clarity is in defining the objectives in terms of markets to be served, their detailed segmentation and range penetration. Why this should be arcane data known only to marketers is mildly curious: it forms the bedrock of strategic intent.

Under the heading of strategic options it is generally helpful to have differentiated plans for three distinctive groupings:

- Existing markets
- Competitor-held markets
- New markets.

They are fundamentally different and demand separate consideration. Figure 2.6 shows a model of these three and how marketers can approach them. It becomes obvious at a glance that

	Friends	Competitor users	Nil users
Generic strategy	Retention	Establish positive differentiation	Establish primary basis of need
Communications focus	Bilateral relationship management	Getting to 'maybe'	Getting to 'maybe'
Customer focus philosophy	Consolidate reward loyalty	Optimize 'safe to try' factors	Manage expectations
Marketing priority	Relationship management plan	Validating basis of differentiation	Segment needs analysis

Established customers (Friends) require a fundamentally different marketing philosophy from that employed in persuading Competitor users to change allegiance—the latter already 'own' the primary proposition, they simply buy from the 'wrong' source. Persuading Nil users to buy is a double dilemma—establishing the primary basis of need and your brand pull.

Figure 2.6 Differential marketing matrix

the most accessible markets are those already held—where the strategy must be retention and organic development—and competitor held markets which at least have the merit of buying your type of products or services, albeit regrettably from a competitor. The last option represents the double assault course of winning the conceptual need as well as the brand argument—not to be lightly enterprised.

Where marketers cannot, I believe, negotiate is in defending (developing even) their home markets. Taking a casual, perhaps disposable view of current customers is still very prevalent. The risk is obvious: if you have lost customers through benign neglect, it is more than likely that someone else has acquired them, perhaps never to yield them up again.

Marketing strategy ought to have at its heart the notion of managing a long-term continuum between the business's core competences (or at least its sources of inspiration) and customer needs. It is, even at its best, a fragile bond and often held only through brand management. If a marketing strategy has nothing else in it, it must have a coherent plan for ensuring that all the customer-impacting resources of the organization are dedicated to the mutually profitable retention of customers. If that can be achieved it is more than likely that organic and incremental development will follow in its wake.

That fundamental coherence applies equally and crucially to the integration of all marketing activities. If a campaign or initiative does not have its roots in this basic strategic intent and is not part of a continuous view of the bond between the business and its current or future markets it should not take place. This puts a massive onus on marketers to integrate the supply-side, so that the powerful creativity unleashed in the range of suppliers to individual campaign targets is cumulative and synergistic to those from other suppliers. Anything less is an unacceptably high risk formula.

In Chapter 3 we take a brief overview of these communications tools and how they might be appraised for their susceptibility to integration within a communications strategy.

3

Sorting the wheat from the chaff

Thus far we have seen the marketer in the role of professional manager, making effective use of resources to improve business performance, understanding the impact of the marketing function on results and striving to achieve high levels of credibility within the management debate. In common with all managers, the marketer operates within a demands, constraints and choices framework. It is the marketer's task to reduce the constraints through developing high levels of competence within the functional team so that more choices can be exercised.

We have also seen the marketer as champion of many aspects of the business strategy, with a direct responsibility for balancing the often irreconcilable aspirations of the principal stakeholders—customers and shareholders. The business strategy is, or at least should be, reliant on the marketer's ability to scan the future horizon for opportunities in the form of sustainable human or commercial needs that can be satisfied by solutions developed from the core competences of the organization. The marketing strategy will, in turn, be a derivative of the overall business strategy, concentrating on specific objective milestones and managing choice using a variety of analytical tools, ranging from Ansoff's Matrix to Porter's Five Forces model.

Subsets of the marketing strategy include clear market segmentation analysis, market research to establish trends of demand and perceptions, brand value development, competitor analysis, pricing policy, product development systems and communications strategy. The latter is the particular focus of *Forensic Marketing*.

In this chapter we shall consider the guiding principles of market communications and their relationship to the marketing process overall. Through summarizing the main tools and techniques we shall appreciate the scope of the challenge to marketers in making sense of this amazing variety of resources. This will be by way of preparation for the subsequent chapters, which take each communications technique in turn and argue the case for its adoption within the communications mix. Each technique's apologist is an acknowledged leader in the field and has been mandated to try to take you by storm. For this is the reality facing marketers: we are the focus for highly sophisticated specialists who believe, rightly or wrongly, that their specialism is the ideal solution to our needs. Having a sound understanding of each will allow marketers to make well-informed assessments of the suitability of each to the particular situation.

Context of the communications mix

At the risk of rehearsing old and well-understood principles it is worth considering both the context for the communications mix and the nature of communications themselves. The former is our old friend the marketing mix or the *Four Ps of marketing* (product, place, price, promotion). Figure 3.1 lays out the basic proposition that there is a powerful interaction between the attributes of the product (or service), its price and other value attributes, the market segment(s) being targeted and the communications used to link them all. While the model is rational enough and demands a

'Customer leading' ——— Push ——→	
←——— Pull ——— 'Customer led'	
Your product or service array and feature attributes/options (PRODUCT)	Market segments you could or do serve and the distribution systems to supply them (PLACE)
The financial basis of your offers and explicit terms of business (PRICE)	The communications mix you deploy to reach and stimulate chosen market segments (PROMOTION)

In using the marketing mix, the sequence will depend on whether a 'pull' or 'push' approach is being used. The mix should not be used in any single linear sequence, but dynamically between all four quadrants

Figure 3.1 Context of the communications mix

thorough understanding by marketers and their suppliers, it is insufficiently analysed from the point of view of its intrinsic dynamics: literally, which comes first?

In Chapter 2 we looked at a very simple model for strategic planning—a basic linear approach in which each stage is a logical cascade from the one before (Fig. 2.1). In reality it is nothing like that, as each stage will have a retrospective effect on the preceding one and groups of stages will have loop-back impact. In practice the strategic planning framework is a complex closed-loop system with many internal loops and exchange mechanisms. The art is to be aware of the whole even when concentrating on one stage: the dependent relationships are the critical factors to manage. It is the same with the marketing mix.

We could start with a product, determine its price to achieve a profit norm, choose a logical distribution system and communicate with the whole chain, from factory to end-user. This simplified linear view is commonly styled product push, since that is what is being done to the distribution chain. In the seventies the acme of product push was the photocopier market wherein box-shifting was the euphemism for pressing the machine on the customer, whether needed or not, so that the long-term revenue stream from paper-supplies and metering charges (the so-called click rate) could be secured. The salesperson's cry was satirized as 'Have I got a deal for you'—deal being the last thing on his or her mind.

Clearly there is a case for product push in certain circumstances, notably when the need for a product or service is so universal that the key task is to ensure adequate distribution, rather than stimulate further demand—the undertaking business comes to mind. We can also sympathize with marketers who are faced with the inevitability of a shipload of product coming over the horizon from some distant factory that is more concerned with production than sales. Here too product push may be the only line to take—moving the product through an established distribution channel and stimulating local demand at point-of-sale—to some extent this is typical of the white and brown goods industries, where distribution channels are well established and retail merchandising is very nearly all, supported by low-level product awareness advertising.

The alternative view of the mix is to start with the segmentation task and identify the needs of specific markets that have prima facie potential, leading to a decision to create solutions for those specific segments or to match existing solutions to them. The aim, overall, is to focus the resources of the business only on those segments with a high propensity to buy. The product pull approach is attractive from this viewpoint—find the need, offer the solution. Now the slogan goes 'Have you got a need for me?'

This approach will include the identification of further needs from existing customers—back to Ansoff again—producing range extensions and upgrade paths, largely dependent on the ability to identify and communicate with those customers and seek a reaction to proactive product propositions. We shall also consider in some depth the ability to clone segments on the basis of understanding the generic attributes of existing buyers—enticingly called psychogeodemographics.

So we have push and pull and combinations of both to manage. But, of course, it is nothing like so clear-cut as all that. The reality is that size of segment, for example, will determine the cost and price of the product and that in turn will have a bearing on the amount of demand that can be stimulated through market communications, which in turn is limited by the amount of resource that the product margin will bear. It is, in sum, a complex web of interdependencies. The questions we need to ask about the marketing mix will include:

- How precisely can I segment my market or potential markets?
- How cost efficient is my means to reach those segments?
- How responsive can I afford to be in meeting the specific needs of segments?
- How will I establish price/volume sensitivity?
- How much influence can I have over demand through market communications?
- How much can I afford to spend on market communications?
- How close to my customers or potential customers can I get?
- What is my competitive environment? How constrained am I on price/performance?
- How well do I understand the buying motivations of the segments I am targeting?
- How much flexibility can I afford to design into my offers?
- Which communications tools will achieve the best response?
- What impact on brand management will this campaign have?

There are, of course, many more questions to answer in deploying the marketing mix, but you will be aware that these questions are closely linked one to another. The overriding consideration is where to start? While recognizing that there are circumstances in which the product and its pricing are largely predetermined for the marketer, I should urge you to consider the merits of concentrating first upon the segmentation and communications quadrants.

This approach ties in well with the concept of being market-led and market-leading, rather than product-led. Better still, if we accept Hamel and Prahalad's (1991) advice, is to be needs-led or needs-developing, so that we avoid the trap of seeking to shoehorn markets to fit our product. Furthermore, if we place a high priority on the effectiveness with which we reach and communicate with our potential sources of need, we may well be able to tap into opportunities currently masked by product-led orientation. For example, take the drinks business: a wine producer tends to think of wine, a brewer of beer, a cola producer of cola and a gin distiller of gin. Fair enough, but what links them all: liquid consumption, bottles of glass or plastic, location, some aspects of production methodology and regulation, consumption environments, distribution needs and so on? There are profound differences too—brands, pricing, image—and high degrees of consumer correlation—beer and crisps, gin and tonic, wine and food, cola and kids—all of which may indicate other opportunities for profitable market development. The art and science of this right-side of the matrix in the marketing mix is to look for commonalties within segments, rather than product niches. Marketing communications are likely to be most effective when the whole buying context is understood rather than the narrower point of purchase.

The relationship between the product and price needs careful management. The ideal is to develop value-for-money propositions that are differentiated in complex ways from their competitors. When the comparison is limited to one or two variables like price and size the scope for value-for-money communications strategies is strictly limited. Value-for-money is increasingly being linked to service quality rather than the intrinsics of the product or service. If we concentrate on functionality and price we run the risk of losing the argument for trivial reasons.

Value-for-money is a proposition rooted in perceptions of benefits received or anticipated: it contains large amounts of irrationality in its make-up, including self-image, prior experience, prejudice and perceptions of risk. The marketer is concerned to establish the belief in the market that the solution offered comprises higher perceived benefits than perceived costs: the latter includes costs to self-image, risk of ridicule, uncertainty.

Where the marketing communications tool-set becomes so vital is in the integration of all the arguments above into a highly targeted, individual promotion of the value-for-money proposition in terms of language and style valued by the prospective purchaser. It is this ability to identify the full range of buyer motivations and to mirror them back in ways that make the individual prospect feel most comfortable that will distinguish the professional marketer.

Siren voices

We have lightly touched upon the marketing mix and the possible positioning of marketing communications within it. For those who wish to look at this subject in much greater depth two books make indispensable reading: Colin Coulson-Thomas's (1983) *Marketing communications* and Malcolm McDonald's (1984) *Marketing plans*. They explore in great detail the step-by-step routines for using the marketing mix and arriving at appropriate solutions.

That is not our purpose here. We are about to start looking in depth at each of the tools available to the marketer to enhance performance, whether of marketing communications as an output process or as contributor to sophisticated segmentation.

The dilemma that we seek to resolve here is how to decide which beguilingly tempting agency's siren song to listen to and which, like the warnings of classical mythology, to remain deaf to if we are not to hit the rocks. The choice is not quite as stark as that, but there are serious difficulties in knowing when one approach is more suitable than another, and how to integrate several techniques to produce holistic benefit and, dare I say it, value-for-money from increasingly restricted budgets.

The first point to be clear upon is that the professional suppliers to the marketing function have high levels of self-belief and a genuine wish to improve client performance. They have an understandable drive to demonstrate that their solution is the best for the particular circumstance and they are, for the most part, competitively aware. Often the choice between suppliers, especially of creative resources, is down to subjective values—our kind of people, for example, whatever that means.

However, each supplier has an axe to grind and it will be done partisanly—above-the-line rather than below-the-line; telemarketing versus direct mail, television versus print media. So what are the criteria that marketers should apply when evaluating the range of options?

In a fascinating book, *Creative people: how to manage them and maximise their creativity* by Winston Fletcher (1990), the myths and legends are explored: are creative people different from the rest of humanity, do they appreciate commercial reality, can they be managed to deliver results within commercial constraints, are they deliberately stubborn and unyielding when challenged? The answers vary from individual to individual, but some key lessons come through. The most important of these poses the question, 'If you want to be creative why hire an agency?' Another question, 'Who owns the brief?', is absolutely fundamental to the effective evaluation of professional suppliers.

These two awkward questions are central to our proposition that the only way to evaluate the supply-side offerings is to be clear what the objectives are. Note the word *objectives*. The marketer must define the outcomes being sought in hard measurements. To this must be added the pragmatic constraints—time, money, *realpolitik*, and brand integrity management. What the marketer does not prescribe is the creative solution—that is what we pay good money to agencies for.

The disputed territory is often creativity, of course, because we are all human and have strong feelings about such things. This we must avoid at all costs: apart from the need to ensure that the resultant solution is legal, decent, honest and truthful (and brand supportive), we should be wary of our subjectivity.

Where we are sometimes negligent is in electing one type of solution rather than another, perhaps because our experience has confirmed our prejudices. We do need to examine why we send for the direct-marketing specialist rather than the above-the-line specialist, or the PR agency rather than the exhibition company.

I argue that if the brief defines the commercial outcomes, the prior history, the marketing strategy and the commercial constraints, the choice of approach and creativity is almost exclusively the preserve of the suppliers. It is up to them to say how the results will be delivered. Naturally the marketer must judge whether the solution will actually work, using objective judgement. Knowing how to evaluate each solution is what we shall examine at the end of each of the following siren's songs.

Thus we must consider, before listening to those 'sublime lays', what leads to the preparation of a quality brief that will, in turn, yield quality solutions from your creative partners? Here we arrive at the origin of the book's title, *Forensic Marketing*. FORENSIC is a mnemonic designed to ensure that sufficient rigour goes into the briefing.

Forensic sciences (or art?)

- Focus on facts
- Observation
- Research
- Evaluation
- Negative indicators
- Strategy compliance
- Inertial barriers/factors
- Check and re-check.

Let us take each of these headings in turn and apply them to the preparation of a brief to a professional supplier of marketing communications resource.

Focus on facts

This is both a broad principle urging an objective stance and a more precise counsel to ensure that you are as well informed as possible through establishing as much hard information as possible about the opportunity being explored. Information comes from the integration or relating of data, and, generally, organizations are data rich—though they may not know it. Sources of factual data include transactional records: what was bought, when, how much, at what price, where, previous purchases, correlative data, credit scores, postcoded address files, decision-making unit records. Other sources of data include press cuttings, surveys, public data (census, electoral roll, etc.), government statistics, industry-produced data, and competitive data. Further internal sources of information or data include the salesforce, service departments, accounts departments, R&D function and operations.

The ability to martial the data assets of the organization is one of the critical competences for marketers, closely followed by the ability to convert data into information. The questions we ought to ask under this heading include:

- What do we actually know about this segment?
- What do we not know?
- What do we need to know?
- Where is the information (or data) we need?
- What interpretation do we put upon it?
- How significant is it?
- How might we validate the assumptions we make?
- Who needs to know what?
- How relevant are the data we have?

- How accurate is our information?
- How do we gather the information we need?
- What format should the data be in for conversion to information?

The list could go on, but the point is made that any new activity is more than likely to be connected with some prior activity and will in turn form the basis of future activity. Every initiative produces a reaction and that will help the organization to get smarter at targeting its resources in the ways most likely to work. If campaign statistics are not gathered in a form that is reusable, ask yourself why not. If you cannot get meaningful market intelligence from your finance function, ask yourself why not.

The focus on facts nostrum is included as the first heading to stress the primacy of objectivity in preparing the brief. There is nothing so dangerous to marketing as the non-validated assumption. Ego-driven enthusiasms for campaigns (including the chief executive appearing in advertisements) are risky to the point of idiocy, when so many hard data are lying around ready to prove the fallacy of the belief. Marketers should be information addicts, endlessly curious about what is known and what are the blind spots.

This does not mean, however, that flair and intuition have no place in defining the opportunity. Far from it. Yet this must be tempered with a search for sufficient information to eliminate the avoidable risk intrinsic to subjectivity. Judgement qualified by fact is worth many times a natural feel for the market. It is not demeaning to the marketer to subordinate judgement to the test of fact.

Observation

This heading is closely related to the focus on facts. Here we are considering interpretation of information, and the conversion to knowledge. The trouble with data is that they are single dimensional—price paid, product code, postcode, payment method for example—and only when they are combined into two dimensional arrays do they become informative—how many paid cash for product x is quite useful, the more so when compared with how many paid cash for product y. Even this level of interpretation falls short of helping the marketer predict behaviour or establish a reasonable prospect view.

What we need are three-dimensional arrays that have time as the continuum. The science of the forensic marketer is to look for underlying trends beneath symptomatic data. The marketer needs to know whether the trends are moving positively or negatively in relation to the planned campaign. More especially we have the need to establish causation behind the symptoms.

Establishing consistent time-series trend analyses for the key performance indicators of the business and the markets is vital to the well-informed marketer. What are the dynamics you need to monitor and what will you do with the resultant information? Regrettably too many data and information are held in isolated pockets throughout the organization, even in people's heads, to be easily co-ordinated into valuable observations. Marketers need to assert strongly for a marketing information system that provides a clear overview of the fundamentals of the business in its markets.

Similarly, the marketer will want to use every new campaign to test out the bases of assumption and to confirm trends. I argue that every campaign should seek to illuminate buyer decision causation and improve the overall knowledge-base of the business. Knowledge is information applied and confirmed.

Decide, in developing the brief, what observations you intend to make—the opportunity is not to be wasted.

Research

Even after scouring the data assets of the organization and developing quality information systems that help the quality of decisions, there will be conspicuous gaps in knowledge. Running live campaigns to gain that knowledge (or experience analysed) may be too expensive an option. You will need to resort to formal techniques of research.

Feelings are very mixed about research, particularly in general management circles—lies, damned lies and statistics is an old and enduring canard—and yet the alternative is even worse: remaining in an assumptive limbo is not acceptable in the professional marketer, nor in a professional supplier. Research that confirms what you think you know is as valid as research that tells you something new. I say this because it is sometimes forgotten that markets are continuously dynamic: unless you are prepared to check that the goalposts are where you last saw them, you could be in for a rude shock, having missed the match altogether.

The art is to be able to ask the right questions that really yield information rather than mirrored opinion. In Chapter 4 on market research you will see the case put with great clarity.

The marketer is relentless in the search for truth—obsessed with root cause analysis—wanting to know the why as well as the what. Naturally, I expect to be challenged in promoting this analytical orientation: there are plenty who will cry 'analysis paralysis'. A perfectly fair comment and well evidenced if the numerative-based analytical obsession with risk management fostered by some US and European MBA programmes is anything to go by. I do not mean analysis paralysis, simply an orientation that says that sufficient risk should be taken when and only when I have avoided unnecessary risk—the latter being defined as risk that was avoidable if I had asked the right question at the right time, or looked at the information assets of the business to avoid needless repetition of old mistakes.

Without a research orientation it is difficult to see how fundamental shifts in the market can be identified and analysed. You may know that something has changed, but not what or why. That strikes me as flying blind, with only one engine left and fuel getting low.

Evaluation

The key question here is how will you and your suppliers know whether the campaign has worked or not and why in either case? It is surprising how often performance tracking systems are not in place to monitor change even when the investment in change is very large. This may stem from deeply ingrained beliefs that it is better to do than to know: action is more valuable than thought.

Whether the aversion to post-facto analysis is anything to do with lack of confidence or accountability problems (as discussed in Chapter 1) is open to speculation, but I would ask you to consider the prize to be gained from adding to the learning and knowledge base of the organization through consciously setting out to evaluate what actually happened.

I hold the view that marketers cannot, by definition, make mistakes, only create experience. Their only potential crime is not to learn from that experience. Admittedly that requires the forgiveness culture discussed in Chapter 1 and a spirit of enterprise that values the deliberately and methodical search for knowledge. Given those conditions the rate at which the marketer can climb the learning curve, through structured experience, is likely to be spectacular.

When a direct marketer talks about a 5 per cent response to a mail-shot all well and good. But always ask what happened to the 95 per cent that did not respond. Think why *Reader's Digest* expensively buys a 'No' response in its prize draw campaigns: certainly it would be difficult to justify on the basis of checking that the addressee was still alive or resident at the address held on file. The real value lies in being able to compare the characteristics of those who said 'No' against those that said 'Yes'—the hidden market lies in the difference. If the negative variables can be eliminated, the proportion of 'Yes' responders can be increased.

Similarly, the ability of marketers to obtain post-facto feedback from customers must not be wasted: they know better than you why they bought and whether expectations built were actually delivered. Without this orientation to evaluation of results, seeking to know more after than before, progress will be limited and rather too dependent on luck—something I would rather leave out altogether. In the same way we need to pick up on complaints and poor payment performance: all are symptomatic of problems we need to understand before we seek to fix them. It must not be seen as threatening to the marketer to confront the truth—self-deception is a dangerous bedfellow.

Negative indicators

I have already touched upon complaints, poor payment performance and the 'No' response solicitation by *Reader's Digest* as a means to establish the gap between the desired state and what happens in reality. When a relationship is weakening behaviours change—for example if you are planning to move your bank account, you may well start by moving part of the account and your salary to the new bank, leaving the direct debits and standing orders to the last moment; your present bank ought to be able to spot these behavioural changes and ask why? How many credit card companies take action when utilization falls off? They are fast enough to move if credit thresholds are breached, but seldom the other way.

Generally, communication declines in quality and value as relationships get weaker. It is, therefore, an imperative for the marketer to know when and why a relationship with a customer or even segment is heading in the wrong direction. It may not, for example, be for any active reason on your part, simply that your competitor has made an offer that cannot be refused—*First Direct* and *Direct Line Insurance* have taken precisely this stance in the UK financial services market—pointing up the difference between what was a satisfactory formula for banking and insurance and what is now possible. Unless this chemical change can be monitored it cannot be remedied.

Negative indicators are arguably the second best condition under which to change the relationship for the better—it is a moment when the customer is ready for change—it is up to you if that change is in your favour or not. The best condition, of course, is when the customer of your competitor is ready to move on.

Strategy compliance

I have made much play in these introductory chapters on the theme of continuity management and strategic fit for all marketing initiatives. The key learning point is that every sale is the gateway to the next, every initiative is an increment in brand development, every opportunity to understand customer or prospect motivations is a step-jump in corporate knowledge.

This continuum view of the marketing strategy is increasingly important as competitors become more and more effective in niche targeting. The critical competence is the ability to gain the customer, retain the customer and develop the relationship for mutual advantage. With this in mind it becomes axiomatic to state that the purpose of the marketing strategy is to acquire valuable relationships that are sustainable and progressive—that is, adaptive over time one to another, as innovations are normalized.

Underlying the marketing strategy for many businesses is the development of the brand. A strong, magnetic, brand is the key to a long and prosperous business life—especially a brand which is not product dependent, but adaptive and generic to enduring needs and rooted in the core competences of the organization. As I have said in Chapter 2, brand values are earned, not created: it is the perception of the customer and prospect that is all important. Brands are developed through quality of product or service delivery and consistency in their application over many years. Since they are perceptions, however, they are necessarily very vulnerable. Any marketing campaign that is at variance with the underlying values is damaging them. An ill-judged enthusiasm may destroy brand values built up over decades. In the UK this has been particularly characteristic of the banking sector, where tactical expedience has undermined traditional values of financial rectitude. With the luxury of hindsight we can see that it might have been wise if the UK banks, and other financial institutions, had repositioned their brands to take account of the effects of competition and the more aggressive marketing stance that that required. Today, these banks do not enjoy strong brands: the gap has been filled with a virtual spot-market orientation by the market-place.

These themes of continuity and fragility of brand management, within the overall marketing strategy, require the marketer to ensure that every campaign is consistent with the brand positioning and will facilitate the development of relationships: it is increasingly difficult to justify a disposable attitude to customers. 'Win some, lose some' is shoddy marketing philosophy.

Inertial barriers/factors

In considering the appropriate communications tool-set for a campaign, you and your advisers will need to take into account just how much are you asking the prospect to do. Is it one small step for man or a leap for mankind? I have referred to the 5 per cent response rate to a direct-marketing campaign as indicative of a 95 per cent failure to respond. The question that must be asked again and again is 'How close did we get to unlocking the hidden market?' Of that 95 per cent who did not respond, what proportion nearly bought: 10–25 per cent perhaps? The figure may be much higher if the quality of research and evaluation of past campaigns led to very accurate positioning of the offer: the only stumbling block is customer and prospect inertia.

All of us have experienced post-cheque-signing tristesse—the larger the cheque the greater the tristesse. For significant proportions of the prospect market the inertial barriers to purchase predate the offer: the desirability is outweighed by perceptions of risk. Whenever perceived benefits are less than perceived costs the inertial barriers get higher. Similarly, we tend to bench-mark intended purchases against other uses for the same disposable income, or commercial budget, so nuances of priority conspire to reinforce inertia. The postponable decision comes in the same category: whenever supply is plentiful the inertial factors are at their highest and the marketer has to work hardest to dismantle them, often through the price mechanism.

No one is a fool in their own estimation: if you are targeting competitor-held customers, because your offering is objectively better, beware of saying anything critical of the original purchase. Your task is to demonstrate the positive differential between what was 'the right buy at the time' and 'what is now available from us'. Inertia can stem from an incomplete decision-making unit: hence the insistence of double-glazing salespeople on both spouses being present for the *coup de grâce*.

In designing the brief marketers will need to look for and clearly identify the range of inertial barriers to purchase. One of the imperatives of tracking 'Yes', 'No' or 'Maybe' responses to a campaign is to find the near misses and why. Consider carefully what would happen to the economics of your campaign if you could convert further increments of the hidden market.

Check and re-check

This piece of advice is, in essence, a reprise of what has gone before. It is a passionate exhortation to make sure that the brief is as complete as it can be, both in terms of objectives and the factors likely to affect the outcomes. The brief needs to be well informed, sensitive to the underlying trends of the market and as well researched as is feasible.

Only on this basis can your professional suppliers optimize their contribution. Be clear what it is that you are asking them to contribute—creativity, solutions, accountability, specific results or advice? Be sure that they are clear what your basis of evaluation of their response is and what they can expect from you in the brief. Too often have I seen agency and client passing each other like ships in the night, not knowing what each other could have done 'if only we had known'. It is, of course, a complete waste of everyone's time if the brief and the expectations it creates are not effectively communicated one to another.

What the well-informed marketer is seeking to do is to find the right solution for the task from among the best tools and techniques available: the first cut at identifying which to use is the writing of the brief.

Now we come to the individual presentations of the major tools in the marketing communications arsenal. Each contributor is championing his or her cause to the exclusion of the others—this is focused advocacy at its best. Read and think about the arguments offered and the claims made. Test them objectively against the FORENSIC checklist.

At the end of each contributor's chapter I pose a number of checklist points and questions. Once you have read each proposition turn to Chapters 13 and 14 in which I shall explore the art of integration of the various tools and techniques and how to prepare a persuasive case for budget. Those readers who are part of the supply-side can compare their arguments to client against this coliseum of gladiators.

4

Market research

The beginning of wisdom

Robert M. Worcester and Peter Hutton (MORI)

Since the mid-eighties, while the British economy has grown by
only a quarter in real terms, turnover in the market research industry
has more than doubled. In this context, though, the term *market
research* is a misleading one because much of the research
commissioned by private companies and, increasingly, by the public
sector has little or nothing to do with researching markets. The
industry goes back to the early years of the twentieth century, but
really began to grow after widespread publicity surrounding
successful attempts to predict the outcome of presidential elections
in the USA and national and by-elections in Britain in the thirties.
The commercial opportunities for understanding mass consumer
markets were soon recognized and led to the setting up of several
of the leading market research companies that exist today.

As the usefulness of the techniques for understanding the public's
behaviour, opinions, attitudes and motivations were more widely
recognized, so they were increasingly employed to assist
management in non-marketing areas in both the private and the
public sectors, including employee attitude surveys, shareholder
studies, corporate image research and the like.

In this chapter we shall be referring to market research to include the
social research which draws on the techniques of the market research
industry. In this context, (market) research might be defined as

> The systematic and objective collection and evaluation of
> information about what people know and how they think about, and
> behave towards, products, services, organizations and ideas.

Most of this activity can normally be divided into one of two
categories: it is either *qualitative research* or *quantitative research*. The
former refers to methods of collecting information which are open

ended and exploratory in nature. The researchers are likely to carry out in-depth interviews or run small discussion groups, normally of around six to eight individuals at a time, in order to understand in some depth how respondents relate to the subject matter under discussion—a new product concept, an advertisement, local council services or a company's reputation. Respondents are encouraged to express their own views, and to react to various stimulus material and (in the case of discussion groups) to other members of the group. The use of certain *projective* techniques, such as asking respondents to describe a product or organization as if it was a person, animal or car, enables researchers to understand how respondents relate to the matters under discussion at an emotional level. An expensive car can signify commercial success, although it can suggest overcharging or exploitation of the consumer in the case of a monopolistic utility supplier. Female figures usually denote caring for the customers; someone who lives in a house at the end of a long drive denotes remoteness from the customer. To be middle aged is usually a good attribute suggesting experience, maturity and reliability.

Many research projects start with a qualitative approach leading to a quantitative survey. As the term implies, the main objective here is to be able to answer the question 'How many people take this or that view or do this or that activity?'

Samples of respondents are normally selected using either *random* or *quota sampling* techniques. These both aim to ensure that the sample interviewed is representative of the population from which it is drawn in so far as it shares the same basic characteristics such as the proportion in each gender, age, and social class category. If the sample shares such characteristics with the parent population, one normally finds that variables which are not controlled also match those of the population. This gives us confidence that we can draw valid conclusions about the population as a whole even though we have interviewed only a fraction of them. The degree to which this is likely to be so depends on the absolute size of the sample (not the proportion of the population sampled) and can be calculated statistically.

As the market research industry has grown, so too have the reasons for using its services. As a generalization it can be said that market research has a contribution to make whenever a manager is planning or making decisions which are likely to affect a sizeable number of people and when information about their behaviour, attitudes or opinions would have a bearing.

Consumer and business marketing

The most obvious areas for market research are in consumer research. In developing new products, for example, research will consist of far more than just developing a product and getting consumers' reactions to it. Market research is likely to have been involved at every stage. First, it has to be established whether there is a gap in the market and what consumer needs the new product will fulfil: how are these currently being met and what sort of marketing messages or selling propositions are likely to attract the consumer? Leading brands and fast-moving consumer goods (FMCG) in general are likely to have their brand shares tracked using data from the bar-codes collected by the main supermarkets and department stores. This information is extremely valuable but it does not tell you *why* one brand is being bought in preference to another, nor *who* is buying, nor whether they are continuing to buy after their first (trial) purchase. Although research techniques are being developed to do this, currently this kind of information needs further research using *ad hoc* (different sample of people each time) or panel (same sample of respondents each time) tracking surveys.

The equivalent research in business-to-business markets is likely to be conducted less frequently and often one-off surveys are used rather than tracking. The reason for this is that companies often keep closer direct contact with the customer base, many industrial products are sold in vast volume at a time to a relatively small number of customers, and tracking research on any meaningful scale would inevitably be going back to the same respondents.

Another application of market research in consumer markets is in pre-testing the effectiveness of various elements of their marketing programmes. A particularly interesting example of this is pre-testing of advertising.

Advertising pre-tests are usually conducted prior to the time when a campaign is used in the market-place, and are intended to check that the advertising works in the manner which is intended. This allows the client to adjust the advertisement, if necessary, to improve its effectiveness before it is exposed to the public. Because of the amount of money that may subsequently be spent on the media needed to run the ad, even a small improvement in advertising effectiveness can lead to significant improvements in the client's profitability.

A typical test will usually involve measures of the advertisement's ability to gain attention, the extent to which it is associated with the product being advertised, and its ability to communicate the desired messages to the audience.

In addition, some techniques, usually proprietary methods, allow the researcher to measure the overall effect of the advertisement on those who see or hear it.

One example of this approach is the BUY© Test (see Fig. 4.1). BUY© Test in an advertising evaluation technique used in some 35 countries. Over 8000 advertisements have been tested using BUY© Test over the last 15 years. BUY© Test is offered in the UK by MORI. In this technique, respondents are classified into three groups, based on their response to the advertising. *Persuaded* respondents (Gp III) are fully affected by the advertisement, and are more likely to act in the way that the advertiser desires as a result of seeing it. *Involved* respondents (Gp II) respond to the advertisement itself, but do not connect the advertising messages and appeal with the product being advertised; this is considered to be a partial effect. *Recall* respondents (Gp I) can remember the advertisement, but are otherwise unaffected by it.

A method such as this one enables researchers to understand what is contributing to good or poor advertising, and give their clients advice which helps them to make their advertisements better.

Similar techniques can be applied to all other elements of the marketing mix, including products, promotional ideas, and pricing.

This area of research accounts for around 57 per cent of the turnover of the UK market research industry (ESOMAR 1993),

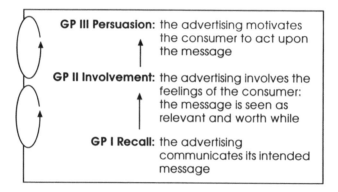

GP III Persuasion: the advertising motivates the consumer to act upon the message

GP II Involvement: the advertising involves the feelings of the consumer: the message is seen as relevant and worth while

GP I Recall: the advertising communicates its intended message

Figure 4.1 BUY© Test Response Model
Source: MORI

though the other sectors are important and growing as their contribution to management decision-making is increasingly being recognized. In sector terms, 33 per cent comes from fast-moving consumer goods, 8 per cent each from media research and customer satisfaction studies, 7 per cent from the financial services sector, 6 per cent each from government and industrial, and 5 per cent each from the pharmaceutical and automotive industries.

Customer satisfaction surveys

In recent years companies have become increasingly mindful of the cost savings involved in retaining existing customers rather than trying to win them over from the competition. Banks, airlines and the utilities as well as major industrial firms have therefore invested heavily in customer satisfaction surveys.

Customer satisfaction surveys fit in well with the focus on total quality which evolved throughout the eighties and with the requirements of the British Standard BS 5750 (and ISO 9000, a system for certifying that organizational procedures comply with the BS 5750 standard of quality) which an increasing number of companies have been applying for in the nineties.

The value of such surveys is not only in providing hard information on how well customers regard your particular product or service and their reasons for rating them unfavourably, but also in sending a signal to customers that you are actually interested in their views and thereby building up customer loyalty.

Corporate image

Some organizations, such as banks and petroleum companies, rely on a strong corporate image to support their market position, frequently when the company *is* the brand. During the eighties the building societies recognized the need to build strong corporate images backed up with a sound range of attractive financial products and services in order to compete with the banks when this market was deregulated. A period of high interest rates and strong competition in this sector has seen the demise of the reputation of the banks while the building societies have held firm, capturing market share (see Fig. 4.2).

For other businesses different audiences are priorities for corporate

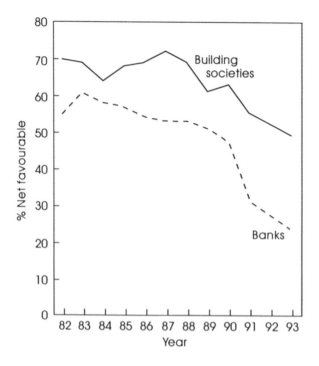

Figure 4.2 Favourability among the general public for banks and building societies
Source: MORI

communications. These might be industrial buyers or institutional investors, stockbroking analysts or Members of Parliament (MPs), business journalists or trade journalists.

Whichever audiences a company decides are important to it, corporate image research has an important role to play in defining the objectives of a corporate communications programme. Research by MORI has, since the late sixties, monitored the reputations of leading companies in a range of sectors among the general public and elite audiences. Two of the key measures incorporated into these studies have been *familiarity*—how well respondents feel that they know a company—and *favourability*—how favourably or unfavourably they regard the company. By allocating values to the question scale points, mean scores can be calculated for each company's familiarity and favourability among each audience. They can then be plotted on a scatter chart. Figure 4.3, for example, plots companies measured among the general public in 1992. Companies plotted further to the right of the figure are better known; those

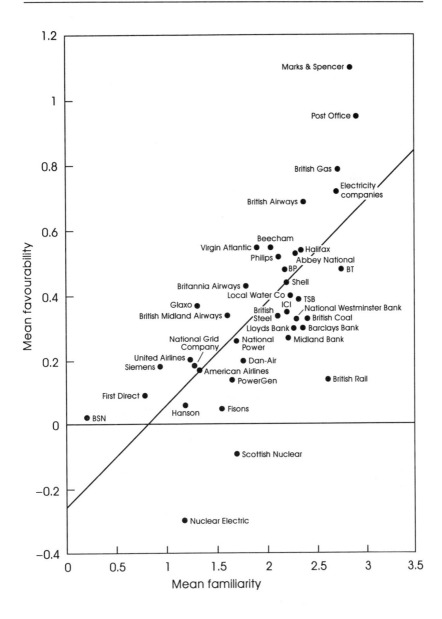

Figure 4.3 Company familiarity and favourability, general public, autumn 1992
Source: MORI

further up the figure are better regarded. It shows how, broadly speaking, the better known a company is the better regarded it is also, although any given level of familiarity can reflect a fairly wide range of favourability ratings dependent upon the company.

In this case Marks and Spencer is in prime position, being both well known and well regarded. Its primary objective is to stay there. British Rail is very well known but relatively poorly regarded and clearly needs to improve its reputation among an audience that feels it knows the company well, warts and all. Glaxo is not so well known but is well regarded by those who think they know it; its main challenge is to increase familiarity and then favourability is likely to follow. Nuclear Electric is little known and those who think they know it regard it unfavourably; it is tarnished by the negative attitudes many people have towards anything nuclear.

Different audiences are impressed by different aspects of a company. It is therefore important to understand what it is that each one is thinking of when making an evaluation of a company. Research by MORI indicates, for example, that City investors will judge a company most by its management, the general public by its product quality, Conservative MPs by its profit and Opposition MPs by its employee relations (see Table 4.1).

Corporate image research is used to diagnose the nature of a company's reputation and determine whether any problems identified are essentially ones which can be addressed by communications alone (e.g. awareness, misunderstandings) or ones which require more radical solutions backed up by communications (e.g. performance).

A strong corporate image takes a long time to build and it is important that this is reflected in the research programme. Thus many companies subscribe to tracking surveys to monitor their corporate images over a period of years. This is done either by using specially designed *ad hoc* surveys for the individual client or by subscribing to syndicated studies, particularly those covering opinion leader audiences.

Public sector

Research for the public sector has not only expanded tremendously since the mid-eighties, but also reflects the enormous changes that have taken place in the way the sector is managed and how it relates to its customers. The Citizens' Charter, introduced by Prime Minister John Major in 1991, followed a decade in which the roles of national and local government had been radically defined. Since the mid-eighties local councils have increasingly used opinion

Table 4.1 Criteria for judging companies—spontaneous

Question: What are the most important things to know about a company in order to judge its reputation?

Answers coded from verbatim responses

	Editors (%)	General public (%)	City investors (%)	Business press (%)	MPs Con (%)	MPs Opp (%)	MEPs (%)
Financial performance/ profitability	42	9	65	80	59	24	30
Quality of management	28	9	91	71	41	15	30
Treatment of staff/industrial relations	11	11	0	11	6	31	40
Quality of products/ services	8	47	20	0	23	16	45
Social/ environmental responsibility	8	5	0	3	9	17	56
Customer services	6	18	0	20	6	8	19
Communications/ reputation	—	0	0	14	12	8	22

Source: MORI

surveys to help them to understand how local residents view their services, their communications and the personal contact they have had with them. In this context surveys have a number of benefits which complement the more traditional kinds of information used by councils to guide planning and decision-making. Perhaps the most important is that they ensure that a representative sample of residents are interviewed; thus they include the politically active as well as the inactive, the interested as well as the uninterested in the correct proportions. Great care is also taken in questionnaire design to ensure the questions objectively measure residents' views and behaviour and are therefore politically neutral. This ensures that the findings are acceptable not only to council officers but also to representatives of all political parties.

A single survey can encompass the needs of several key areas of service provision such as housing, transportation, leisure, and waste collection and disposal. Issues which may not warrant the commissioning of a survey in their own right can therefore be incorporated into a survey designed to meet a broad range of needs.

It is now common for councils to commission research into local residents' views, and also to commit themselves to repeating the exercise in future years to monitor their performance and gauge what impact, if any, council policies are having. The London Borough of Richmond, for example commissioned 15 such surveys between 1984 and 1994.

Hutton and White (1993) followed the experience of Colchester Borough Council in commissioning and responding to surveys of its local residents. The research was fairly typical of that being commissioned by local authorities. However, the case study is particularly interesting because it illustrates how normative data collected by the research agency, MORI, over a number of years, have provided management with bench-marks against which the council can determine whether it is achieving its defined purpose. This has been stated as: 'to maintain or improve the quality of life through the provision of protection, regulation and amenities for those who live in, work in, trade in and visit Colchester and the surrounding area'.

One of these normative questions, which measures satisfaction with the way the local council is doing its job, has been asked in over 70 local authorities since the mid-eighties. A survey conducted in Colchester in 1988 found a net satisfaction score (per cent satisfied minus per cent dissatisfied) of + 36 per cent. The council set itself the target that it must not fall below the average for local authorities in England and Wales and to move into the upper quartile of such authorities by the continuing improvement of services, thereby leading to an increased level of satisfaction. In practice that meant the net satisfaction level should not fall below + 27 per cent and, in future it would be striving for + 44 per cent or more.

A follow-up survey in October 1992 showed that, with a new satisfaction score of + 65 per cent, it had easily surpassed its goal. This had been achieved by responding to a number of findings in the research which had identified problem areas, not least in respect of traffic control, road maintenance housing, and communications (see Fig. 4.4).

The suggestion that *how* services are delivered can be as important as *what* is delivered was brought home in an analysis of two

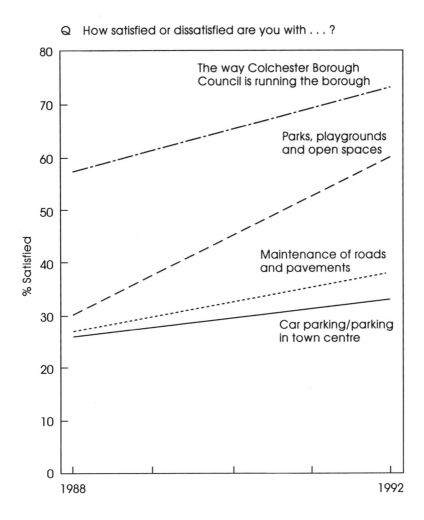

Q   How satisfied or dissatisfied are you with . . . ?

Figure 4.4 Colchester residents' satisfaction ratings, 1988–92
Source: MORI

councils (MORI, 1987 and MORI, 1988) representing similar areas
though in different parts of Britain. It was notable that while the
residents of Richmond upon Thames (near London) rated individual
key services somewhat higher than the residents of Solihull (near
Birmingham), the latter gave a somewhat higher rating to the
overall service provided by their council. One clue as to why this
should have been the case came in the ratings that residents gave to
the contact they had had with council staff. On their last visit to the

council Solihull residents rated the staff they had contact with as markedly more helpful, efficient and easy to get hold of than did the residents of Richmond. There are potential lessons here for retailers wishing to attract people back to their stores.

With the setting up of Next Steps Agencies to implement the Citizens' Charter, a demand has been created for improved understanding and measurement of customer needs and priorities with respect to the provision of services by national government. Research has an important role to play in this process of reorientation. Without the pressure of market forces, feedback from market research surveys provides some kind of measure of customer satisfaction and indications of which aspects of service need to be improved. This is an area of research which still has a long way to go before it reaches the level of sophistication of research conducted for the private sector.

Utility services

A similar process has been going on in the utility services sector. Although most of these are now in the private sector (telecommunications, gas, electricity, water) they are still largely monopolies in their respective markets. The terms of their regulation, however, mean that they are required to undertake research to understand customers' views about their services and, in particular, their willingness to pay for improved levels of service. For British Telecom and British Gas, which have long been subject to a certain degree of competition, market research is no new experience. For the water and electricity distribution industries such research is a new departure. As in local and national government, the value of such research lies in the new perspective it provides, not only on the individual services provided, but also on the whole business. In these sectors the trend and pressure from the regulatory authorities is towards greater customer orientation in every aspect of the business. Market research is one of the most reliable and indisputable means of collecting information to provide the necessary corporate focus.

Research for the Water Services Association (International Water Supply Association, 1992) in the first few years following privatization is a salutary reminder that public perceptions of service and reality can diverge opening up a major communications gap. Despite one of the heaviest investment programmes ever undertaken by the industry, public perceptions on a range of service measures drifted relentlessly down in the first few years following privatization.

Employees

Normative data bench-marks are also used in the field of research among employees. MORI has collected information in Britain from a very wide range of companies and other organizations since the late sixties (see Fig. 4.5). Companies commissioning research can find out whether the attitudes of their employees are above or below current norms on measures such as overall job satisfaction, and the company as a place to work, amount and credibility of information, understanding of organizational objectives and commitment to the job.

Because of the extent of the database it is possible to measure trends over time. This can provide interesting and sometimes surprising information such as the fact that, despite the major developments and initiatives in the internal communications field, perceptions of communications has increased by only 2 per cent since the mid-seventies.

Further perspective can be provided by comparisons within public, service and financial sectors so that organizations can measure themselves against others in their field. To be just average is increasingly not enough for some companies which bench-mark

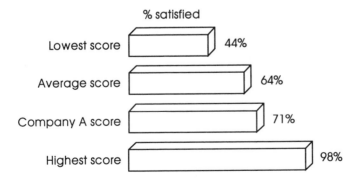

% satisfied

Lowest score — 44%
Average score — 64%
Company A score — 71%
Highest score — 98%

Figure 4.5 Job satisfaction norm
Source: MORI

their performance against top performers in specific areas such as communications and people development.

Another trend in the employee research field is towards the development of an Employee Satisfaction Index, a composite score of satisfaction indicators. This is measured on a regular basis against set targets. Although still relatively rare, this index can be given to managers in relation to their own department as a target built into their assessment in line with other hard targets.

Twinned with the Customer Satisfaction Index, these monitors provide both continuous measures and targets, which have been used by such organizations as the RAC (Royal Automobile Club), TSB (Trustee Savings Bank) and London Underground.

The fact that employee research can be used as a management tool to help bring improvements to an organization is reflected in the impetus behind an employee research programme. Issues at the heart of the business such as quality, customer service, communications, culture and change are all prime movers in these initiatives.

Research in the employee field has, therefore, developed so the reporting structure provides not only data but also perspective and recommendations for a positive way forward to address the issues identified, as well as building on the strengths of the organization.

Social change

As market research has evolved, so too has our understanding of the power of the techniques involved for helping us to understand social change and spot the marketing opportunities of the future. While the better market research agencies already work alongside their clients to interpret the data correctly, there is a move now to undertake ever more sophisticated research to understand businesses and other organizations within the context of the deep-rooted but evolving values of the societies in which they operate. Socioconsult, for example, is an international, research-based consultancy working in Europe and North America. It advises businesses and policy-makers on the implications of socio-cultural change for organizational development and communications. It employs extensive programmes of qualitative research to understand the various social milieux which make up a given society, then large-scale surveys to measure the core values of that society and how they are changing. The results provide the backdrop for understanding any particular client's business, what this rests on in terms of social, cultural and international patterns, and how this could change in the future (see Fig. 4.6). Part of the purpose of such research is to identify the seeds of social change early on before they become apparent through other means, and to assess their likely implications. Such research provides a valuable link between consultants who are employed to advise on organizational change, though often without research to support their recommendations, and researchers who are specialists in organizational and social change and also understand the nature of the information they collect at a fundamental level.

Costs of research

Compared with other elements of the communications mix, research is not particularly expensive. Normally the research buyer buys a complete project according to an agreed specification. There are not usually any add-ons apart, perhaps, from some additional computer analysis. Interpretation is usually given for free not as additional consultancy.

Some surveys are set up to cater for the needs of several buyers thereby spreading the overheads. These include general public omnibus surveys on which clients can buy individual question units for a few hundred pounds a time for samples which normally range from 1000 to 2000.

Syndicated surveys also cover specific markets such as financial services or motoring and MORI runs a range of studies among opinion leader audiences, such as MPs, business and trade journalists and the City. These are specifically designed to measure corporate images and the effectiveness of corporate communications and to monitor how these are changing over time.

Ad hoc survey costs depend on size and complexity and the audience being researched and can therefore range in price from a few thousand pounds up to several hundred thousand pounds for multi-public multi-country tracking surveys.

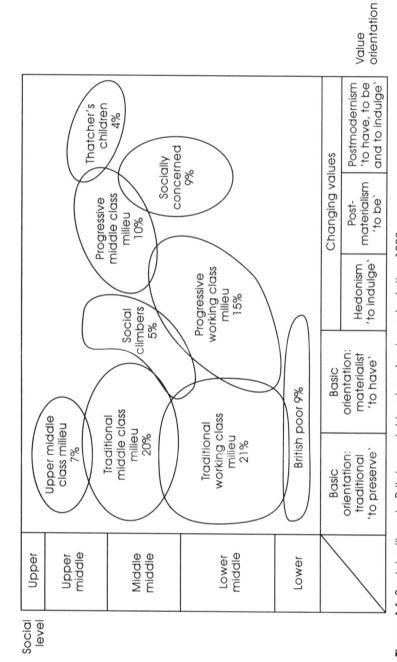

Figure 4.6 Social milieux in Britain: social level and value orientation 1990
Source: Socioconsult

Checklist

Peter Hutton and Robert Worcester have reviewed a wide range of applications for research techniques in both public and private sector marketing. We now need to consider how their propositions are evaluated. Remember, the key premise for research is to become better informed, so that decisions contain only sufficient risk. Confirmation of what you know, or believe you know, may be as valid as discovering what you do not know.

Questions to consider

4.1 What are the current assumptions on which the marketing proposition is based?

4.2 How valid are those assumptions?

4.3 How recently have you checked your customers' buying motivations?

4.4 What do you need to know about buyer perceptions of your business?

4.5 How well do you think you rate in comparison to your competitors?

4.6 What factors are you using to make that comparison?

4.7 How do you know who your competitors are?

4.8 What are the strengths and weaknesses of your competitors?

4.9 What do other stakeholders, besides your customers, think of your business?

4.10 Why does their opinion matter?

4.11 What are the macro factors influencing your business environment?

4.12 How will you establish the market potential for an innovation?

4.13 What innovations are your market(s) looking for?

4.14 What are the bench-mark standards of performance in your sector?

4.15 What do you know about interpretation of research data?

4.16 How credible are the various forms of research in your opinion?

4.17 How credible are they in the opinion of your general management team?

4.18 How much should you spend on research as a proportion of revenue?

4.19 How much do you know about the professional agencies in the research field?

4.20 How much research on your sector is already published/
    available?

4.21 What priority should you give to customer satisfaction
    research?

4.22 What priority should you give to new product development
    research?

4.23 What priority should you give to a corporate image survey?

4.24 What priority should be given to a staff attitudes survey?

Those 24 questions will be easy to answer if you are a significant
user of research techniques, whether in-house or out-sourced, but
they will be more challenging if you are not. Knowing where to
start and how to secure acceptance of the value of research in the
management team are critical points.

Give careful thought to what information you already have from
internal systems, such as the transactional data from accounts, and
what information you could get for yourself: postal customer
attitude surveys are relatively easy to distribute with corporate
literature, for example. Be aware that low response rates from a self-
selecting sample means results often have to be treated with
caution. Then, taking Porter's *Five Forces* model (see Chapter 2),
consider what you need to know about each of the forces—
suppliers, customers, substitute products or services, potential
entrants and your current competitors—and on what scale—
national, zonal, global. A particular one to watch is the impact of
technology on your business: the rate of change is so dramatic that
it is easy to miss the innovation that is going to change your world
forever.

Whatever you do, make sure that you are sufficiently well informed
to retain some control over your destiny.

5

Six ways to make advertising more productive

(Instead of just creative)

Robin Wight (WCRS)

I spoke to a wise client the other day about the worldwide recession. He said that originally he had seen himself as hanging on to a window ledge with his fingernails. Eventually, he hoped that when things got better he would be able to climb back into the room from which he had fallen. Now he recognizes that when he does the party will be over. The decade of the eighties was the exception not the rule. And that he and his company will have to find a way to be profitable in an era of flat economic growth.

Many agencies have been slower than their clients to recognize these changes. Too many have felt that the good times will come back again. That this is just a nasty blip on the radar screen of economic prosperity.

The fact is, taking a 25-year perspective, one can see that the pressure has been tightening for advertising agencies and their clients for a long time. For a long period, the gap between the amount of advertising a brand *needed* and the amount of advertising a brand *could afford to buy* has been growing bigger and bigger. Consider a few facts. In the USA, in 1965, three-quarters of all commercials were 60 seconds long. They actually called 30 second commercials 'half length commercials'. In 1995, nearly half of all American commercials were 'quarter length' or 15 seconds.

There has been a similar trend in Britain. In the mid-nineties 43 per cent of all commercials are under 30 seconds. But shortening is only one way to pad out an advertising budget shrunk by media inflation. Another is to cut the television ratings, and here we can see the most dramatic impact on major brands.

In 1965 Persil had 9000 television ratings (TVRs); in 1990 it was reduced to 2273. Kellogg's had 7125 TVRs reduced to 2691, Cadbury's Dairy Milk Chocolate had 4111 reduced to 627, Quality Street had 2466 reduced to 1073, Guinness had 4716 reduced to 1415.

Over that period these leading brands had their television ratings reduced by three to four times. It is clear, then, that advertisers are having to ration their ammunition. But what makes all these trends worse is that the evidence suggests that the advertising bullets are not hitting the targets like they used to.

If we look at the market for cars, be it in Australia, Britain, the USA or Germany, we find a rather salutary fact. Even allowing for inflation, it took twice as many dollars to sell a car in Australia in the late eighties than the late seventies. The same is true in the USA. In Britain it took three times as much.

And the story is no more encouraging if we look at beer. Across the world it is taking two to three times as much advertising to sell each barrel of beer as a decade earlier. The evidence, then, points to a reduced productivity for advertisements. Partly this comes from the reduced weight of advertising that has forced brands to operate on inadequate advertising expenditure. (And agencies behaving as though their advertising had far bigger budgets behind it.)

Those big brands of the sixties that I listed above averaged about 5000 TVRs a year. That produced 28 minutes of television advertising a year per consumer for those brands against each of their target consumers. Today, a typical brand is closer to 600 TVRs a year. And that generates just 3.5 minutes of advertising. If 28 minutes of advertising a year could be argued to be a needless extravagance then 3.5 minutes is certainly too little.

New competitors in the battle have added to the problem. In the lager market in Britain, for example, between 1988 and 1994 the number of brands increased by 67 per cent. Each of those new brands is bidding up the price of the existing brands' television air time, and so reducing the amount of expenditure per brand. The net result is a fragmentation of the total advertising market for lager in the mind of the consumer, whose brain—please note—has not expanded in proportion to the number of brands competing for a place in his or her memory.

In this confused fragmented situation, the existing brands have an enormous advantage. Because as the battle rages consumers have tended to stay loyal. In established markets, from lagers to baked beans to soup to detergents, we see that most leading brands in the forties are still the brand leaders today (*International Journal of Advertising*, 1984) (see Table 5.1). Even in newer markets, like lager, the original brand leader in Britain, Carling Black Label, is still brand leader in the mid-nineties. Much as I would like to put this down to brilliant advertising by WCRS, the fact is that brands established when quality differences were more easily perceived are harder to subsequently displace with basically parity products.

Table 5.1 Leading brands: comparison over 50 years

Leading UK brands	
1933	**1984 position**
Hovis, bread	No. 1
Stork, margarine	No. 1
Kellogg's, cornflakes	No. 1
Cadbury's, chocolate	No. 1
Rowntree, pastilles	No. 1
Schweppes, mixers	No. 1
Brooke Bond, tea	No. 1
Colgate, toothpaste	No. 1
Johnson, floor polish	No. 1
Kodak, film	No. 1
Ever Ready, batteries	No. 1
Gillette, razors	No. 1
Hoover, vacuum cleaners	No. 1

Leading US brands	
1933	**1984 position**
Swift Premium, bacon	No. 1
Eastman Kodak, cameras	No. 1
Del Monte, canned fruit	No. 1
Wrigley, chewing gum	No. 1
Nabisco, biscuits	No. 1
Ever Ready, batteries	No. 1
Gold Medal, flour	No. 1
Gillette, razors	No. 1
Coca Cola, soft drinks	No. 1
Campbell's, soup	No. 1
Ivory, soap	No. 1
Lipton, tea	No. 1
Goodyear, tyres	No. 1

Source: International Journal of Advertising, 1984

The annals of marketing are littered with new product failures that demonstrate the truth of this. Only 15 per cent of grocery products sold in the USA come from brands introduced since 1970—the rest are over 25 years old. In that period, North America has changed dramatically, as has virtually every advanced society, with new types of products pouring into the market. Many of these products are ones which consumers were not yet used to buying and were far more complex to evaluate such as hi-fi equipment and video cassette recorders (VCRs).

Faced with an explosion of choice, consumers can simplify their decision-making by staying with the brands that they know and concentrate their evaluative skills on the product categories that they do not know so well. As a result, in many markets, the dominant brand leader has got stronger and stronger.

We have now moved to the era of the giant super brands, the new *haves* of the marketing world. The *have-nots* are the new minor or declining brands with their 3.5 minutes of television advertising every 365 days struggling to keep on the supermarket shelves.

With the relative failure of above-the-line (i.e. broadcast or display advertising—all media) advertising to help them, it is not surprising that more and more of them switched their marketing funds into below-the-line. It is something that has been reported particularly in the recession of 1992. It happened again in the recession of the early eighties, but then was abandoned as marketing companies discovered that the new forms of promotion didn't work any better than the old forms of advertising.

Studies amply demonstrate how most below-the-line (i.e. literature, direct marketing, PR, sales promotion and point-of-sale) campaigns at best bring forward sales among existing users. They certainly fail to build the brand values that provide the long-term basis for a premium position in the market-place.

Of course, what is the good of a long-term strategy if the company goes bankrupt in the short term? The challenge for advertising in the mid-nineties is to recognize how the world has changed and create new strategies to help brands in very different situations from the golden years of the fat cat eighties. We need to remember the words of the great Lord Rutherford, who split the atom on a shoestring: 'We have no money so we shall have to think'.

The creative *renaissance* has been replaced by the more demanding creative *reformation*: a new tougher creative framework that needs more imagination, not less. For the business goals will be higher.

But the production budgets will be less. And the media budgets will be less. So we face a difficult task of producing masterpieces with much smaller canvasses to paint on and far fewer colours in our palette.

We have moved to the era, in short, where the creative mind has to be wider than the layout pad. We have moved from the era of advertising *creativity* to the era of advertising *productivity*.

There are no simple formulas that can transform advertising. But I do believe there are some frameworks that can help make advertising's imagination more productive. Six of these are described below.

Interrogating a product until it confesses to its strengths

All products are not created equal. Research shows that 74 per cent of new products that succeed outperform their rivals in consumer tests, compared to the 24 per cent superior performance among those new products that fail. Yet for how long has the advertising industry believed that they just had to put a new coat of varnish on the product to make it succeed in the market-place?

Now we have to go back to the product and seek to find the strengths that impress consumers and find a way to encapsulate them in advertising. This means going back to the fundamentals of advertising that we had forgotten when we slipped into the big budget entertainment business of the glittering eighties.

Remember 'Washed in live steam' that transformed the fortunes of Schlitz beer in America in the thirties? Product interrogation will not answer every advertising problem, but it will add a layer of extra knowledge that can make advertising more effective. BMW in Britain is probably the classic case history. Since the mid-eighties we have produced over 200 advertisements, most of which have used the grit of product knowledge to create a pearl of persuasion.

It is interesting how companies, like Heinz, have so effectively gone back to telling the basic facts about their products. The fact that their Tomato Ketchup comes out of the bottle more slowly because of its higher quality. The fact that they don't add sugar to their ingredients. In the same way, agencies need to get back to basics instead of relying on what is now an unaffordable creative soufflé to fluff up their clients' sales.

Advertising archaeology

Many clients have a powerful asset that they are not exploiting: a past advertising property that has been prematurely abandoned. Media costs today mean that advertising properties will increasingly need to be adapted, optimized and modified by agencies.

This goes against the grain of most agencies' beliefs. Danish Bacon, for example, had not used the line 'Good bacon has Danish written all over it' since the early eighties, yet we discovered that 60 per cent of shoppers recalled it. That meant that at today's media prices, there was a £40 million media investment of the past waiting to be reused. And that is why we spent £2 million doing that rather than trying to invent a completely new advertising property from scratch.

We did the same for Sanatogen, in retaining the 'Do you feel alright?' theme rather than abandoning it. Advertisers should now be reviewing their old larder of advertising ideas to see if there is something in it that could be revived. Agencies should be helping them.

Television posters

One simple way to get more out of your advertising budget is to use shorter length commercials. Most agencies describe this as a *cutdown* which clearly implies that something has been left out.

An alternative way of looking at it is to do what our French colleagues do. Instead of doing it as a commercial that has had something removed from it, they see it as a *poster* that has had something added: sound and motion.

The result is 10 and 20 second commercials that are purpose made for length. In the last six months of 1991 more than three-quarters of the commercials we produced were under 30 seconds in length. It helped clients such as Lunn Poly dominate the airwaves in a way that conventional 30 second commercials would not have allowed. It helped clients like Canon use television which they could not otherwise afford.

Short length commercials can't do all that a 30, 40 or even 60 second commercial can do. But neither are they the second-class advertising citizen too many agencies believe.

Publi-tising

Publi-tising is a cross between publicity and advertising, and though ugly, it is productive. It means designing your advertising to get media coverage, rather than exploiting it as an afterthought.

Like the way the electricity privatization used the Frank N. Stein character with the expectation that newspaper cartoonists would not be able to resist the temptation to use the idea in their cartoons. The extra visibility this gave the campaign was not paid for by the taxpayer, and helped make the campaign the most cost-effective privatization ever.

Virgin have used publi-tising effectively with their new 'mid-class' by tying in with current events. Heineken and Carling Black Label have made something of a tradition of it. It will be a technique that more advertisers will need to use in the next decade: and that will require a far closer alliance between advertising agencies and PR companies.

Creating ten-year advertising properties

The ad is dead, long live the campaign: that has to be the maxim for the nineties. The zig-zag of advertising campaigns that gave creatives and clients their chance to leave their mark upon the brand are no longer practical (and they were never desirable).

Creating long-term advertising properties is not easy; it is made even more difficult by the creative pitch that tends to be an advertising zig-zag factory. Our own humbling experience is that great campaigns often have false starts: the first two years of Carling Black Label showed that it was a potentially great campaign but the advertisements were not working. Happily the wise client had the courage to stay with the idea and help develop it.

Agencies will need to learn to be more open, to be more modest and to be more straightforward to create a relationship that has the maturity to support a long-running campaign and not stifle it prematurely at birth.

Advertising needs to be more than just advertising

Agencies need increasingly to focus on adding value to their clients and not just look for added commission. New opportunities in sponsorship, sponsored programmes and other traditionally non-agency areas create opportunities for agencies.

Like the sponsorship by Sega of the advertising coverage of the European Cup, where 70 different *tops* and *tails* for commercial breaks were created linking Sega into the world of football in an effective way. Conventionally agencies would not have been involved in such a process. But if they are going to serve the needs of their clients they must be involved in them in the future.

People who do not like change will not like the advertising industry of the nineties. Formulas that proved effective in the sixties, seventies and eighties will need to be thoroughly adapted and developed to be of value to clients in the very different and harsher world.

In doing this, there is the possibility that trust, which has been severely eroded in client–agency relationships, can be revived. Without that, and without some of the adaptations—not all of which are new—which I have described has been about, advertising will diminish in importance to more and more clients.

Which would be bad news for more and more agencies. But agency people are nothing if not adaptive. The fittest will survive and the smartest clients will find agencies that have adapted best.

Checklist

Robin Wight, ever one to break a tired mould, has spoken the unspeakable—the good times are over. Put another way, the ease with which the decision to spend above-the-line used to be taken is no longer possible: the risks accelerate with time, the duration of useful effect from campaigns is reducing and the certainty of beneficial payback can no longer be taken for granted.

Yet the myth is not quite dead. Heavy above-the-line spend remains favourite for fast brand build, despite the decrease in signal-to-noise ratio for each competitor and the consequent increase is cost against effectiveness. Robin Wight makes the salutary point that in spite of the frenzy in competitive up-spend in key, brand-dependent, sectors, no real change in brand positions seem to come through.

The forensic marketer is, at the very least, restless about the continuing low hit rate for new products, especially those brought fast to market with above-the-line fanfare. The truth is that most new products fail. While accepting that there is some inevitability in this, I am convinced that with the application of more science and less (ego-fuelled) art, the forensic marketer can sharply improve the odds of a first time strike for new products—and, in the process, enhancing the probability of costly above-the-line spend producing effective results. How this transition can be attained is very much centred around attitudes to the vaunted claims of above-the-line techniques. The myth of its Utopian power lives on.

We must practise the rigorous disciplines of forensic analysis well in advance of arriving at the range of solutions in the communications tool-set. It may seem a statement of the obvious, but it cannot be avoided none the less, that as the risk factors rise—such as the exponential growth in production costs for TV commercials—so must the preparation effort. After billions of advertising spend over the decades it might be thought that the key learning points had been established to the point that most are taken as axiomatic. Yet it is not so. We reinvent the wheel with prodigious zeal, time and time again.

I am convinced that the root cause lies in the generic resistance of marketers to think long, as well as tactical. Given that every marketer wants to make an impact, and a personal one at that, it is predictable that trying something new is seen as the best way. It is inconvenient, at best, to think incrementally, consolidating gains and seeking improvements at the margin. Admittedly the very best brand-led organizations are spectacularly consistent over time and enjoy the rewards of cumulative communications. They are enviable and Robin Wight's examples merit close study. That said, the majority of marketers I meet have great difficulty in discerning between valuable experience to carry forward and well-identified factors that are positively known to be negative that must be dropped.

It is certainly true that with such powerful media as radio, television and national print, identifying the critical variables in performance is difficult, but not impossible. As Robin Wight argues, a good deal of systematic reflection before new campaigns are even outlined is not just a 'nice to', but the minimum standard of professional behaviour—applying equally to the client as well as the agency. 'What do we know, how do we know it or how can we confirm what we think we know?' are questions heard less frequently than they might be. Is this perhaps a symptom of solutionitis?

Thus, in this the heartland of marketing communications we need a catechism embodying a good deal of rigour in helping us to approach and evaluate each opportunity. The following checklist provides a start-line, upon which readers will almost certainly wish to build their own systematic, and forensically oriented, criteria.

Questions to consider

5.1 What is our prime motivation for above-the-line spend?

5.2 What criteria do we apply to judge whether that motivation is justified?

5.3 What do we believe the roles of above-the-line communications are?

5.4 What is the evidence that these roles are deliverable?

5.5 What are the risks that we must appraise prior to initiating above-the-line campaigns?

5.6 What are the core strengths of our product/service?

5.7 What is the evidence that the market(s) see the same strengths as we do?

5.8 What is our motivation for considering above-the-line spend?

5.9 How does this approach fit with every other aspect of the communications mix we deploy?

5.10 What are the core values that every campaign must contain in order to avoid positional shift (unless wanted)?

5.11 What elements must be included in the agency brief before creative work is commenced?

5.12 What is the competitive environment for above-the-line in our sector?

5.13 Are we adding to the market-place *noise* or achieving a distinctive *voice*?

5.14 What are the performance measures for above-the-line campaigns?

5.15 How objective are those measures and what systems are in place to deliver them?

5.16 What are the alternative communications strategies (or tactics) that could deliver similar performance outputs at the same or higher cost-effectiveness?

5.17 How will we determine what *critical mass* is in terms of impact from above-the-line—will we spend enough?

5.18 How well are we able to identify variables in the above-the-line campaign so that we can positively learn in order to contribute to our cumulative knowledge?

5.19 How well integrated are our other communications with the messages in our intended above-the-line campaign(s)?

5.20 What are our objectives in terms of market retention?

5.21 What are our objectives in terms of new business?

5.22 Are these objectives compatible one with the other?

5.23 How rigorous should our agency be in challenging the business case behind the brief and will we listen to and respond to those challenges?

5.24 How clear are we who owns the business brief and who owns the creativity—does your agency agree?

5.25 How objective are you really being about your use of above-the-line?

Robin Wight makes a generic call to marketers to consider the maturity of their approach to this, the most dramatic of communications tools. Because of the glamour and the perceived power it is understandable that perceived competitive pressure to use above-the-line, let alone internal pressure, is overwhelming. The forensically oriented marketer will build an objective argument for its use, and will be determined to derive cumulative learning from each campaign as well as tactical advantage. The risk factors are becoming so high that to have any other orientation is, arguably, to take an unacceptable career risk too. Perhaps that is enough to straighten out our thinking.

6

Corporate image

Credo or convenience?

Wally Olins (Chairman, Wolff Olins)

The death and rebirth of the British motor industry

Since the mid-sixties the bulk of the British motor industry, operating under a succession of anonymous corporate names—BMC, BMH, British Leyland and BL—and remorselessly shuffling together an increasingly tired and worn set of brands—Austin, Morris, Triumph, Rover, MG and so on—managed to achieve the unique distinction of becoming simultaneously a national joke and a national disgrace.

During its apparently interminable period of crisis, which derived from a combination of every malaise afflicting British industry of the period, it suffered inevitably from bad marketing. Many of its marketing weaknesses can be attributed to a total lack of comprehension or control of corporate and brand image.

There were constant changes of image policy. A volume car division, called Austin Morris, and a specialist car division called Jaguar Rover-Triumph (JRT for short) lasted a year or so. Austin Rover turned up, only to disappear again. MG badges were stuck on to Metro cars for a bit. A new brand name, Princess, appeared and was then dropped. And so the whole frightful charade went on. Beset by every known corporate disease the corporation did not have time to examine, let alone comprehend, the power of the images with which it was so frenetically playing.

Then gradually everything changed for the better. Jaguar, under a new and vigorous regime, honed its image, became independent and got a quotation on the London Stock Exchange. Eventually, despite the fact that Jaguar was losing money, was wrestling to improve an archaic factory, and that its cars were still plagued with unreliability, Ford paid $2.5 billion for the company. Ford bought Jaguar for its image. Its purchase of Jaguar was a tacit admission that Ford with all its muscle and skills believed that it could not internally generate a brand that could fight on even ground with BMW and Mercedes.

The British Leyland part of the story is also interesting and instructive. BL became Rover. It hived off Land Rover into a different division, and using Honda mechanicals, opted for a niche in quality cars. Gradually its passenger cars started to look like lineal descendants of the old Rover. In this way Rover went back to its roots as the doctor's friend. Cynics might say that the current Rover 400, 600 and 800 series are simply Japanese products with olde Englishe radiator grilles. They are; but it works. Rover dealer showrooms, publicity material and products all reflect the same coherent, corporate image. Rover cars, which look and feel like English cars but with Japanese product quality built in, are now marketed successfully against Volvo, Saab and BMW not just in Britain, but in major international markets as well. In fact Rover has become so successful that it has now been bought by the company whose image it has envied and admired for so long—BMW. These two examples reveal a lot about both corporate and brand image— its management and its mismanagement.

Brand and corporate image in the struggle for markets

Jaguar and Rover are now as good as their competition. They are reliable and perform well. But nowadays, all cars are reliable and perform well—that is taken for granted. Success comes only when the product is as good as the competition and the image is better. Rover is not taking business away from Volvo because it is a better car, but because it is just as good and offers an alternative image which some people find more seductive. In other words its appeal is both rational and emotional.

The lesson: choice and the rational/emotional mix

The image issue in marketing is largely based around this

characteristic human mix. When other things, like price, quality and service, are equal or unquantifiable, most of us will buy the product/service which we like better. Emotion is the key.

We all as consumers like to think that we are able to choose between one product/service and another on some kind of rational basis, such as on price, or quality, or service. But price for price, in most areas of the market-place you get what you pay for. In about 80 per cent of the product/services that are marketed today, rational choice is simply not possible. How can you make a rational choice between competing brands of petrol, between the offers of different financial institutions, even between the products of competing chemical companies?

The vision/core idea

In order to be successful every company has to market products that are as good as the competition in price, quality and service, that encapsulate a clear, simple idea which emotionally differentiates them from competitors, and which some consumers will prefer. Burberry raincoats are sold in the international market-place not only because they keep you dry in wet weather, but also on the basis of a kind of rural upper-class Englishness.

While it is true that the products of most companies are pretty similar, the companies that make them are not. Each company is unique. The vision of the brand or the company has to be rooted either in history and tradition, or in its aspiration. The vision has to ring true and be individual. The vision is what differentiates the company or the brand from its competitors. The vision has to be communicated clearly, consistently and coherently through everything that the brand or company touches.

Four channels: product, environment, communication, behaviour

There are four channels by which the organization can project a clear idea of what it is and what it stands for. All of these are important, but they vary in significance according to what is being marketed; they are product, environment, communication and behaviour.

Product

Products and services are what you make or sell. Sometimes the product and how it performs is much the most significant factor in influencing how the brand or company is perceived. It is, for example, the appearance and performance of a Jaguar car which largely influences the way we perceive Jaguar as a brand and a company. The image of Jaguar is product dominated.

Environment

Environments are where you make or sell your products or services. In some organizations, like retail stores, hotels and leisure centres, the environment is crucial in presenting the image. The core idea of Holiday Inns is most clearly perceived through the environments of the hotels themselves. The way they look and feel is the key to the way in which the Holiday Inns' organization wants its hotel products to be perceived.

Communication

There are some companies whose brands derive their image from the packaging, advertising and other promotional material which enfolds them and through which they are presented. In these cases advertising and other forms of communication largely convey the core idea. Many consumer goods from Persil to Pepsi fall into this category.

Behaviour

Finally, there are those organizations whose personality and style emerge not so much through what they look like, what they make or where they live, as through the way in which they behave.

These are, for the most part, service organizations like banks, airlines, police forces, health authorities, and so on. A common characteristic of such organizations is that it is the most junior staff who have the most contact with the outside world and are therefore largely responsible for establishing how the organization as a whole is perceived. The RAC get-you-home service is for example dependent upon its roving mechanics for its image.

Four definitions: image, identity, corporation, brand

Image and identity

Although the differences between image and identity are largely semantic they can create some confusion so it is best to get them out of the way. The identity is what the organization projects. All organizations carry out thousands of transactions every day. The people in them buy things, sell things, make things, promote things, write, telephone, meet and otherwise carry out a multitude of activities with customers, suppliers, collaborators, governments and inevitably with their own staff. The totality of the impact of all of these transactions adds up to its identity.

So the corporation projects an identity whether it is aware of it or not and out of this its publics build an image. Even if the corporation makes no attempt to control all its manifestations of identity, its publics will still build up an image, although this image is likely to be both negative and confused. The image then is everything that the audience perceives.

Corporation and brand

Now let us look at the differences between corporation and brand. A corporation exists in three dimensions. First, it employs people, second, it owns buildings, third, it has relationships with customers, suppliers and collaborators. It makes and sells things, sometimes under its own name and sometimes under other names.

The brand exists only in two dimensions. It exists for the benefit of one audience—the customer. It is the puppet of the marketeer within the corporation who in turn acts as the ventriloquist, manipulates the brand and determines its actions. Sometimes the brand has the same name as the corporation, in which case, when the corporation deals with the customer, it is for practical purposes the brand. More often, though, the corporation operates through a number of brands, which it may or may not endorse with its own name and identity.

Developing a clear identity structure

In order to sustain a clear, coherent and consistent image, every organization has to develop a logical identity structure. There are three models: monolithic, endorsed, and branded identity. Each has advantages and disadvantages. None of them is intrinsically superior to any of the others. It is possible to find examples of different identity structures among successful competing companies in the same industry.

Monolithic

This is where the organization uses one name and one visual system throughout. Companies with a monolithic identity have usually grown mainly organically, and they tend to operate in closely related activities. The strength of the monolithic identity is that because everything that the organization does has an identical name, style and character, the organization and its products can be clear, consistent and mutually supportive. In three quite different fields, BP, Porsche, and Tesco exemplify the monolithic identity type.

Endorsed

This is where the organization endorses companies and brands which it owns with its own name. Sometimes this happens because a company makes acquisitions and finds itself with a number of names, many of which have high value in the market-place. The acquiring company is anxious to preserve the goodwill associated with these acquisitions, but at the same time to associate its own name with theirs. Nestlé, in the consumer goods field, is an example of such a company. It bought Rowntree, whose brands are now also endorsed by Nestlé—the ultimate owner.

Another example is Forte, which endorses hotel brands of various levels of price and quality—Forte Grand, Forte Posthouse, Forte Travelodge, and so on. It does this to show that Forte standards are applied to all of its activities.

Branded identity

Some companies, especially those in consumer products, separate their identity as corporations from those of the brands and companies they own (e.g. Unilever). So far as the final consumer is concerned, the corporation does not exist. What the customer perceives is the brand. Brands have names, reputations, life cycles, and personalities of their own, and they may even compete with other brands from the same company.

Issues

Although each of these identity structures is equally legitimate depending on the marketing circumstances faced by the corporation, most organizations, bound by tradition and orthodox practice, tend to follow one or other of these structures almost regardless of evolving circumstances. However, there are some signs that things are beginning to change.

Banks, for instance, have traditionally followed the monolithic route. They still tend to use one name wherever they go. When they merge or take over other banks they usually keep the old name or create a single new name. For example, the merged Banco Central and Banco Hispano Americano in Spain produced Banco Central Hispano. However, with a widening range of financial services—insurance, pensions and mortgages—and the increasing technological opportunity, leading to banking by telephone and similar developments, there is pressure upon banks to develop separate brands which have none of the traditional banking baggage. Hence Midland's First Direct or Union Bank of Finland's Solo are both advanced technology brands deliberately created to be distanced from the image of the traditional banks which devised them.

While a distinct brand like First Direct can be created completely from scratch, with a clear, brand idea of its own, an endorsed identity shares much of the endorsing corporation's image.

The same effect can also be observed the other way round. Some major marketing organizations traditionally dedicated to the branding route, like Unilever and Nestlé, seem to be inching towards endorsing brand ranges because it appears in the long run to be more economical to operate with a corporate endorsement.

Creating a corporate brand

Although many brands are created, their failure rate is high, and they often sink without trace. New corporate brands are created less frequently, and even then, the success rate is low.

Q8

The case history of the creation of Q8 is interesting; first, because it is big, second, because it is successful, third, because it is both a corporation and a brand, and fourth, because its development mainly followed an orthodox methodology but ignored it when appropriate.

To join the big league in the international oil business you have to be rich and brave. Kuwait Petroleum is both. In 1984 the company decided to go into the retail petrol business worldwide, which made it the first OPEC (Organization of Petroleum-Exporting Countries) country to move in that direction.

The basis for development was for Kuwait Petroleum's international arm to acquire the greater part of Gulf Oil's European network. By agreement KPI had to get rid of the old Gulf Oil name and symbol. The company opted for an entirely new name and identity, intended for possible eventual worldwide application, linked—and this was another brave decision—to a pricing policy aimed at the same level as the competition.

The images projected by all the major oil companies were studied in detail. As each of them was carefully examined, it became clear that the differences between them were not very great. It seemed clear that there was an opportunity for a major new brand aimed at a younger quite affluent well-educated audience.

Working with Wolff Olins, KPI introduced a new name, Q8 (based on the English pronunciation of Kuwait), and a new symbol, based around the idea of sails and sailing, like traditional Kuwaiti trading vessels (see Fig. 6.1). The name, visual style and overall design of the stations was unlike the competition and clearly aimed at the international market-place of younger, well-educated English-speaking (or reading or writing) audience.

The programme was introduced in the orthodox fashion: first to staff and then to dealers, through seminars, teach-ins and so on. The staff and dealer network, who had become apathetic after years of uncertainty under Gulf Oil, responded enthusiastically to the programme.

The changeover from Gulf Oil to Q8 took place in 1986. Over 3000 petrol stations were involved in six European countries. Just before the change took place the Gulf Oil share in the six countries was a shade under 4 per cent. After the change to Q8 the market share rose to 5.5 per cent. This represents a volume increase of nearly 50 per cent. The market was static so the increase came at competitors' expense. In succeeding years Q8 has sustained its position.

Although there has, of course, been some advertising, the company

Figure 6.1 The Q8 logo

attributes the success of its programme largely to the impact of the new corporate image programme.

Developing a clear corporate or brand image

Q8, Rover, Jaguar, First Direct, Forte and other relatively recent corporate and brand image successes all have certain characteristics in common. They are based around a clear idea—a vision—and they are executed with obsessive thoroughness through the complete spectrum of activities in which the consumer perceives the brand.

Four lessons to learn from these successes

First, be clear about where your product fits in the identity structure. Is it monolithic like Porsche, branded like First Direct, or endorsed like Forte Posthouse?

Second, be certain that your product is at least as good as the competition in terms of its performance, price and quality—the rational factors.

Third, get the emotional elements—the elements which will enable you to win—right. Be clear about the vision or the core idea. Be certain about what your brand is trying to say and to whom. Try to understand what competitive brands are saying and make sure that your brand says something which is different, attractive and above all credible.

Fourth, pay attention to all aspects of the product and its delivery system. Where appropriate see that environments, communication and behaviour are coherent and cohesive. Most brands fail because they do not deliver. If you manage a friendly and efficient telephone banking brand, be sure that you train your staff so that their behaviour reflects the claim. There is nothing more likely to cause sudden death than a brand that does not deliver.

If you get all of these things right your brand may have a chance, just a chance, of success.

Working together

The corporate and brand image activity is in the nature of things the result of collective effort between people working in a wide range of disciplines—marketing, advertising, communication, manufacturing, sales, purchasing, finance, organizational behaviour and others.

The rules involved in creating a successful image are strict, but straightforward. They are based, like so many of the rules in business, on the application of common sense to experience and to sound training.

Good luck.

Checklist

The winner of the British Quality of Management Awards in 1993 was BTR plc (one of the UK's largest industrial conglomerates, including brands like Hawker Siddley and Dunlop), with Marks and Spencer and Glaxo as the runners-up. Besides being voted the best managed company in the UK for sustainable growth in shareholder value, BTR is massively profitable and sufficiently diversified to have a good counter-cyclical capability—enviable and, to all but institutional shareholders, invisible. On the other hand, Marks and

Spencer, besides being highly rated for its management capability, is arguably the most consciously corporately imaged UK business.

Two successful businesses and two profoundly different approaches to image and brand management. That is a key learning point and one well established in Wally Olins's thoughtful observations: we must not think of corporate image purely in terms of street-level visibility. Corporate image is a complex amalgam of factors that include the product performance, the personality of the organization and its voice or communications style. It is open to each organization to decide where its image potential lies, but, as Wally Olins points out, product image differentiation is becoming harder to achieve as more and more products/services become commodity-like. I am particularly keen to emphasize the style or personality attributes of the organization because these have a massive bearing on the way customers feel about doing business with us. When, in Chapter 9, we come to look at relationship marketing, the connection between positive identification with the personality of the brand image and a willingness to remain a loyal customer is absolute.

The challenge of corporate and brand image for general management, not simply the marketing function, is how to develop them in ways which are responsive to changing customer needs and perceptions without having to completely re-engineer them every five years or so and run the risk of losing some of the accumulated values in the process. I have stressed that the business and marketing strategies must, above all, allow for an adaptive approach, sensitive to market, competition, technology, organization and societal factors. The corporate image requires a broad consistency that values the long-view, while allowing dynamic response to changing environments. This is what puts the issue in the realms of general management responsibility.

There are, however, times when an old, and perhaps long-established image is no longer appropriate and requires a complete redesign. That is a moment of truth for the organization and fraught with risk—hence the value of understanding the professional criteria for image management offered by Wally Olins.

Questions to consider

6.1   What are the product attributes of our corporate image?
6.2   What are the environmental (point-of-sale) attributes of our corporate image?

6.3 What are the communications attributes of our corporate image?

6.4 What are the behavioural or personality attributes of our corporate image?

6.5 What ought each of these to be to meet our overall business, as well as marketing, strategy objectives?

6.6 How consistent are we in the application of our corporate image across all functional areas of the organization?

6.7 How consistent are we in the use of our brand images?

6.8 How well do we understand the brand attributes as perceived by customers, prospects and other, strategic, stakeholders?

6.9 What brand attributes are we trying to project?

6.10 What are our competitors' strengths and weaknesses in corporate image terms?

6.11 What aspects of buyer motivation, rational or irrational, are we consciously targeting in our marketing mix?

6.12 How fragile is our corporate image?

6.13 How appropriate is our corporate image to today's market-place?

6.14 How appropriate is our corporate image to tomorrow's market-place?

6.15 How do we know the answers to Questions 6.13 and 6.14?

6.16 What aspects of our brand attributes do we wish to develop?

6.17 What are the critical success factors for achieving the brand perceptions we seek?

6.18 What impact on our key performance indicators does the management of our corporate and brand images have?

6.19 How will we establish progress in brand development?

6.20 What is the significance of our corporate image to each stakeholder and why?

6.21 How well does our corporate image meet the expectations of each stakeholder?

6.22 What are the core attributes of corporate image that we must manage for all stakeholders?

6.23 Should we commission a corporate image survey to establish our current position *vis-à-vis* our competitors?

6.24 Where should the responsibility for brand and corporate image lie within the organization?

6.25 What could we do to develop each of the four dimensions of image (product, environment, communication and behaviour) to achieve first choice status in our chosen markets and what is the correlation between these dimensions and our core competences (see Chapter 2)?

The corporate general manager, as well as the functional specialist, will be highly sensitive to the prize to be had from achieving a strong magnetic brand and corporate image: they attract business to you and away from the competition or even other applications for disposable income. Corporate image and brands are the tireless ambassadors for your business—they never sleep. They are, however, fragile and prone to premature death if tactically abused: the 'fourth quarter fire fight', chasing any sale at any price, is more fatal than a 'flu epidemic in killing off brands and customers. Arguably it is the responsibility of forensic marketers to ensure that the issues of brand and corporate image are fully understood by, and are responsibly enhanced by, the full gamut of functional areas, whether purchasing, sales, engineering, R&D finance, personnel or production. No other issue is so critically a shared accountability: there can be no opt-out or inconsistency. How much of a battle that statement will create in general management circles I am not sure, but Wally Olins and I are unrepentant in giving it exceptional emphasis in the forensic argument.

7

Public and media relations

Well-informed publics?

Jeffrey Lyes (Good Relations, Lowe Bell Communications)

If you run any kind of business you are in public relations. Or rather, you are subject to public relations. You don't need to have a formal public relations policy or programme nor do you even need to make a conscious spending decision. Like it or not, people—customers, staff, shareholders, trading partners—are forming opinions and making decisions on the basis of what they perceive of you: what they perceive of your public relations. So far as they are concerned the perceptions are real. You may agree or disagree—or be completely unaware. But all the time the real experts on the subject, the public, are weighing up who you are and what you stand for. Then they are voting with their pockets (see Fig 7.1).

The decision you have to make is twofold: Do you care? If you care, how much do you care? To those of us in the communications business it is still astonishing to see how little effort some companies put into controlling and directing their public relations. Until, that is, they hit a real problem and then desperately cast around for a quick fix.

It is no coincidence that many of Britain's most successful companies are run by people who take communications seriously and understand the advantages they gain from good public relations. This applies equally in bad times as well as good. A well-known example is that of John Egan, who went into Jaguar and used his public relations skills to great effect to address the product quality issues with staff and customers alike and so turn necessity into a virtue. But when the *Financial Times* runs a story headline 'Good PR gives GM Chief the edge' (as it did when espionage allegations at General Motors' German offshoot flew thick in the air in the summer of 1993) you had better believe public relations has

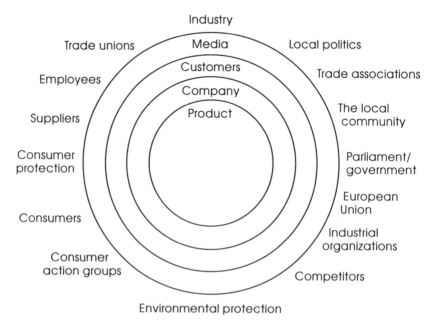

Figure 7.1 Evaluation of public relations needs to work like a radar—continuously sweeping audiences to monitor reputation and gather intelligence on opportunities or concerns

well and truly arrived as a strategic discipline. Especially as two weeks later the *Financial Times* even front paged complaints by British Gas that the industry's regulator had been 'manipulating the media' rather than minding its own monopoly. Everybody, it seems, can be a PR practitioner.

In the routine running of a business you may feel that you will rarely have the opportunity for such grand gestures or great campaigns. This may be true. But it does not need a big event to sway customers in a buyer's market. A critical press item about a product can begin a process of steady sales erosion magnified by the insidious word of mouth condemnation that follows as sure as night follows day.

A flattering press item, on the other hand, can position you ahead of the game and create a positive and productive climate for sales. It follows, therefore, that a marketing strategy that ignores public relations is at best incomplete and at worst greatly weakened. On a competitive basis major opportunities may be overlooked and on a defensive basis loop-holes can exist through which the opposition can undermine you.

Akio Morita, the late chairman of Sony, reminds us that
'Communication is the most important form of marketing'. Public
relations is all about accurate, considered and persuasive
communication delivered in a way that is relevant to the recipient.

At Good Relations we formally define public relations as 'the use of
third party endorsement to inform and persuade'. The third parties
may be either media or relevant experts. The persuasive power of
public relations comes from this independent endorsement. In
separating public relations from advertising it is not unfair to say
that advertising is what you claim about yourself, whereas public
relations is what other people accept and understand about you.

The skill in public relations, therefore, is in winning the acceptance
of the most influential media or commentators. The audience is
convinced because they know you have not bought the
endorsement but won it on merit. As a result, an editorial item in a
newspaper or on television is reckoned to be several times as
valuable—as persuasive—as an equivalent size advertisement. This
equation becomes more interesting when one takes into account the
high cost of paid space or air time in the first place. Not to mention
the signs of *advertising fatigue* that some consumers are already
displaying. The video 'zapper' was a wonderful liberator for the
advertisingly oppressed.

An independent qualitative researcher, Tim Reid (1993), points out
that today's consumers are *marketing literate* to a terrifying extent.
His report is entitled (refreshingly or frighteningly, depending on
your vested interest) 'They know what you are trying to do'. It
shows that when consumer products perform more or less
identically, as so many now do, the deciding factors on purchase are
the beliefs held about the brand or manufacturer by the purchaser.

Consumers are now looking beyond the packaging and into the corporate values of the brand or company. Anita Roddick's Body Shop
is a classic example of the success that can *be built* (if not held) from
timely identification with consumer values. But Reid's research also
emphasizes that it is not just what you communicate, but *how* you
communicate, that the consumer is sensitive to. He suggests that
both the content and form of the communication are closely checked
out by our enlightened consumer to see how closely they relate to
the individual consumer's tastes and values. In this context advertising faces a huge challenge to hit its targets sympathetically and cost
effectively. Public relations, on the other hand, can be economically
structured to utilize a spread of selected publications with a message
tailored in each case to the particular interests of each publication's

readers. Public relations thus becomes increasingly useful in fragmented markets where the wastage and weaknesses of advertising become a serious problem. So let us assume there is a prima facie case for public relations and move on to the second part of the question, which was 'If you care, how much do you care?'

Let us put the question another way. How do you want your company and its products to be perceived in the market-place? How important is this to you? Which groups of people matter most to you?

These questions set your objectives and should immediately throw up the parameters within which to consider the role of public relations and the priority to attach to it. Add to your answers a list of opportunities you can see and the possible threats you might face and you are well on the way to quantifying your needs. It is not always easy to be objective and this is one reason why public relations consultants have emerged into the mainstream of business life since the mid-eighties. The perspective of a well-informed independent adviser can be invaluable; the adviser will also bring creative ideas and the benefit of hard-won experience as to what works and what does not.

In addition to your general public relations needs the analysis will probably reveal specific instances where public relations techniques are particularly appropriate. Some of these will now be discussed.

Exploiting news value as a competitive edge

Your product may have a unique topicality or a performance advantage over the opposition. So you have to make the most of it. Getting in quick via the trade and consumer media will consolidate your lead and create a productive climate for your salesforce or retailers. There is now an enormous range of titles through which to target your audience and a well-organized public relations plan will do this cost effectively.

For example, to mark the fortieth anniversary of the Queen's Coronation, the Royal Mint produced collector versions of the Coronation anniversary crown. Public relations techniques were used to support sales to the public and businesses in addition to an advertising campaign. News releases were tailored to appeal to gift columns in the press and in women's magazines; the product was shown on television and described by radio; a national competition was staged through a Sunday newspaper to award silver

Coronation crowns to babies born on the anniversary. The
Coronation crown coins sold exceptionally well and the Royal
Mint's sales tracking system proved that many tens of thousands of
pounds worth of sales were directly attributable to the public
relations campaign.

Dealing with sensitivities

Being seen to recognize and respond to public concerns rather than
burying your head in the sand can turn a potential problem into a
demonstration of corporate responsibility.

For example, a US company, specializing in waste recycling,
discovered the vagaries of the British town planning system and the
power of NIMBY-ism (Not In My Back Yard) when it started
building a new plant in Yorkshire. A popular local resident began a
Toxic Waste Out campaign and, as press and public support
mounted, it was alleged that the local authority had breached
planning laws in approving the plant. The case was directed to the
High Court and construction work was forced to a standstill. At this
point the company sought public relations advice and a four-point
plan was devised, to stop the rot in the local press; to get the
company's message into the community; to seek endorsement of the
scheme from local civic leaders; to propose a constructive way
forward for the company and the community.

As facts gradually neutralized media hysteria, newsletters were
issued to every household, civic and media open days were held,
and a joint monitoring committee was proposed by the local MP.
Although the local authority was found by the High Court to be in
breach of planning regulations, the judge ruled that the
development could proceed.

Educating the consumer

Public relations techniques can convey a great deal of information.
A programme of editorial features and placed articles can, for
example, help explain the role of new products and ideas to
consumers.

For example, NutraSweet is a branded sweetener and the vital
ingredient in the highly successful low-calorie varieties of soft
drinks that contain no sugar and virtually no calories. NutraSweet

also forms the basis of Canderel, the biggest selling table-top sweetener. A branded ingredient is in itself an unusual marketing strategy and since its launch in 1983 NutraSweet has used public relations on a consistent basis to create and maintain awareness and confidence with trade customers, such as Coca Cola and Pepsi, and millions of their consumers.

In addition to an ongoing programme of consumer and trade media relations, NutraSweet has established links with consumer groups and special interest groups, such as diabetics, and operates a telephone information service for consumers. The core values of the brand lie within a healthy lifestyle and in 1993 NutraSweet decided to reinforce this positioning by sponsoring the London Marathon. New facets were added to the sponsorship by NutraSweet, including the adoption of the Snowdon Award Scheme for disabled people and the production of a London Marathon Book as a photographic record. A media relations team was dedicated to ensuring that the event received the widest possible media coverage.

Although the NutraSweet London Marathon was to some extent a mature promotional device and had enjoyed previous big name sponsors, research by NutraSweet after the event showed that extensive media coverage had sent brand name awareness levels to a record high.

Adding value to your marketing strategy

Other ways in which public relations can add value to your marketing strategy include the following.

Projecting leadership

A company or brand that is always in the news is more likely to be perceived as the market leader.

Changing legislation

Using publicity in conjunction with lobbying can be an effective way of projecting your case—and illustrating the support that you have.

Promoting corporate values

Embarking on award schemes, giving speeches at conferences or launching community involvement schemes can be effective ways of underpinning corporate philosophy.

Preparing for the worst

Crisis preparedness is a must, not just for FMCG (fast-moving consumer goods) companies, but all manner of service companies. You will be judged by the public not only on what caused the crisis but also on how you dealt with it. The golden rule is to be as well rehearsed as possible and have your allies well briefed before there is a crisis. This will establish authoritative support for your policies and a helpful response when you need it.

Opening channels of communication

As can now be seen, a public relations programme is likely to be a mix of the strategic and the highly tactical. But as flexible as it is, you cannot expect to turn public relations on and off like a tap. As we saw at the start of this chapter you are living with public relations, of a sort, all the while. What you do when you formalize it is to open a series of channels of communication. It can take time to get complex messages understood and your audience will expect consideration in return. If you say to the press one day that you are a good source of material they will expect a professional standard of service and ready access to your people thereafter. And they will expect this even when it does not quite suit the marketing plan. So you should enter into the use of public relations with your eyes open.

You might also be tempted by the notion that public relations is a free type of advertising. Certainly the gains in media coverage can be extraordinarily high for the right idea. And, odd as it seems, public relations consultancies frequently undersell their own value. Developing and managing a productive media relations campaign can be very time intensive. This is because different publications like to have exclusive angles relevant to their readership. So the programme becomes a series of tailormade packages targeted to specific journalists, their publications and their readership. The days of a standard press release are all but gone.

Similarly, you must be realistic about the nature of press relations.

The press loves—and needs—its heroes. But it also loves—and needs—to see them occasionally fall. The press loves to be spoonfed an exclusive diet of tasty news morsels, but it also delights in biting the hand that feeds it, particularly when the line between good communication and self-serving publicity is crossed.

This appetite was once prevalent only in the popular tabloids. But it is now visible throughout the press and even in specialist trade press that once slavishly reflected the self-interests of the sector they serve.

Investigative journalism, born out of consumerism, fuelled by political scandals from Watergate onwards and buoyed up by media competition, is now a fact of life. Accountability via the media can come as a shock to the unsuspecting chief executive. Reputations that have taken decades to grow can be threatened overnight, justly or unjustly. In media relations there is no carpet under which to sweep unpleasant truths so it pays to recognize the problems and develop in advance the arguments that justify your actions. Equally, if a company is open to ill-informed comment or mischievous disinformation then anticipation is half the battle. The other half may well be in practising and polishing television interview techniques to ensure you are able to present your case coherently under pressure.

The journalist is an opportunistic sort of animal and as much as it can be a nuisance, this curiosity also provides an ever open door for the topical idea. Your public relations programme, therefore, needs to be linked not only to the marketing programme and the position as seen by your company, but also to the wider events in the market-place and the community as a whole. This will also help ensure that you can readily identify corporate platforms in keeping with the values you wish to be seen sharing with your customers.

Managing public relations

By now you (hopefully) have a general appreciation of what can be involved in a public relations programme. But two questions probably still remain: How do you manage it? How do you measure it?

On the management front there are basically three options.

First, do it yourself, with the possibility of learning the tricks of the trade the hard way and at some considerable distraction to your other duties.

Second, hire specialists and bring them in-house. They can then get to know the business and the key press very well indeed. But they may tend to become a little sterile on the ideas front with the passage of time. They may also need outside reinforcement for particular issues such as large-scale events or expert assistance on activities like lobbying.

Third, hire consultants and get the benefit of wide experience, an ideas pool, lots of useful contacts and true objectivity. That is, if you pick a good consultancy. The sad facts is that not all consultancies are the same and there are still ex-clients around who have ended up dissatisfied and disillusioned after a consultancy experience.

Interestingly, very few prospective clients seem to ever ask to talk to other clients of a consultancy before they engage it. The formal process of presentations, short-listings and proposals still seems to be viewed as corporately the way to do things, but it clearly has its shortcomings, especially if left as a mechanical procedure. Getting to know a consultancy and its people on an informal basis will probably reveal more useful insights as to their likely fit. Buying some of their time to work with you on a strategy or particular task will give you a much clearer impression with little risk of making a long-term wrong decision.

Whichever option you choose you should always bear in mind that a public relations programme will make demands on management time. It cannot all be left to the public relations team, be they in-house or consultants, as the media will always want to talk to the people who make the decisions. A good public relations team will ensure that the time used of top managers is kept to a minimum and well spent by providing background briefs, hints and tips and doing all the follow-up work for you.

Measuring public relations

So now your team is in place and you want to measure their effectiveness. First return to start. Judging effectiveness of a public relations programme stems from the precision or otherwise with which its objectives were set, coupled with a clear assessment of the starting situation.

There was a time when the progress of a public relations campaign was measured in column inches. All different forms of coverage in all media were lumped together in a single and completely meaningless statistic. Happily most clients have moved on from the plastic ruler approach, but many still baulk at the additional expense of the more sophisticated research and analysis techniques now available. It is a bit like buying a car without a speedometer.

The true measure of a public relations campaign is not simply how much coverage it got but rather did the coverage have the desired effect? Did it inform and persuade people? If so, how many and how much?

Computerized media analysis techniques can give you bench-marks on 'How many?' and the audience reaction, if you set out to capture it, will answer the 'How much?'

If the campaign was intended to convince people of an argument, then you need to find out if their opinions have changed. If it was designed to encourage them to buy a product, then you will need a mechanism to identify the sales gains involved.

Random sampling can yield useful insights and a consumer information service, for example, can pick up valuable feedback. A small extension to ongoing market research programmes can also capture relevant information. However, the ideal solution is a regular qualitative research exercise which should be provided for in the budget at the outset.

Often one of the most telling side-effects of a public relations programme is the most difficult of all to qualify—a visible increase in confidence of the management team, a feeling that they are a little more in control and recognized as such by their peers.

Well, your overview of public relations is now almost complete. By now some of the fog is hopefully lifting and its relevance to your situation may be more apparent.

The public relations adviser has come a long way since the sixties or seventies. The great corporate take-over battles of the eighties were as much a battle of the headlines as anything else and did much to register the strategic value of public relations with the chairman's office.

At whatever level it is utilized public relations involves a cocktail of ideas, intuition and personal contacts. But be reassured it is susceptible to the disciplines of the marketing world, except perhaps for attaching any sort of unit cost/benefit ratio to it. Then you are dealing in an area that depends on the application of that most mysterious of all management attributes—judgement. And who can put a price on that?

Checklist

Jeffrey Lyes has made a strong case for public relations as being an all-embracing framework in which the stakeholders of the organization are seen as proper targets for planned and sustained communication—where possible bilaterally. Central to the thesis of Forensic Marketing is the concept that marketers have a strategic plan for the organization that reflects the needs of all stakeholders. The question then arises as to whether their needs should be accepted at face value or be informed by the marketing communications plan—of which PR is likely to be a significant component. By informed I mean checked, understood and balanced one against another so that the resulting plan is sensitive to real needs, perceived or actual, in the entire stakeholder community— rather than an internalized, even paternalized, view of what is best for them.

We need to consider the extent to which PR represents the strategic platform for communications in so far as one definition of it that I use states 'PR is about gaining and holding the high ground of positive image'—clearly a critical condition for any form of relationship management with any of the stakeholders. Another factor that is worth reflecting upon is the role of PR in the earlier stages of the customer development hierarchy:

- *Suspects* possible interest in your goods and services
- *Prospects* probable interest in them
- *Customers* people who have bought once, but with whom there is no dependent relationship
- *Clients* people who have bought more than once and who regard the supplier as first choice—there is mutual dependency
- *Advocates* people who provide unqualified endorsement of the goods or services offered—the great unpaid salesforce.

Arguably, in the suspect to customer development phase, PR is the most cost-efficient tool for the development of primary awareness.

Long-standing users of the PR tool-set regard it as central to their brand development strategy, particularly effective in managing the gap between transactional activity—as one wag puts it, 'keeping the bed warm'.

Questions to consider

7.1 How many publics does the organization have?

7.2 What do we want each public to know, feel and do?

7.3 What do these publics think of us?

7.4 What are the strategic messages we want to keep in front of stakeholders?

7.5 What are the opportunities and threats (if any) we need to address?

7.6 Who are the third party endorsers who can support us?

7.7 What third parties would help reinforce our brand position?

7.8 How strong is our network of contacts and influencers?

7.9 Where are the weaknesses in our network and how can we remedy them?

7.10 What public platforms are open to us?

7.11 What are the key positive discriminators between us and our competitors?

7.12 What are our policies towards the media?

7.13 How proactive are we in maintaining continuous relations with the media?

7.14 How competent are we in media relations?

7.15 How clear are we about what we will say and what we will not?

7.16 How much do we know about the techniques of PR?

7.17 What performance measures of the business are we seeking to impact through PR?

7.18 What performance measures of the business are directly impacted through PR?

7.19 What is the relationship between market research and PR?

7.20 What are our priority uses for PR in the marketing mix?

7.21 What is our ethical stance on external communications?

7.22 What value do we put on column inches/centimetres compared to their content?

7.23 What do we know about the specific professional areas of interest of individual journalists?

7.24 How complete is our knowledge of the media that monitors our sector(s)?

7.25 What is our policy on the release of factual data?

7.26 What is our policy on the release of opinions?

7.27 What are the boundaries of our PR agenda?

7.28 How many of our staff are capable of meeting the media effectively?

7.29 What is the relationship between PR and shareholder relations?

7.30 What do we know about assessing PR consultancies/agencies?

7.31 How well qualified are we to write a brief for a PR supplier?

7.32 What ought our PR budget be?

7.33 Where should PR report in our organizational stricture?
7.34 How should we evaluate the PR programme each year?
7.35 By when will we have a PR strategy and programme?

Here again, the checklist is not designed to be exhaustive, but in it you will perceive that it is a subject far wider than mere media relations—a graveyard to which it is too often confined. I should argue that PR is one of the most powerful and cost-effective communications resources open to most organizations. It is particularly appropriate in the management of relationships with the so-called minor stakeholder group comprising, *inter alia*, the general public, schools, local authorities, environmental lobbies, local media, prospective employees, suppliers and staff. I make the point because if it were not for PR techniques and resources I doubt whether these particular stakeholders would get serious attention within the marketing plan.

Where organizations sometimes go wrong with PR is in allowing a belief that it is a tactical, even defensive, mechanism only to be deployed in fending off a problem—such as a hostile bid or a serious environmental infraction. First, this would suggest that it is seen only as media relations (which it is not), and second, a tap to be turned on or off at will. Both attitudes are completely wrong. PR is about sustained, quality and, as far as possible, bilateral relations with all the publics we value, or ought to value.

8

Below-the-line literature

Indulgence or lifeline?

John Drewry (Drewry Marketing Communications)

The problem for below-the-line literature is that it lacks sex appeal. The very fact that it is often categorized inside organizations as 'print' exemplifies the problem. Indeed, in many cases the funding for below-the-line literature comes from the print budget rather than advertising or promotion budgets.

For lack of sex appeal read lack of funds (when was that ever not true, of anything?). Generally, literature is an area where one side of Parkinson's Law rules supreme: £5 million will be allocated to a television and press campaign with barely an eyebrow raised— major investigation when a sales brochure goes £5000 over budget.

I shall be scoping four categories of literature in this chapter:

- Sales literature
- Information literature
- Internal sales communications
- Corporate literature.

Above-the-line is where all the sex appeal resides. Like films, it is in the public domain, which is where everyone wants to be. If you are on television or in the national press, you are famous, at least for a moment. You expect it to be expensive, which it is. The industry measures up to that expectation in the way it presents itself to you and handles your business. In short, above-the-line is an industry which is based on and functions on big money. No wonder it is sexy. Which is not to decry it in any way. My case is not to bash the advertising industry, but to position literature in your mind as a neglected species, often entirely outside the advertising and promotion strategy, doing a fraction of the job it is capable of, and perhaps even working against you.

Let me give you a simple example of literature working against you. Let us imagine that the product you advertise to end-users is actually supplied, fixed or fitted by trade channels. Let us imagine you spend a zillion pounds a year above-the-line raising awareness of your product and your brand to end-users. Unfortunately, at the trade counter, the contractors cannot understand or cope with your lousy price list, whereas your competitors have sunk some money into making theirs easy to follow and friendly. At this stage (the classic switch-sell, engineered entirely by yourself), not only can all your TV spend go out of the window, but also your competitor mops up the extra market demand you have just created. And what is worse, you are probably not even aware of it. You just spend more money above-the-line.

The reason you are probably not aware of it is because it is extremely difficult to measure even if it occurs to you to measure it. Only sexy things get measured. The effectiveness of your TV campaign, for example, is measured and tested beyond reproach. The response figures are excellent. Conversion, however, is another matter, as you well know.

The price list analogy is easily extended to all below-the-line literature. It is terribly obvious, really. You just have to believe in the significance of it to get worried.

Let me help you. It is a generalization, but basically above-the-line is concerned with awareness, below-the-line with decision. This has little to do with the advertising industry. It is simply the way people behave in an understood cycle of events. At the front end they are susceptible to impression and persuasion. Downstream, at the purchasing decision, is the below-the-line work (or the lack of it).

And here is another poignant fact. You can turn above-the-line on and off like a tap. True, you can leave a lasting impression after the campaign, which is difficult to control or alter. But at least you can withdraw it, or produce a new campaign. Below-the-line, once distributed, is often impossible to retrieve or control. What is more, it can survive an awful long time. It is a physical entity, outside the laws of extinction of tomorrow's air time or yesterday's newspaper.

Literature is there at the decision, the point of sale. It is often the medium through which your company, or its products, are ultimately judged. It is rather like the secret ballot. The opinion polls tell you everything is fine, but what matters is the vote.

I would ask you, then, to view literature as your representative on earth. Earth is where the buying decision is made. But there is no reason why your literature cannot be made in Heaven, alongside your above-the-line work. All it needs is your understanding and your will.

The first rule is to make literature a conscious, integrated and planned part of your overall programme, with a clear view of the job it has to do, and its position in your selling cycle. It is normally the last part of the cycle. Which is why it is often left to the last minute, and left out of the overall planning. And yet, if it is the last part of the cycle, it must be in the most important part. I trust the irony is by now very clear.

In helping you to produce effective literature, some expanded definitions of my four categories will provide a short-cut.

Sales literature

Literature which sells? Well, yes, but surely everything commercial and non-administrative has to sell, or what is the point of it? There is nothing new about the idea, for instance, that the people who answer the telephone are the most important salespeople you have. Equally, as we shall discover in these categorizations, information literature does a good or bad selling job, depending on how accessible and understandable its information is.

Most organizations I have met have no clear idea of the role of sales literature, or what they mean by sales literature, principally because there is no clarity around the different categories of commercial literature.

If you are to integrate literature into your overall programmes you will need to be clear about the role of each category.

You may discover that you do not need sales literature at all, but that you are sadly neglecting some of the other categories.

My definition of true sales literature is a piece of print which either replaces the salesperson or supports the salesperson. Either way, it is a highly tactile and motivating animal. Its primary purpose is not to look pretty but to shout.

Good sales literature, in my experience, is not handled particularly well by graphic designers. Their role is far stronger in information and corporate literature. Good sales literature is noisily constructed by art directors and copywriters. Just like ads. And only has one basic function. DRY DEM(onstration). In two dimensions, and in silence, successful sales literature has to demonstrate its wares to you.

Now it is interesting how inhibited people get about this. No one would be surprised to see a salesperson hold a product up and say 'You'll be impressed how quickly I can replace the cartridge. Just watch'. Neither would that be surprising in a TV commercial. Or even a press ad. Yet when it comes to literature, clients tend to become very formal and serious. As though it is bad taste or sacrilege to stray outside some invisible decorum (meantime the TV campaign features a man dressed as a jelly, blowing raspberries at a giant rubber duck).

If you really mean sales literature, then get it to talk and manipulate. There is no reason why your copy and graphics should not say 'You'll be impressed how quickly you can replace the cartridge. Look!' That very type of messaging will drive the visual treatment in a dynamic and forceful way.

All too often, however, such an approach will be superseded by a neat square-up in a sea of text and photos, and a little caption which says 'Easily replaceable cartridges'. Now there is nothing wrong with that, *per se*. But it is not sales literature. It is information literature. Information literature is also a powerful selling device. So which do you use, and when?

Basically it is to do with positioning in the selling hierarchy. There's nothing profound about the classic selling hierarchy:

1 Grab attention
2 Make aware
3 Create interest
4 Create enquiry
5 Respond to enquiry
6 Provide information
7 Close the sale.

It could well be that the first four steps are taken care of by above-the-line advertising. In which case you may not need sales literature, because that is also concerned only with steps 1–4. Not all above-the-line advertising, of course, covers all four steps. It may cover 1, 2 or 3 of the first steps. In which case, you may need sales literature to complete some of the first four steps.

Or you may wish to use a combination of above-the-line and below-the-line to create steps 1–4.

In either of the above cases, your sales literature must crucially be themed with your above-the-line campaign. For this to be so, it has to be part of your campaign briefing, not something you can expect the print department to slap together at the last moment.

In summary, therefore, good sales literature concentrates on grabbing attention, creating awareness, creating interest, and creating enquiry. It does not attempt to close the sale. It is not a response device. It is not a detailed information provider.

So whether cartridge replacement is part of it or not depends on whether cartridge replacement is a major benefit or USP (unique selling proposition), rather than an additional piece of, albeit useful, information.

And essentially, real sales literature talks and gesticulates—a demonstration, not a comprehensive thesis.

Information literature

Most so-called sales literature is actually information literature. But because this is not understood, it rarely performs well as information literature either. The most common hybrid is sales literature without the right uninhibited punch, masquerading as information literature with some ineffective sales subheads cluttering up the information. If you believe you have now understood what sales literature is, then also remember that information literature does an equally powerful selling job, but at a different stage of the sales hierarchy, and therefore with different rules.

Let me sow a seed in your mind. There is no such thing as a 'data sheet'. There is no such thing as 'user instructions'. There is no such thing as 'further information'.

Information is dynamic. It is what people want. Especially at the buying decision. And afterwards, too, when they become loyal and continuing customers.

Information is your most powerful deliverable because, successfully delivered, it results in a sale. Information literature needs to be clear, uncluttered, devoid of gimmicks and smart copy (reserved strictly for sales literature) but—and this is why there is no such thing as a data sheet, etc—its driving purpose must be to inform. Obvious? Maybe, but most information literature does not fulfil this function. Because there is more to it than simply laying out information. There has to be a conscious desire to be helpful. This makes information literature the domain of copywriters. Yet this is not often enough perceived, because copywriters are terminologically associated with sales literature and advertising.

We come back to the same basic irony. Good information literature is often neglected, regarded as an ancillary piece of print unconnected with any promotional drive, and yet is at the very coalface of the decision-making process. Because, going back to our selling hierarchy, information literature is in the second phase— respond to enquiry, provide information, close the sale.

If you doubt this, look at the way a travel brochure works, and the way you relate to it as a reader. Good travel brochures are information-driven, not sales-driven. But they construct their information in layers. Like a gradually focusing telescope, you start by flicking around the world, narrow it down to a country, then a resort, and by the time you are at the buying decision you are studying the 6-point type to see how many yards from the beach the hotel is. You become concerned with the minutiae, the detail. And there is a magic moment when a whole set of facts convinces you.

If that is you at the buying moment, then bear in mind that so it is for most people. Study your experience and work out what it was that made you press the button. Then apply those principles to your own selling situation. What are the facts that really matter? Where is the emphasis? What is useful to know? And avoid trying to sell. Let the pleasure of concise, carefully structured, plain-English information do the selling for you.

And if you want to mark out your information literature from the rest, remember to close the sale. Not with a bland piece of hype, but with a summary of all the reasons to buy. Now there is a data sheet with some bite.

Internal sales communications

If you think I have already gone on too much about neglected literature, the greatest and most common crime is yet to be exposed, and the lost opportunities.

Let us be clear what we mean by internal sales communications. I mean the literature that (sometimes) gets produced which explains the product, its functions and its benefits to your salespeople, whether they are on the road or on the telephone. It is sometimes called sales support or sales briefing.

Now I have always been fascinated by the nature, and often lack, of communications between marketing and sales. I believe we can identify a genuine phenomenon that has grown up certainly in large organization cultures over a number of years. It is the phenomenon of total about-face. For, incredibly, sales briefing is produced last or not at all, at minimum cost, and as a spin-off to all the other activities.

A proper understanding of sales briefing material will reveal it as the most important of *all* your communications. And I do not particularly mean because it will keep your salespeople better informed, although there are a lot of points to be won there, too. Is it not the land of topsy-turvy to articulate at the end of the marketing and promotional process what all the sales benefits are? Does this mean we did not know what they were during product development, during all the marketing meetings, and briefings to the agencies?

Yes!

Now before you throw your hands up in disbelief and derision, what I mean to say is that articulation comes late in the day. And so, therefore, does a clear understanding of why the product exists, inside and outside your organization. Agency copywriters should not be searching for the benefits and plus points. They should long ago have been identified. Inside your organization.

I am a great believer in scripted demonstrations. For products and services.

It is not just because I believe salespeople work better through training with scripted demos (even if they subsequently improvise, but stay with the structure and the emphasis). It is much more fundamental than that.

I wonder if it has occurred to you that the discipline of having to produce a scripted demonstration provides the embryo for your whole marketing communications programme. I guess it is obvious when you think about it. Working, honing and practising a scripted demo forces out into the open key benefits, personality, emphasis, product knowledge, customer reaction and working messages. You can write your agency briefs from that, let alone your sales briefs. You can produce customer-friendly user guides. You can construct and dissect sales messages and information messages.

I honestly believe that internal communications are the key to external communications. You know the metaphor—the outer person is a reflection of the inner person.

Corporate literature

Once again, definitions are important. My best definition of corporate literature is literature which promotes the provider, not the provision. If you like, it is a story about the company. Its products (including service and other non-material products) are featured, if at all, only as part of the company's persona, not as products for sale. I think this is safe territory for most people, and the recognized corporate pieces comfortably drop into the definition—annual reports and accounts, company histories, case histories. (People notoriously find case histories difficult to position in their literature hierarchy. I think they are corporate literature. Even though product is mentioned, sometimes in great detail, the thrust of any case history I've ever seen is 'How the company solved the client's problem'.)

There are some fairly simple rules around corporate literature, and you are probably aware of them.

Every established company has a corporate brand image. I am not talking about your logo or your house style. I mean the perception your market-place has of you.

I suggest you research that perception. Among your clients, your prospects and your staff. It may or may not be the image you have of yourself. But you need to know. Because the graveyards are full of failed attempts to change corporate brand image. It is excessively expensive, and usually a waste of time.

The reason research is so necessary is that if you are perceived as a dinosaur, there is little point in producing literature that pretends you are a cheetah. Sure, you may have a bit of a problem, because dinosaur errs on the derogatory. But as a cheetah you simply will not be recognized. Or worse, you may be laughed at. Which would be a pity, because even dinosaurs have their good points.

Dinosaurs, like everyone else, should extol their good points in the way they approach their messaging and imagery, while accepting what they are.

Corporate literature, then, can be said to be about respect, self-respect, reality and truth. Your designers and writers must under-stand that. Use your research agency to help you with the brief. And try to remain objective about it: quite difficult, because corporate literature touches all the sensitive spots inside an organi-zation, and there are great temptations to meddle. Tone of voice and graphic approach should be dictated by your research findings.

Checklist

John Drewry's championship of the unfashionable but familiar friend, literature, provides cautionary warning against taking any one element of the communications mix for granted. While familiarity and favourability are highly correlated in brand positioning terms, so too are familiarity and contempt when marketing budgets are being prepared. The almost tacit assumption that we shall do a brochure or two, some sales presentation material and the annual report under the loose heading of 'print' is to paper over the fact that this key area of the communications mix is often treated as an also-ran, rather than a fundamental pillar of the marketing communications plan.

Why marketers think so relatively casually about literature is one of life's mysteries. John Drewry argues that it is its lack of glamour and sex appeal. That is almost certainly true. But I believe that the purposes and impact of literature are too little appreciated. While its role is, at one level, simple—to provide structured information that is accessible to the reader independent of any other constraint, such as time or location—its overtones are much more profound. Consider the brand impact. How well does your literature complement and enhance your brand attributes—performance, personality and promotional effectiveness? Great care is generally taken with high spend elements, such as above-the-line campaigns, but literature items, like the poor, are always with us: their durability or shelf-life expose their fundamentals to scrutiny as no other element in the mix. Yet do we think about it in those terms? Arguably not.

Literature is the embodiment of accessibility to an organization. It ought to be exemplary—representative of the highest values you aspire to. As John Drewry trenchantly puts it, below-the-line literature exists to secure decisions: it is the point at which the whole communications proposition comes to the crunch. To buy or not to buy, that is the question.

I sometimes wonder if marketers actually want prospects to say 'Yes'. Is it better to live in an ideal world than to have to face reality? The literature is the last stage in the development of the decision cycle and, thus, it seems remarkable that the ball can so often be dropped at this eleventh hour. Marketers need to think long and hard about the whole relationship continuum if they are to see below-the-line in its proper context.

The four conceptual types of literature offered in the chapter open up the wide realm of possibilities as well as the limitations of each. The single-mindedness that John Drewry advocates for the deployment of each format flies in the face of the widely held view that literature can be multifaceted—serving both the sales and the corporate role simultaneously. Please think again. It is in the focus on the specific objectives for each format that the key to success lies, not some notional omnibus view.

May I urge you to think long and hard about the ways in which literature works: the multilayered process, the cumulative effects, the drill-down to the point of decision. A good start-point is to test your own uses of, and views about, literature you receive: are you led purposefully forward, or taken on a roller-coaster of discovery, including wide detours, or even blocked in your attempt to garner the information that you and you alone want?

Like all good facilitation, literature should blend authoritative fact with creative persuasion, with stimulus for the imagination and gentle nudges towards the right decision. High-level facilitation, practised by great advocates in the judiciary for example, is a seemingly effortless blend of all four approaches; it is, in fact, supremely difficult and, rather as in music, it is risky to improvise if you lack a profound foundation of technique. The same applies to below-the-line literature. Knowing when and how to provide emphasis, and when to back-off is something of an arcane mystery, though susceptible to detailed evaluation and measurement.

John Drewry ends with a clarion call for objectivity—the very heart of the forensic approach. The checklist below may help achieve that.

Questions to consider

8.1   What decision(s) do we want at the conclusion of the communications cycle?

8.2   What is our evaluation of the specific roles of literature in general in our communications mix?

8.3   What have we learned from our prior use of literature—the positives and the negatives?

8.4   How well do we brief our below-the-line agency on the macro objectives of the communications strategy?

8.5   What do we see as the linkages between above and below-the-line campaigns?

8.6   What proportion of marketing spend should we target at decision-support materials?

8.7 What distinctions do we make between one sort of literature and another?

8.8 Do we apply research techniques to the development of literature solutions, such as consulting the salesforce on their need of literature support?

8.9 Do we put conformity of look in our literature before effectiveness?

8.10 Why might we do this?

8.11 What should the consistent elements in all our below-the-line literature be?

8.12 What are the roles of literature in relation to each other element of the communications mix—such as PR, direct marketing, shareholder liaison, etc?

8.13 How do we measure the effectiveness of each type of literature?

8.14 What is the nature of the brief to our agency—measurable outcomes or subjective criteria or something in between?

8.15 What do recipients actually do with our material—whether internal or external recipients?

8.16 How important is literature in helping us achieve an integrated, customer-focused organization, through enhancing *internal* communications?

8.17 What are our strategic objectives in publishing corporate literature?

8.18 Who are the stakeholders in corporate literature and to what extent should they be consulted in the development of the brief?

8.19 What are the purposes of the Annual Report?

8.20 What are the purposes of our price lists and catalogues?

8.21 What other uses could we put below-the-line literature to?

8.22 What structured testing can we do to isolate the critical variables in our literature?

8.23 What pre- and post-facto research ought we to do to optimize the performance of our literature formats?

8.24 What do we admire in our competitors' literature and why?

8.25 Where should responsibility for below-the-line material sit in the organization?

If below-the-line literature is as potent in its effect as John Drewry has claimed in the chapter, why does it remain the poor relation within the mix? Its associated subject of direct marketing literature is enjoying a fashionable vogue, due, almost certainly, to the high levels of precision with which it can be deployed and measured. It is the burden of this chapter to say that the same level of precision is available to below-the-line material given sufficient forensic orientation in marketers. The gap is still wide, but it is bridgeable.

9

Relationship marketing

It takes two to tango

Stewart Pearson (ADAMAS Partners)

The business imperative

The concept of direct or (preferably) relationship marketing (RM) is fundamental to business success. It is the aspect of marketing which manages and develops the individual customer relationship. It is crucial to marketing's role as a strategic business function. It has a profound effect on the organization of marketing. It demands new skills for the able direction and management of business.

Relationship marketing operates at a higher level (involving all management functions) and at a deeper level (touching all levels of the business) than the other aspects of the marketing mix. The role of advertising is increasingly limited to creating the backdrop of awareness and image. Advertising agencies—Toffler's (1980) 'image factories'—are dinosaurs ill-equipped for the new interactive world of media diversification, market segmentation and multi-media communication. Sales promotion is the last refuge of the desperate, sacrificing margin to customers and/or the trade for short-term sales. Not only do many promotions not develop long-term share increases (Ehrenburg, 1988), but also in many cases they damage customer perceptions of brand value.

- Only relationship marketing can effect and manage sustained change in customer behaviour.
- Only relationship marketing can target marketing investment for maximum pay-back.
- Only relationship marketing can integrate and focus the corporate effort where it matters—towards the customer.

Today's major business priorities—total quality management (TQM), business process engineering (BPE), customer satisfaction

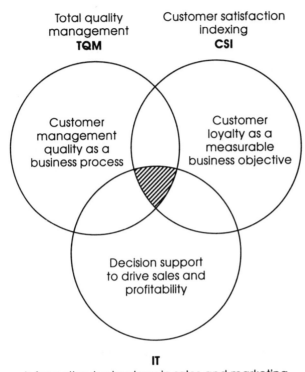

Total quality
management
TQM

Customer satisfaction
indexing
CSI

Customer
management
quality as a
business process

Customer
loyalty as a
measurable
business objective

Decision support
to drive sales and
profitability

IT
Information technology in sales and marketing

Figure 9.1 TQM, CSI and IT

indices (CSI) and information technology (IT)—are all concerned
with the desire to reorganize the business towards the customer (see
Fig. 9.1). Relationship marketing unlocks the sales potential in these
developments, and redefines marketing as an investment in the
future, not a current expense.

Direct marketing—and its roots

The term direct marketing (DM) is unhelpful. As coinage the words
are debased by association with junk mail and mail order. We need
new language for this most dynamic business concept.

Its roots do lie in mail order as a channel of distribution, and direct
mail as a communication medium to support this channel. The
pioneers of DM in the fifties were *Reader's Digest* and the mail order
catalogues. Then in the seventies financial and business marketers

(from American Express to IBM) recognized its potential. In the nineties the degree of commitment of any business to the concept is a measure of its forward thinking—and of its chances of survival.

Every business needs DM—because every business needs customers.

Relationship marketing—and the new language

DM is the fastest growing force in marketing. You cannot measure DM, because it is a concept, and not just a medium or a channel. But you can measure the explosive growth in direct mail, in direct response advertising, in customer databases, in the use of the telephone in marketing, and above all in the new focus on customer retention and loyalty. And the movement is not unique to the USA, but is now gathering momentum throughout Europe (EDMA/NTC Research 1993) (EDMA is the acronym of the European Direct Marketing Association). Expenditure on DM is estimated at 27 billion ECUs (growth rate 8 per cent per year) against media advertising at 37.4 billion ECUs (set to decline).

One simple idea drives all these developments. The role of marketing in business is to create and deliver to customer needs. Business success rests on customer relationships. Marketing's objective is to generate business value by developing the value of customer relationships.

As Levitt (1983) puts it succinctly: 'the purpose of business is to make and keep a customer'.

The value of the customer—and what you must know

The value of the customer is the contribution to profit which flows from the revenue streams generated from customer relationships. The concept is best illustrated by example, and the calculation is guaranteed to challenge your imagination. Do it now—even if only on the back of an envelope.

Think of yourself first, as a customer perhaps of your favourite restaurant. Think of the value of your custom—how much you spend each month, each year, in the last five years. Then think about family and friends you might have recommended to it. Then think about what might happen if you stopped visiting, if you had an unpleasant experience, if you told others about it. Just how much are you worth as a customer over five years? (Tom Peters (1987) uses this example to telling effect.)

This is your value as a customer.

How much might you be worth if you went more regularly? Do you receive the service you deserve? Do you feel special? Do they talk to you about changes? If they advertise do they talk to you first? Do they create special events or experiences for you?

How much will it cost them if they upset you?

Keep thinking about yourself as a customer—but now of your bank, your insurance company, your supermarket, your fashion store—the manufacturers of all the products you buy from day-to-day, from week-to-week. Think of the major suppliers to your business. How much were you worth to them over the last five years—and how much might you be worth over the next five?

Then think about the value of your customers.

The value of relationships—and the implications

All business revenue flows from customer transactions. The quality and reliability of this revenue depends fundamentally on the quality of customer relationships.

Value is sometimes attributed to brands, with some companies putting the value of their brands on their balance sheet. But the accounting value of a brand is only the discounted cash flow from anticipated future purchases of the brand by today's customers. What counts is customer behaviour, and it is changes in customer behaviour (towards new brands and own label) which threaten any brand, from soap powder to computers.

The value of a brand can only be attributed to the value placed by the customer—and the effect on future purchase choice.

Value lies in customers, not brands. And marketers who calculate the value of the customer for one brand or product ignore the potential value of all household or business transactions for all their brands, products and services.

Value is sometime maintained by personal relationships. Salesforces and retailers deliver the products and services, and are the immediate interface with the customer. But it is customer information, and signals relayed from the personal relationship which matter in retaining and developing the customer. These signals become the basis of the dynamic customer databases which increasingly drive marketing actions.

Value lies in the feedback from the relationship, not simply the personal contact. So marketers who rely on salesforces, agents, dealers and re-sellers are vulnerable if they do not receive the flow of information and signals which will enable them to own the customer.

The value of the customer has profound implications for marketing strategy. The message is clear, that retention of customers and development of relationships is the business priority—not only because it is essential to ensure business survival, but also because it pays. Indeed nothing pays quite like it.

The evidence is everywhere. Price Waterhouse (1993) has calculated that a 2 per cent increase in customer retention is equivalent to a 10 per cent reduction in costs—and is a much better way of surviving recession. In the US, TARP (1988) (Technical Assistance Research Programmes) has researched customer satisfaction and report that addressing a customer complaint raises re-purchase rates even where the complaint is not fully resolved. Bain (quoted in Reichfeld, 1993) reports re-purchase rates rising uniformly with the length of a relationship—and concomitantly that bank branch profitability rises with the length of tenure of the manager.

We need a new perspective—that of the customer.

Any business that studies its sales from this new perspective finds that it costs from four to twelve times more to sell to a new customer as to an existing one. A shift in focus to customers can transform marketing effectiveness at a stroke.

Relationship marketing—the business model

The business model for relationship marketing can be best represented as a Spiral of Prosperity, in which the organization creates and generates value from customer relationships (see Fig. 9.2).

Customer prospecting—opening the relationship

Customer prospecting is the highly targeted recruitment of

Figure 9.2 Spiral of prosperity

customers—not just any customers but market segments with high lifetime value potential. Prospecting replaces the mass advertising approach to new business with strategic identification of the most profitable parts of the market, the competitive customers who are worth attacking cost effectively, and the segments with real long-term futures. Prospecting generates a database of potential recruits for today and tomorrow.

Increasingly marketers are using direct response advertising and direct promotions to prospect and to build databases. A famous example is the 'World's Biggest Offer' by British Airways. By creating a motivating proposition prospecting has been used in markets as diverse as pet foods and computers. The critical success factor is a motivating proposition to 'engage' the prospective customer.

Customer sales

Customer sales matches message, offer and channel to customer. The database system of potential recruits drives the selection of the right message at the right time, delivered with the right offer through the right channel, to maximize cost-effective sales. Communication is managed by the design of a cost-effective contact strategy which selects customers for appropriate cost-effective contact which is timed, targeted and triggered by the system. The process involves both 'pull' (targeted messages to customers) and 'push' (tailored support packages to the field, to the trade, and to retailers). All channels of distribution can be supported, with direct distribution (home shopping) offering the exciting potential in any market for incremental sales through a new channel.

Increasingly marketers are identifying their end-customer directly, however the sale is ultimately made. A famous example of a business founded on a direct channel is Dell Computer. Markets as diverse as entertainment and financial services are developing new direct channels and new revenue streams, complementary to their existing distribution networks.

Customer cross-selling

Customer cross-selling begins the process of developing the customer relationship by determining in partnership with the customer—and driven by the customer—the future products and services which the customer needs and might buy. Cross-selling is driven by learning about the customer, identifying needs, and choosing the right timing to address these needs. Not only is selling more to existing customers (as noted above) highly cost effective, but also it is essential to move from a single transaction or product relationship.

Increasingly marketers are redirecting their creativity and spend, away from general advertising, and to their customers. A famous example of commitment to customers has always been American Express. By moving from isolated mailings to a series of messages that identify and meet the needs of selected customers, any company can create more profitable relationships and more satisfied customers.

Customer loyalty

Customer loyalty is whatever locks-in the customer to the business. Loyalty is another term in danger of debasement to nothing more than a promotional scheme. Loyalty has two levels. At the first level the rewards are *functional*—the financial rewards and additional product benefits the customer receives for repeated and frequent buying. But there must also be a second *emotional* level to loyalty, arising from recognition of the customer and enhanced levels of service and customer care. Loyalty will demand that the business treats the customer as an individual, with all that this entails, and that the customer recognizes the human touch.

Increasingly marketers are differentiating their proposition and adding value to their service to regular users, to enhance loyalty. The successful loyalty programmes are more than elaborate promotions or discounting. Customer tracking studies, just like advertising tracking, can be used to evaluate the return on investment from loyalty, as well as the incremental sales.

Relationship marketing—the art

The concept of a brand has three dimensions—features, benefits, and added values. The relationship with the customer now becomes an essential fourth dimension. The nature of and motivation for the relationship defines and develops the brand position and role in the customer's life.

There is a magic moment when customers make direct contact with a business, and learn that the business is organized and willing to treat them as individuals. The creative process in relationship marketing then becomes a development of general or brand advertising, but now the customer is directly involved or (better language) engaged, and no longer the passive onlooker at broadcast and space media. The brand personality is reaffirmed ever more strongly when it reacts directly with the customer.

The engagement creates the opportunity to sense customer needs and to select appropriate messages. Once the customer responds, future communications become solicited, and ideally welcome. Any response—no matter how modest—becomes the start of a relationship. Companies who put the customer first can enjoy a genuine advantage over more passive competitors.

Relationship marketing—and the integration of other activities

In the business model relationship marketing may exploit the high awareness and positive image created by general advertising and public relations. But even this is only a model appropriate to mass brands. It is increasingly inappropriate in the new media environment, and less and less economic for a broader range of businesses.

Increasingly the role of advertising is to recruit: it is a matter of observation that the majority of advertising now carries a response device, and direct response television is a wave of the future. Targeted customer communications carry the responsibility not only of selling but also of achieving advertising objectives— generating awareness, fostering a positive image and creating preference.

And the new proliferation of media channels—only just underway in Europe—will change the very nature of the media. A visit to the USA is no longer needed to observe how 'junk' television is an increasingly inappropriate environment for brand-building, and how media choice makes buying your target audience impossibly expensive and complex.

In the business model the role of promotions is also to recruit. This means that promotions must become targeted to segments with profit potential. They must discriminate between user and non-users. They must be designed as the first step in a customer relationship and not as a one-off transaction. They must be planned to generate return-on-investment. Promotions are not a separate activity but an element of the relationship marketing process.

Relationship marketing—and organizational resources

Business faces a bewildering choice today in selection of its marketing agents and suppliers. Advertising agencies of all structures and philosophies vie with direct marketing agencies, sales promotion agencies, public relations consultants, management consultants as well as a new range of service bureaux specializing in data processing, mail and telephone. There must be consolidation, and the shape of the consolidation will reflect the imperatives of business.

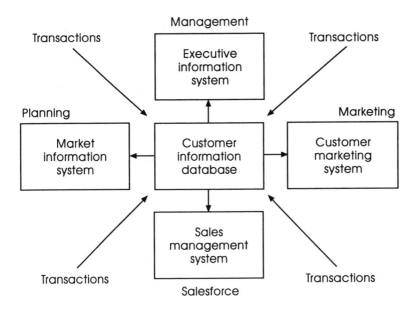

Figure 9.3 Customer support system

The first development will be that business will internalize more and more of the process functions of relationship marketing. The organizational structure will develop to accommodate two major functions—the customer support system (CSS) and the customer contact centre (CCC).

The CSS is the evolution of the customer database concept towards a system in which all functions in the organization access and manage customer information (see Fig. 9.3). Increasingly the customer too will access the CSS (which is just what is happening, for example, in the rapid trend towards more cost-effective remote banking).

The CCC is the integration of the customer response concept with customer communications so that it becomes practicable and manageable to respond to customer needs on an individual basis. The CCC will encompass telephone and mail response management. In the future it will offer on-line access through electronic media. It will be cost-justified on the basis of increased customer retention (by satisfying the problems of customers) and of increased customer cross-selling (by providing customers with direct access). It will become a source of competitive advantage, winning and retaining customers by providing easier access and superior service.

Relationship marketing—and service sector structure

The advertising industry sector in the USA and Europe is struggling to respond to the changes in client needs which are eroding its value to business. Since the early seventies it has attempted to retain its hold on client relationships by diversifying, and in particular by acquiring other marketing services functions.

That strategy has failed. In particular the attempt by advertising and promotion agencies to hijack direct marketing, with its totally different skills and philosophies, has set back development by years. There was no client benefit in the one-stop shop.

In the future business will work with two forms of external agencies. First, the advertising agency will survive, alongside an autonomous but dependent media buying service. The role of the agency will be much curtailed to a source of creative ideas, and its assignments will be mass market brands.

The second form of agency will be the relationship marketing agency. The services of this agency will be direct response advertising, sales support, customer communications and customer loyalty. The value added will be deep and objective customer understanding, derived from a balanced tool-kit of qualitative and quantitative skills. Communication programmes will be designed through a new data-driven planning system.

This agency and its clients will both have on-line access to customer information, and the tools to use this information to guide decision-making and to manage marketing programmes. There will be no separate account, creative, media and production departments: clients will have dedicated business teams with an integrated set of planning, communication, sales and project management skills (see Fig. 9.4).

This agency will be specifically skilled in the development of interactive communications between business and its customers using the new interactive media, through satellite, cable and telephone lines into the customer's business and home.

Relationship marketing—and business organization

Relationship marketing will have significant effects on marketing

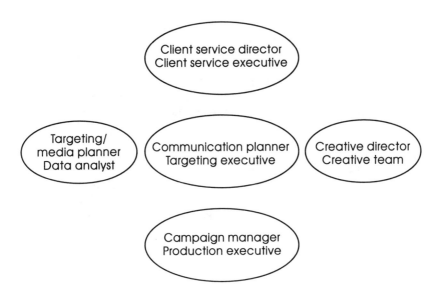

Figure 9.4 Relationship marketing agency business team

organization and on business communication. The traditional marketing organization consists of marketing communication specialists arrayed opposite marketing management responsible for product communication (see Fig. 9.5).

Here no one owns the customer. Product or brand management may deliver different (and conflicting) messages to the same customer at the same time. Advertising, promotion or direct marketers may deliver different (and uncoordinated) messages with different themes. The process makes no sense to the customer.

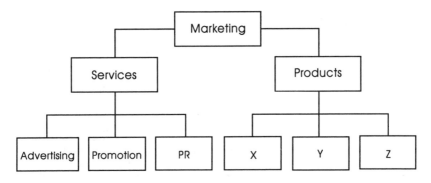

Figure 9.5 Traditional marketing organization

Cross-selling opportunities are missed. Traditional organization wastes marketing money, and it is a barrier to any initiative designed to develop the customer.

In the new form of marketing organizations, communications will be run by generalists, and marketing managers will become customer relationship managers—responsible for the total customer relationship (see Fig. 9.6).

Relationship managers will be responsible for deployment of all organization resources to plan, to contact, and deliver to their customer segments. Business process engineering will develop new working practices to pull together in cross-functional teams, and to focus on customer service with marketing at the hub of each.

Customer relationship management can be the focus for the whole company—the banner to rally the troops. But the practice means the daily, nitty-gritty care for the customer. It means that everyone will have to work together. And it means that your front-line people are as important as your head office management. Ultimately the promise to the customer must be fulfilled wherever and whenever the customer deals with the company.

So relationship marketing is a starting-point for change. And feedback from the market-place should drive a re-engineering of the company and of its organization, to bring all the people closer to their customers.

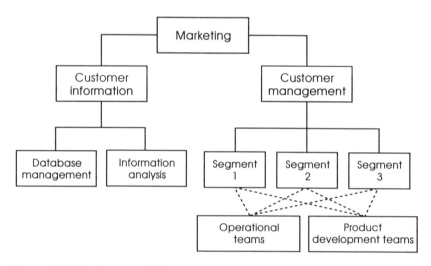

Figure 9.6 Modern marketing organization

Relationship marketing—and the barriers to change

The adoption of relationship marketing practice has been slow but steady. Growth has accelerated in Europe not only with recession but also with the fierce competition from the USA and Japan. There are still significant barriers to change.

The first barrier is *technological*. Investment is required in the resources required to manage relationship marketing. But new technology has resulted in a rapid fall in computing and telecommunication costs, bringing customer information systems down to desk-top PCs (Fig. 9.7). Customer systems are for the first time feasible and practicable propositions, and they can be managed directly by the marketing function.

The second barrier is *economic*. The real costs of reaching target audiences through mass media are escalating. Retail markets are becoming saturated, and salesforce costs are subject to sustained inflation. But falling costs in print, postage, and interactive, electronic media make direct communications and distribution increasingly attractive. Relationship marketing is for the first time a cost-effective proposition.

Figure 9.7 Marketing workstation

The highest barriers are *cultural* and *educational*. Professionals trained in traditional marketing methods cannot but be wary of the new concept. Management faced with recession and competition cannot but be cautious about the investment. Businesses developed to deliver product to customer cannot but be challenged hugely by the prospect of becoming customer-driven.

Relationship marketing will demand enhanced skills in project planning and management, and higher levels of numeracy, as well as a deep understanding of interpersonal relationships. What matters is not what management says—but what the customer wants.

Relationship marketing requires new language and new tools. The business needs to think share of customer before share of market, and will need a new framework to plan and to evaluate marketing expenditure.

Relationship marketing—and the financial pay-back

The objective of relationship marketing is to address and deliver directly to quantitative and qualitative business objectives.

Quantitatively, investments in customer relationships generate rapid pay-back and long-term revenue and profit streams. These processes of calculating and allocating the marketing budget can be modelled. Marketing expenditure should be treated as a business investment, and its allocation among different customer segments and different communication media and channels should be optimized, for maximum profitability (see Fig. 9.8).

When subject to this rigour most marketing functions will be pleasantly surprised that their budgets will rise. And most business management will be equally and pleasantly surprised to find themselves renewed advocates of the marketing cause.

Investments in customer relationships generate measurable improvements in customer satisfaction and retention rates—and (what is critical) in active customer loyalty. The great interest in customer satisfaction should not obscure the reality that this is a backward-looking measure. In relationship marketing we evaluate active loyalty, which looks forward to the potential future value of the customer.

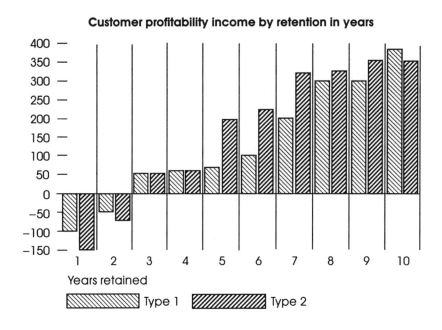

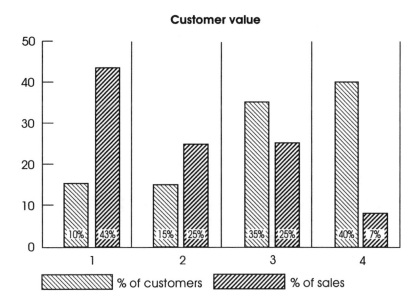

Figure 9.8 Customer profitability and customer value

Relationship marketing—and the quality of business

Relationship marketing also delivers qualitative benefits which enhance the quality of business through relationships both internal and external.

Ownership of customer information and customer relationships ensures the future by allowing the business a new degree of control. We can directly communicate to customers. We can observe their behaviour, listen to their signals, learn from their actions and address their concerns and needs.

Customers are people—not market share points, not faceless revenue streams. Relationship marketing simply fosters a better relationship between a business and its customers—a relationship based on a greater degree of open dialogue, mutual understanding and a basic level of honesty.

Customer honesty test

Now test your own business for your customer honesty, with Stewart Pearson's four customer honesty tests:

1 Do you say thank you to customers?
2 Do you listen to your customers?
3 Do you learn more about your customers?
4 Do you compete aggressively for your customers?

Checklist

Stewart Pearson's assertion that relationship marketing is the critical functional competence today, far exceeding in significance advertising or sales promotion, will raise a few eyebrows, particularly of those with vested interests in the more traditional forms of the communications mix. The special significance of relationship marketing is its focus on the individual customer as an individual, with unique needs or perceptions of needs. Within the orthodoxy of the marketing mix, the individual becomes a self-contained micro-segment and requires marketing focus at that level of precision. Direct marketing, in all the forms described by Stewart Pearson, certainly aspires to individual focus, particularly through personalization of the communications media, but the dilemma for all of us is to sustain the reality, or dare I say illusion, of individual values throughout the organization—at every point where the customer is impacted; accounts, after-sales-service, and operations, for example. Relationship marketing is fully integrated marketing and demands the culture of a marketing organization.

Stewart Pearson also argues with great conviction that we must be sensitive to the value potential of each customer and prospect. This powerful concept means that we must sign on to the notion of continuity rather than opportunism in our attitude to customers—hence his challenge to the world of sales promotion. In earlier chapters I have repeated the mantra that an existing customer is many times easier to sell to than a prospect, hence the need to invest time and effort in creating sufficient bonding to facilitate the continuity of sales.

This, as I have stressed, requires the management of the gaps between sales, as much as the sales pitch itself.

Questions to consider

9.1 What are the potential uses for relationship marketing in our business?

9.2 What data do we have that allows us to identify customers as individuals?

9.3 What is the lifetime value potential of each customer?

9.4 What are the life-stages of customers that we can appeal to in particular?

9.5 What is the role for relationship marketing in business-to-business sales?

9.6 How do we store transactional history for each customer?

9.7 How able are we to analyse the transactional history of customers for indicators of future potential?

9.8 How well do we reward customer loyalty?

9.9 What do we do to promote customer loyalty?

9.10 What do we do to manage the gap between sales?

9.11 How well integrated are our business processes to ensure that the customer perceives coherent individual treatment?

9.12 How well do our information systems support relationship marketing?

9.13 How good are we at targeting only high potential prospects for specific offers?

9.14 How good are we at single-variable testing to establish the optimum offer?

9.15 How consistent with our strategic aims are our tactical direct marketing campaigns?

9.16 How supportive of brand development is our use of direct marketing?

9.17 What measurement systems have we for establishing the effectiveness of our relationship management?

9.18 What measurements ought we to have in place for relationship management?

9.19 For business-to-business sales, what is the potential for direct marketing?

9.20 What use could we make of direct marketing in developing relationships with influencers within the commercial customer's decision-making unit?

9.21 What criteria should we use for managing the frequency and regularity of contact with existing customers or prospects?

9.22 What are our ethical policies for telemarketing, direct mail and direct response advertising?

9.23 Where will we find bench-mark standards of performance in relationship marketing?

9.24 How well organized are we for integrated relationship management?

9.25 How knowledgeable are we about the tools and techniques of relationship marketing so that we can brief suppliers to a professional standard?

Unlike many other aspects of the communications mix, relationship marketing makes particular demands on both suppliers—agencies, post office or distributors, mail shops, telemarketing agencies, geo-demographic systems, IT vendors and handling houses—and the marketing organization. No aspect of marketing is as scientific in its methodology or as demanding of disciplined systems for success. Because it can be deployed on a large scale it is perhaps easy to forget that its focus is always upon the individual—a critical success factor to be stressed internally and in all briefings to suppliers. There can be no doubt, however, that relationship marketing will be the dominant theme for some time to come.

10

Geodemographic segmentation

You are where you live

Richard Webber and Jim Hodgkins (CCN Marketing)

Segmentation is becoming an increasingly key issue for marketers as the focus of their activities shifts from macro to micro marketing. To market products and services effectively it is necessary not only to define and quantify a target audience but also to access information on the ability of localized media to reach it. The system that is used to do this must be robust, so that decisions can be made based on its findings. These decisions may vary from the location of outlets through to the selection of the audience that receives promotional literature.

Geodemographic modelling provides a valuable solution to businesses wishing to segment consumer markets. Whether the distribution channel is retail, mail order or through a field salesforce, for products from food to financial services, magazines to motor cars, geodemographic modelling is now used by most of the UK's larger consumer marketing organizations.

The assumption that underlies geodemographic modelling is that neighbourhoods attract similar sorts of people. If we can define a set of neighbourhood types that are broadly similar across a wide range of demographic indicators, then they are also likely to offer similar levels of opportunity for any widely advertised products or brands. These types are defined by statistically analysing a wide range of demographic measures for each neighbourhood in the country. The classification is independent, as all audiences, areas or lists of customers are analysed by the same classification. This avoids the problems that occur when different marketers describe customer characteristics using categories specific to their own application.

Geodemographic modelling allows marketers control through the provision of a data analysis system that enables much better understanding of customer and market characteristics. Applications have expanded greatly fuelled by the growth in application software, personal computer power and the demands of users.

Key benefits offered by classifying consumers in this way are as follows:

- *Coverage*   Every consumer in the county can be classified whether he or she is a customer, a respondent to a market research survey, a name and address on a mailing list or simply a person living in a particular area.
- *Flexibility*   The system can be used to link different types of data held on separate databases.
- *Convenience*   Coding data with the model is quick, easy and inexpensive. There is no need to interview people to find out their characteristics; their addresses are all that is needed to classify people.
- *Local detail*   Geodemographic modelling enables national research findings to be projected down to a very fine level of local detail enabling marketers to improve decision-making and achieve better results in all applications relating to local market segmentation.

This chapter explains how a geodemographic model is built, examines the applications of geodemographic models, gives a brief history of the discipline and looks at future trends.

How geodemographic models are built

Objective

The actual process of building a geodemographic model involves applying a range of statistical techniques to a vast quantity of spatially organized data. There are relatively few individuals or businesses in the UK with the training, resources and experience to enable them to build successful models. However, the ingredients and methods of building a system can be explained without excessive technical references.

Before examining the ingredients and method it is wise to look at the objective. What does a geodemographic model aim to achieve?

The main objective is to create a series of easy to interpret consumer types which each contain a reasonably homogenous population and that are as distinct as possible from each other. Separating the wealthy from the financially dependent, families from singles and young from old may appear a simple task. However, deciding precisely how best to combine information so as to produce an optimal set of consumer groups is not a simple process.

Ingredients

Britain is a consumer market containing around 45 million adults in 23 million households. No two individuals are identical but characteristics can be identified that correlate highly with their behaviour. Of these characteristics demographic data supplied by the Office of Population and Census Statistics decennial census offers the largest available volume of information on a local area basis.

Demographic data are used in geodemographic modelling to infer likelihood to behave in a particular way, for example

- To own a particular product, e.g. a dishwasher
- To have a set of values or an attitude, e.g. voting preference
- To participate in an activity, e.g. playing bingo.

The census publishes counts for over 10 000 individual characteristics. However, the data are available only as statistical counts for neighbourhood areas, termed enumeration districts. These contain 180 households each, on average. Some geodemographic models use just these data while others supplement it with other data such as electoral roll information, data from the Postal Address File (PAF) and data held by credit reference agencies.

In all cases these data will be anonymized by creating statistics that relate to neighbourhoods. These will be either areas similar to the enumeration districts that the census data are released for or individual postcodes averaging 15 households each.

Method

From all of the available data a series of statistical processes are used to discover which pieces of data are most predictive in measuring consumer behaviour.

The statistical process that all geodemographic models use is cluster analysis. It is clustering that creates the neighbourhood types that make up each system and give it an identity. Cluster codes will then be applied to all postcodes in an enumeration district, or if additional sources of data are used to each individual postcode.

Geodemographic models typically have a structure containing 30–60 distinct cluster types which are then grouped into 8–12 broader groups. Figure 10.1 illustrates the MOSAIC geodemographic model.

Groups		Types		Description	
L1 High income families	L1	High income families	1	Clever capitalists	
L2 Suburban semis	1	Clever capitalists			
L3 Blue-collar owners	2	Rising materialists	Clever captalists are typically wealthy people involved in management of companies and in broking, commercial trading, importing and exporting	
L4 Low rise council	3	Corporate careerists		
L5 Council flats	4	Ageing professionals		
L6 Victorian low status	5	Small-time business		
L7 Town houses and flats					
L8 Stylish singles				The areas are characterized by company directors living in large detached houses, though not necessarily with extensive grounds, in well-established residential areas within reasonable reach of city centres	
L9 Independent elders					
L10 Mortgaged families					
L11 Country dwellers					
L12 Institutional areas					
				Children are typically of secondary school age or students and there is a higher proportion of foreigners than in the more suburban types within high income families	

Figure 10.1 Structure of geodemographic system illustrated by MOSAIC
Source: CCN Marketing MOSAIC database 1993

The model is then adapted to the applications discussed in the next section in two forms, as a postcode directory for appending codes to name and address files and as a database containing the number and proportion of households and population falling within each code for each neighbourhood. However, a critical factor in the growth of geodemographic modelling is that software modules for analysing areas and individuals, reporting on them and mapping them are an integral part of the geodemographic solution. Figure 10.2 illustrates how the various components of a geodemographic software and data system combine.

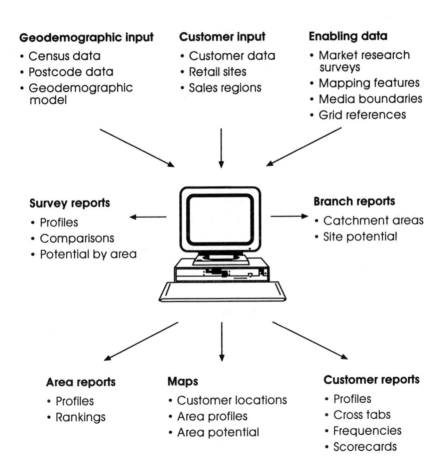

Geodemographic input
- Census data
- Postcode data
- Geodemographic model

Customer input
- Customer data
- Retail sites
- Sales regions

Enabling data
- Market research surveys
- Mapping features
- Media boundaries
- Grid references

Survey reports
- Profiles
- Comparisons
- Potential by area

Branch reports
- Catchment areas
- Site potential

Area reports
- Profiles
- Rankings

Maps
- Customer locations
- Area profiles
- Area potential

Customer reports
- Profiles
- Cross tabs
- Frequencies
- Scorecards

Figure 10.2 Configuration of a geodemographic software and data solution

Geodemographic applications

This section describes implementing geodemographic modelling within your business to help improve performance. It explains what a geodemographic profile is and how it can be combined with other data and systems to achieve marketing advantage. Examples are based on the MOSAIC geodemographic model.

Profiling

In all applications profiling is used to provide an objective analysis of a product, medium or area. Having examined the way that geodemographic models are built it is necessary to understand how profiling works. It is a simple method for comparing the distributions by MOSAIC of two different sets of data. The first set, the target, is commonly the MOSAIC distribution of customer addresses, responses to a question on a research survey or a geographic area. The second set is the base for comparison. In a simple profiling exercise this may be the MOSAIC distribution of all adults or all households in Britain or, in the case of a research study, it may be the MOSAIC distribution of all respondents. However, the decision of which base to use is an important one as it affects the results greatly.

Table 10.1 shows a profile of all credit card owners against a base of all households. It has been obtained from the Target Group Index market research survey. The geographic model shown is MOSAIC, which has 12 Groups and 52 types; only the Group level data are shown in the table. Looking at the profile in Table 10.1 it is easy to see that credit card owners are over represented in particular groups. What makes geodemographic modelling so important is the ability to develop actionable marketing programmes from these data. There are three main areas of implementation of geodemographic models which cover between them many applications of data in marketing. These are planning and research, database marketing, and customer acquisition.

Planning and research

Market research

Geodemographic models can be used to build structured sample frames for market research purposes. When postal, doorstep or telephone research is to be undertaken the identification of neighbourhoods and individual households which meet the required criteria for interviewing can save survey costs.

Table 10.1 Profile of credit card owners

MOSAIC Group	Credit card owners[a] (%)	Adults (GB)[b] (%)	Adults with a credit card[c] (%)	Index[d] (GB = 100)
L1 High income families	15.96	11.23	61.0	143
L2 Suburban semis	16.32	12.93	54.2	127
L3 Blue-collar owners	15.75	16.03	42.2	99
L4 Low rise council	9.67	16.43	25.3	59
L5 Council flats	2.41	4.94	21.0	49
L6 Victorian low status	7.03	8.49	35.5	83
L7 Town houses and flats	10.96	10.48	42.9	100
L8 Stylish singles	4.35	3.68	50.6	118
L9 Independent elders	5.27	4.97	45.6	107
L10 Mortgaged families	5.27	4.40	51.4	120
L11 Country dwellers	6.72	5.67	50.9	119
L12 Institutional areas	0.27	0.23	49.0	115
	100	100	42.7	100

Source: TGI (Target Group Index—a quarterly consumer survey available by subscription only).
Notes:
[a]Credit card owners gives the percentage of all credit card owners that fall within the MOSAIC Group. The sum is 100% as all cardholders have been allocated to a group.
[b]Adults (GB) gives the percentage of all British adults that are in the MOSAIC Group. Again this column sums to 100.
[c]Adults with a credit card states the percentage of adults that are credit card owners. The figure of 42.7% for each group is the average for Britain.
[d]Index shows the extent to which each MOSAIC Group is under or over represented compared to the national average. L1 High income families has an index 143 meaning that there are 1.43 times the national average representation of High income families among credit card owners.

Geodemographic models are frequently used to analyse *ad hoc* or syndicated research surveys enabling marketers to identify the types of areas in which concentrations of particular types of individuals live.

Potential buyers of new products can be identified and profiled by a geodemographic model and their geographical distribution examined, enabling the best test markets and outlets to be identified.

Local media owners wishing to improve their professionalism of display advertising presentations often use geodemographic profiles of their distribution areas to show the suitability of their title for the target group of the advertisers whose budget they are bidding for.

It is the combination of the client's information with geodemographic data that enables an effective solution to be produced.

Network planning

Major companies with networks of stores, branches, restaurants, franchises or direct salesforces use geodemographic models to improve the location of their outlets and to adapt concepts and merchandise to the requirements of the local communities that they serve.

Geodemographic data are often combined with other data for analysing and forecasting. For example a bank wishing to change the profile of its branches by appointing specialist consultants in selected branches to sell mortgages and retirement planning may appoint a geodemographic modelling company to

- Analyse what types of people buy these services.
- Assign a market opportunity value to each branch in the network for each type of specialist.
- Suggest the best sites for locating new branches containing these specialists.

The analysis will involve

- Using customer data to calculate the outer limits of branch catchment areas.
- Using customer and research survey data to determine the profile and spend of buyers within that area.
- Calculating total potential for each branch catchment.
- Creating a model to analyse market share, by examining local competition.

- Producing a management report and detailed statistical reports advising the results.
- Providing an in-house system for producing 'what if' models for a range of scenarios.

Database marketing

The use of geodemographic modelling in database marketing depends greatly on the volume and relevance of the data held on all individuals on the database.

The geodemographic codes are frequently used for the following purposes:

- Examining the differences between customers buying different products and services.
- Analysing changes over time in the composition of new customers.
- Finding groups of customers that are best suited to the cross-selling of different products.
- Analysing customer spend, profitability, bad debt, stability and payment methods.
- Examining the difference between the profiles of customers of different branches.
- Analysing the response to promotional campaigns of customers on the database.

An example of database analysis over time is shown in Table 10.2 using data on credit card owners.

A credit card company wishes to analyse who is currently applying for credit cards to estimate future spend patterns. It takes data on those who have taken out a card in the last 12 months and compares this to all owners of credit cards. From the profile in Table 10.2 it can be seen that Group L8 Stylish singles has the greatest penetration of applicants and the highest index although in Table 10.1 it was ranked only fifth for credit card ownership. This change in the customer database will affect the marketing strategy immediately. It may also affect the volume of spend on cards, the types of products purchased using them and the expenditure on credit cards at different types of outlets. Over time this will have great impact on the credit card operator's turnover and profitability.

With databases that contain little detail about each individual the geodemographic codes are a vital analysis and selection tool. On databases where large volumes of customer data are held, including

Table 10.2 Database analysis over time of credit card owners

MOSAIC Group	Acquired credit card last 12 mths[a] (%)	Credit card owners[b] (%)	Penetration of credit card[c] (%)	Index[d]
L1 High income families	17.48	15.96	5.6	110
L2 Suburban semis	14.72	16.32	4.1	91
L3 Blue-collar owners	15.19	15.75	3.4	97
L4 Low rise council	8.41	9.67	1.8	89
L5 Council flats	1.50	2.91	1.1	63
L6 Victorian low status	8.70	7.03	3.7	125
L7 Town houses and flats	9.35	10.96	3.1	86
L8 Stylish singles	6.15	4.35	6.0	143
L9 Independent elders	4.58	5.27	3.3	87
L10 Mortgaged families	6.67	5.27	5.5	128
L11 Country dwellers	6.94	6.72	4.4	104
L12 Institutional areas	0.23	0.27	3.0	88
	100	100	3.5	

Source: TGI (Target Group Index—a quarterly consumer survey available by subscription only).
[a]Acquired credit card last 12 months gives the percentage of recent successful applicants that fall within the MOSAIC Group. The sum is 100% as all new card holders have been allocated to a group.
[b]Credit card owners gives the percentage of all credit card owners that are in the MOSAIC Group. Again this column sums to 100.
[c]Penetration of credit card states the percentage of adults that have acquired a credit card in the last 12 months. The figure of 3.5% for each group is the average for Britain.
[d]Index shows the extent to which each MOSAIC Group is under or over represented among recent credit card acquirers compared to all credit card owners.

individual demographic characteristics such as age, length of residence, marital status, home ownership and income, the codes are most useful for two purposes. First, they provide a quick analysis of any set of individuals, and second, they enable database information to be used for purposes such as research and planning and customer acquisition modelling.

Customer acquisition

Geodemographic models are regularly used to improve the cost effectiveness of customer acquisition using direct mail and door-to-door leaflet distribution. They are also increasingly being applied to media selection for print and broadcast media and poster sites.

Direct mail

Using the geodemographic profile, names and addresses can be selected which are in the types that have the highest indices on a profile. Many local promotions such as store openings, leisure events, home improvement offers, product launches and charity fund raising use this approach.

National advertisers usually organize local campaigns centrally and geodemographic modelling gives centralized marketing departments the ability to accurately analyse local market characteristics that they are not familiar with.

Geodemographic models are also used in more complex selections often involving the use of multiple regression models to select the best individuals to mail using a wide range of data combining geodemographic models with the data available on electoral register based lists enables the more accurate selection of prospects. Other factors analysed often include an individual's gender, household structure, length of residence, likely age (estimated from electoral register information) and their credit profile.

Leaflet distribution

Most of the country's leading door-to-door distributors now use MOSAIC applications software to improve the level of targeting they offer their customers. Having MOSAIC-profiled each of their distribution blocks, the companies match their users' products to the profiles of their distribution areas so as to restrict distribution to areas where there is likely to be product demand.

Table 10.3 shows a ranking of all the postcode sectors in a store catchment by their potential to buy. The marketing manager can

Table 10.3 Brick ranking report by postcode sectors

Zone Name: Guildford
Target: High Income Families
Base: Total households

Rank Brick	Brick description	Target	Base	Penetration	Index
1 KT24 6	West Horsley	737	1499	0.492	216 ***
2 GU 1 2	Merrow	1723	3833	0.450	197 **
3 GU 4 8	Shalford	785	2095	0.375	164 **
4 GU 3 1	Compton	269	726	0.371	163 **
5 GU 4 7	Bushy Hill	1333	3805	0.350	154 **
6 KT24 5	Effingham	515	1809	0.285	125 **
7 GU 2 5	Guildford Park	987	3971	0.249	109
8 GU 5 0	Bramley	574	2404	0.239	105
9 GU 3 3	Worplesdon	458	1998	0.229	101
10 GU 1 3	Epsom Rd	330	1666	0.198	87
11 GU 5 9	Gomshall	203	1448	0.140	62 – –
12 GU 1 1	Bellfields	575	4202	0.137	60 – –
13 GU 2 6	Stoughton	304	6880	0.044	19 – – –
14 GU 1 4	North St	1	2257	0.000	0 – – –
	Zone total	8794.	38593.	0.228	

© CCN Marketing, Talbot House, Talbot Street, Nottingham NG1 5HF
Tel: 0115 9410888 Fax: 0115 9344903
Source: CCN Marketing MOSAIC database 1993
Note: Brick = level of geographic area analysed, in this case postal sector

decide to prioritize sectors to deliver a certain volume of leaflets or
to distribute to all areas where potential is above a given limit.

Print and broadcast

Local media such as regional newspapers and independent local
radio are often prioritized using a similar ranking to that shown for
leaflet distribution. The areas analysed in this case are broadcast
coverage areas rather than postal sectors.

National media profiles can be matched to those of products to
show which titles offer the best sales opportunity (see Table 10.4).

History and trends in geodemographic modelling

The first commercial application of geodemographic modelling in
Britain was in 1977 when the British Market Research Bureau

Table 10.4 Ranking of national daily newspaper titles by their similarity to the profile of Volvo car buyers

Newspaper	Match index (AV = 100)
Daily Telegraph	133
The Times	126
The Independent	115
Daily Mail	113
Daily Express	109
Guardian	104
Today	101
Daily Record	85
Daily Mirror	84
The Sun	84
The Star	77

Source: TGI (Target Group Index—a quarterly consumer survey available by subscription only).

(BMRB) used CRN (Classification of Residential Neighbourhood), a ward parish classification, to improve the representativeness of their Target Group Index (TGI) survey. When analysing product and media fields on the TGI by CRN, Ken Baker and John Bermingham (1979) of BMRB discovered that geodemographic data were more effective discriminators of readership of the *Guardian* and *Daily Telegraph* than the most commonly used indicators of status such as social class.

In 1980 an American consultancy, CACI, adopted the system, which had originally been built for public sector analysis of areas of deprivation, rebranded it ACORN (A Classification Of Residential Neighbourhoods) and sold it as a system for analysing the potential of retail sites.

In 1981 the system was linked to all postcodes enabling the coding of geographic areas, the TGI and of customer files by direct marketers. The ACORN codes were also added to the electoral register belonging to CCN Systems, part of Great Universal Stores, and used to select mailing lists which provided commercially worthwhile response rates.

The number of classifications expanded following the release of 1981 census data and in 1986 CCN Systems launched its own classification, MOSAIC, which was the first to use significant volumes of data from sources other than the census.

In the late eighties the systems on offer included PIN from Pinpoint Analysis, Super Profiles from CDMS, Define from Infolink as well as ACORN and MOSAIC.

Important advances that aided the expansion of geodemographics included the growth of direct mail volumes, with a requirement for targeting names and addresses, and the dramatic fall in the costs of computer processing.

Geodemographic suppliers now offer PC systems in which to run customer and geodemographic data and CCN Marketing and CACI are the main suppliers with around 300 installations in Britain.

The use of other data in the PC systems, particularly that generated from mass consumer surveys such as the National Shopper Survey by CMT Ltd, is a trend which is likely to continue in the nineties. Marketers require more detail about buying patterns and, now that profitable methods of distributing questionnaires containing over 100 questions that generate up to 1 million responses annually have been achieved, marketers can satisfy this need.

Within the core discipline of geodemographic modelling trends in the mid-nineties include

• Extension of geodemographics into other European markets and the construction of pan-European segmentation systems such as EURO-MOSAIC.
• Building models to suit individual markets such as Financial MOSAIC and Investor ACORN.
• Creating more detailed models for areas within Britain such as Scotland and London.

The growth of geodemographic modelling and the market analysis business is strong and the only cloud on the horizon is the threat of control on the use and application of certain types of data by the Data Protection Registrar in Britain and the European Union.

During the nineties it is our expectation that the growth of micro marketing will intensify the use of market analysis and databased marketing and that software tools will satisfy an ever widening range of applications with the marketing departments of British and European companies.

Checklist

In a perfect world marketers would communicate only with prospects they know are going to buy—no risk, no waste and no brickbats. In the less than perfect world we inhabit how close to perfection can we get? What prospect to sale ratio would we regard as satisfactory? The answer will vary with the sector being considered and the offering, but the principle holds good, whether we think of multi-million pound capital investment projects or circulation of a daily paper, that we should seek to communicate only with high propensity prospects and avoid promoting those who would, almost certainly, never buy. Marketing budgets are, after all, finite: it makes sense to use it to maximum effect on the prospect base most likely to respond.

Richard Webber and Jim Hodgkins have described the logical and experiential basis for MOSAIC and its derivatives and have demonstrated that the correlative links between one or more types of activities and a propensity to buy something else are commonly high. While geodemographics may have started as a housing-based classification system, we are today dealing with very powerful regression analyses of millions of purchase transactions in almost every sector of consumer expenditure. This is the key to understanding: we are able to add the prior behavioural history of prospects to behaviours we have observed from our own transactional experience. We have access to lifestyle indicators rather than the narrower focus of our own sector.

This ability to target more cost-effectively is the financial pay-back. The greater prize comes from being better able to understand what makes our customers tick and how best to stimulate them. As geodemographics grows in international markets the ability to achieve large savings on brand development and general marketing communications becomes obvious. However, the subject is highly specialized and, like direct marketing in all its forms, repays very careful study. There are few specialists in the market, so it is wise to use only the leading firms in the field which besides CCN include CACI and CDMS. Geodemographics are one of the most potent tools available to the consumer marketer and, like all toxic remedies, they need to be handled with care.

Questions to consider

10.1 How confident are we that our distribution network is appropriate for the real distribution of our end-users?

10.2   When did we last check this distribution pattern out?

10.3   What are the criteria we use for geographic marketing?

10.4   How effective are we at geographic analysis of our markets?

10.5   What would the benefit be of being able to conduct market research at micro-segment level rather than macro?

10.6   What do we believe the correlative lifestyle factors are in our customer buying motivations?

10.7   How might we establish those correlative links?

10.8   What is our current prospect to customer ratio?

10.9   What difference would it make to our cost-of-sale if the prospect/customer ratio were improved?

10.10   What are the underlying demographic trends in the markets we serve?

10.11   What are the demographic trends in the lifestage segments we serve?

10.12   What correlation is there between credit score and geographic location?

10.13   What impact could geodemographics have on media targeting to prospect markets?

10.14   What do we have to do to our customer records to be able to profile them using MOSAIC or comparable systems?

10.15   What are the key indicators in our customer behaviour we wish to analyse for their significance?

10.16   How might we segment our customers differently using systems like MOSAIC?

10.17   How might we test geodemographic profiling?

10.18   What part does direct marketing play in our customer strategy?

10.19   In what ways do mail-order customers differ from retail customers?

10.20   What else do our prospects and customers do with their disposable income?

10.21   What other marketing organization might we collaborate with in promoting to prospects we both value?

10.22   What added-value services and products could we add to our range as a result of geodemographic profiling?

10.23   What market segments, revealed through geodemographic profiling, might represent attractive potential markets for strategic investment?

10.24   What is our definition of the ideal prospect or customer?

10.25   How will we integrate geodemographic profiling with our market research, direct marketing, product development and marketing communications processes?

Those organizations who have substantial consumer markets will, without doubt, acquire significant competitive advantage from systems like MOSAIC, ACORN, *et al.*—the ability to focus the marketing effort and to be more certain that hidden markets are not being ignored, are large prizes. The relationship between geodemographics and other aspects of the marketing tool-set is of prime importance today—it will be one of the critical competences for marketers in the near future.

11

Telemarketing

Getting ever closer to home

Wendy Aldiss (Inbound Outbound)

Telebusiness is a more appropriate term than telemarketing for most companies today. Telebusiness can be defined as any part of a company's business which is carried out primarily over the telephone in a way that is planned and controlled, and which is designed to open up lines of communication between a company and its customers or prospects and to give or gather information. Telephone marketing (telemarketing) has attracted a somewhat limiting definition as the telebusiness executed solely as part of a marketing strategy.

Telemarketing started in the USA, which enjoys a far more innovative business culture than the UK. Among some of the earliest users were the Ford Motor Company and Coca Cola, who saw the potential value of making outbound calls. So successful have the telebusiness innovations been in the USA that they have been gradually adopted in the UK albeit with certain essential adaptations to suit the British market-place. Germany and France have also followed the US example, and gradually the rest of Europe, then the rest of the developed world. Japan is a keen user too.

As the costs of other sales and marketing tools have grown, so telephone usage has increased. It is generally accepted that telemarketing agencies alone generate revenue of around £75 million each year in the UK.

Like all telebusiness procedures, telemarketing enables person-to-person communication on a small or mass scale. It is an extraordinarily powerful marketing tool. Comparing telemarketing to most other marketing methods is like comparing a laser beam to torchlight.

Advertising, however good the research it is based on, is essentially a broadcasting media: ads send out your message to a wider audience, but the communication is only one way, transitory and shallow. Because telemarketing relies upon two-way communication with each person, it enables you to penetrate and exploit your market by creating a personal interface—the most personal interface you can have short of meeting your target in the flesh.

Uses of telemarketing

Typically, telemarketing is used for

- Taking requests for company literature
- Taking, creating and upgrading orders
- Customer care
- Service calls
- Customer retention
- Increasing loyalty
- Making appointments
- Introducing new services or products
- Encouraging people to attend events.

All the above telemarketing activities enhance your marketing mix by bringing you closer to the customer.

Part of the secret of telemarketing's power, the element that elevates it above other ingredients in the marketing mix, is its singular ability to create a one-to-one relationship with a customer or prospect. It makes the connection that lies at the very heart of all business—the dialogue between buyer and seller.

Let us follow, for example, Acme Ltd, a fictitious company considering launching a new product. Enjoying a healthy cash flow it wishes to increase its range of goods or services. An idea for a new product has been kicking around for some time. But how big a demand for it is there?

Market research begins: conversations, conducted either on the telephone or in the flesh, with people either individually or in groups. The feedback is good. A few sample designs are produced and reaction is tested, again on a one-to-one or group basis. The results are positive. The money is there, the demand is there, and production and supply pose no problems. The signal is given. Lights turn to green and minds turn to the launch.

Having scrutinized the market research, creative teams begin designing the advertising. Which publications? Where in the publication will it attract most attention? At what price? What about mailshots? Coupons? Trial packs?

It is at around this time that Acme Ltd says 'goodbye' to the responses of individuals and 'hello' to what it perceives is the market. Computer predictions take precedence over research reports. Reality is replaced by virtual reality. Certainly, Acme's marketing is slick and professional and based on accurate research, but it acts like a blanket; while intending to cover the market the company has inadvertently smothered its voice. Acme's direct marketing will yield a response rate of around 3 per cent; the remaining 97 per cent will remain silent. It is a poor reward.

The additions of two telemarketing practices to the marketing mix could make all the difference and ensure that the investment in time, effort and money yields its full potential.

Dedicated telephone numbers

First, by including a dedicated telephone number in its marketing output, Acme Ltd could easily begin re-establishing the individual link with its customers that it enjoyed during its fruitful days of market research. It will gain more responses, from those people who would not normally write but will phone; in addition it can impress its customers or prospect in a way that no mass-produced letter (however carefully worded) can.

Through telemarketing, Acme can project an image of caring professionalism, while finding out much more information about its market. It can find out why people responded; if they have used a similar product or not; how suitable it is; whether they usually use a competitor's product; how easy it is to buy; how much they spend on the product per year; how often they make that purchase. Ask the right questions and listen to the answers.

Telemarketing also lets Acme introduce the customer or prospect to other lines which the call reveals are relevant to their needs— something it would never know by simply putting things in the post or on the page of a journal.

Non-responders and lost subscribers

Second, outbound telemarketing made to a selection or all of the non-responders (subject to industry restrictions) will establish why this percentage remained silent, convert some to customers and point the way forward towards more effective marketing in the future.

Not only is telemarketing a powerful medium in its own right and when enhancing the effectiveness of other aspects of marketing but also, unlike some other ingredients you find in the mix, telemarketing is a friendly medium. It combines well with the other ingredients and can either lead or support them in creating a successful strategy. In fact, so dependent has marketing become on the telebusiness that if you take the telephone out of market research, or erase the freephone number from the above-the-line advertising (to give just two examples) you would seriously impair many marketing strategies.

So the question when to use telemarketing is almost academic: you are probably already using it and have been doing so for years. In short, you could use telemarketing whenever it is advantageous and cost effective to have controlled and planned one-to-one communication with a targeted audience.

One true success story involves a company who used the telephone to lower attrition. This finance organization decreased their attrition rate by 70 per cent by making a single phone call to selected subscribers. They were already doing regular communication mailings, encouraging members to use their product more, some with incentives. They undertook a lot of market research to keep in touch with their members and to find out what they wanted in terms of new services. They were very proactive, conscientious in providing what they knew their general member profile wanted. Yet it was when they introduced telephone calls, carried out three months prior to the date when the subscription was due, that attrition dropped by 70 per cent. Through the calls they could provide what the individual member wanted.

Care lines

Care lines generate customer feedback and brand loyalty. In the USA 83 per cent of FMCG (fast-moving consumer goods) products carry a care line number. Companies are well aware that if a problem arises within the company and it is dealt with in a positive way, even if it is not totally solved, the customer can be converted to be an advocate of the company. Left unsolved a bad image spreads very quickly. Telebusiness can be used to raise your company's profile or to reinforce product awareness. Certain activities will be performed on an ongoing basis, year in, year out; others tactically. While the instances where you should use telebusiness would fill an entire book, it would not be wise to use telebusiness when it is not cost effective.

The difficulty with defining the cost efficiency of telebusiness is that there is so much you achieve through the telephone that it is hard to quantify. For example, if you run a customer service department it is difficult to tell on a week-by-week, month-by-month basis what sort of additional loyalty you are building up with your customers which itself will increase sales. Even in instances where telemarketing is, at first glance, clearly inappropriate, it may have a role to play later in the sales cycle. For example, telemarketing cannot be used where your sales team have to physically be there to see the stocks on a shelf or the physical environment of a company. However, it could be used to maintain contact between personal visits or as an inbound facility for additional orders to be placed. It is ideal to bridge gaps in sales territories.

Some people are still wary of making commitment over the phone and need a personal visit. These can, however, be arranged and followed up by phone. Standards of service and/or delivery can be monitored through phone calls.

Thoroughness and versatility

It is known that telemarketing can increase the size and detail of the response from the usual direct marketing mailshot, but it has many more strengths than that. By its very nature—being a planned and controlled exercise in one-to-one communication—it can replicate the function of a personal visit from your company's representative, which is an increasingly expensive exercise and not always the best way of dealing with the client or customer.

Probably most salespeople would find it hard to maintain a rate of five appointments per day. A good telemarketer should make contact with around five decision-makers *per hour*, and will face less risk of initial rejection. How many sales are lost in face-to-face meetings because of some prejudice on the part of the customer? It does not happen on the telephone. Not only is each call tailored to the objective but also a good telemarketer becomes just the type of person that the customer on the other end of the phone wants them to be.

Flexibility and immediacy

To the qualities of thoroughness and versatility we can add a third: flexibility. Let us suppose that something happens in your marketplace that needs an immediate response. You probably cannot afford to put out a new television campaign or intercept your direct mail deliveries nor to recall your salespeople from the field, retrain them, then send them out again in the space of a few hours. But you can change the wording of your phone calls and start spreading the message almost straight away. No other marketing medium lets you do this.

This flexibility allows you to improve your own performance as well. Perhaps you have started with a style of approach that works, but as time goes on it becomes inappropriate. (You can tell by monitoring the success of the calls when or where something is going wrong.) With telemarketing you can simply change the presentation—easily, cheaply, effectively, immediately.

This leads us to the fourth and probably the most important contribution that telebusiness will make to your marketing mix. Telebusiness will make you think more deeply about the objectives, structure, expectations and results of the campaign than any other method because of the immediacy of its response. Once you have opened up a phone line to your customers or prospects—inbound or outbound, it does not matter which—you will not be able to avoid hearing both their opinion of you and their real requirements. A company may advertise an 0800 prefix telephone number, offering a particular car or software bargain in the belief that this will form the sole topic of conversation. Some hope! They will get everything, and they will start learning very fast exactly what their customers think of them. So telebusiness should force you to think about the whole business you are in and you should be prepared to take that on board.

Advantages of telebusiness

Is this an advantage or a disadvantage? I firmly believe that the company who makes itself accessible in this manner—through planned, controlled professionally executed telebusiness—holds a permanent and distinct advantage over those of its competitors who are not using telebusiness. If you open up a customer services line, that will be the number where your customers know that they can get a decent response; where they will always be listened to; where something will always be done. No other form of marketing has the same ability to give customers and prospects the feeling that their complaints or suggestions will be followed through so well or that the company is on their side.

This concept of being accessible and friendly to the customer is still alien to too many companies in the UK who continue to prefer the brutal certainties of operating as hunters and gatherers, rather than putting the extra effort required into cultivating their customers. Their primitive view of the customer begins and ends with a quick kill at the point and moment of sale. Quite frankly, once they have taken the cash, they lose interest in the customer; or worse, the customer is regarded as trouble and brushed off. Why this should be is unclear, especially in the light of the American business experience. Perhaps it is just another example of the difference between the more open manner in the USA and the chillier, more reserved way that such matters are dealt with in the UK.

Disadvantages of telebusiness

Naturally, telebusiness has what for some people will appear to be drawbacks. Professional telebusiness is not easy and it does not come cheap. You have to have the right environment, expensive equipment, all the staff overheads and, above all, be prepared to pay for professional training. Badly performed telebusiness will be seriously damaging to your company's health. We have already seen how telebusiness makes you look long and hard at your marketing basics. There is no short-cut to good telebusiness: you have to take it step by step. It is like any other marketing campaign: if you do not sit down and target your people properly, design your creative approach and think what you are trying to achieve, you will not achieve half the results that you could have expected if you had planned well.

If you choose to use an external resource, you have to put just as much thought and planning into what you are trying to achieve—if not more—than if you are doing it in-house.

Tailoring outbound calls

It is quite possible that for your company to get value for money from telebusiness and enjoy the benefits outlined above, certain corporate attitudes will have to change. All your calls—inbound or outbound—must be handled professionally by well-trained staff using suitable telephony and working to achievable and cost-effective targets.

Outbound calls should be carefully tailored to each particular customer or prospect. Their form and content merit serious thought. It should be obvious to companies (but often it is not) that a good call guide is more than just a replication of the same words you might use when meeting customers face-to-face, or in a brochure. Telephone communication is just not like that. Besides ensuring fluency, a well-written call guide means you can handle a wide variety of attitudes. Even if your customers or prospects say that they are not interested because their budget does not come up for review for another six months, it is not just a 'No'. It is an indication that in four months' time it is worth ringing the customer. So, whereas from direct marketing you had only a 3 per cent response and the remaining 97 per cent you know nothing about, with telemarketing, even if you increase response by only 5 per cent on the first call you know *why* the other people are saying 'No'. You define the people who said 'No' into different types of 'No' and communicate with them again at the optimum time, with a history of contact and exactly the right message for that person.

Handling inbound calls

For some companies, *maximizing value* means reducing the costs of calls to a minimum, often by shortening inbound calls in a frenzied bid to increase productivity with little thought for what you or the caller are gaining. I would argue for a more sophisticated balance and prefer to think in terms of optimum cost for the maximum return.

Why have so many inbound call centres concentrated their attention on shifting inbound calls as fast as they can? Because they do not want to keep people waiting? Well, if they employ a few more staff they will not have to keep people waiting. But, you might argue, that puts up the cost of the operation. Okay, well let us see what a company stands to gain from those calls if a bit more time is spent on them.

Take the example of someone ringing up and asking for a particular holiday which is already fully booked. What would the usual response be?

'I'm sorry. That holiday is fully booked now. Thank you for calling. Goodbye.'

Excellent. The telemarketer has got rid of the customer quickly and reasonably politely. Call duration was within target. Everyone is happy. But how about, when the customer is on the phone showing an interest in a product, the company representative —for that is what the telemarketer is—shows some interest in the customer and suggests another date or another destination, which may be just as viable for the customer. They may make a sale. Is it not worth employing an extra person to take the calls that were not answered because they were taking the time to deal with calls in this way? A sale has been made and the company may have gained a loyal customer. Loyal or not, the customer has not gone to a competitor who may bother to take the time.

Always bear in mind how much pressure you are putting staff under to get rid of calls the minute they are answered. Staff absenteeism and turnover are themselves a cost. Maximizing the value of each call means attaining the correct balance between costs and the results you get as a business.

Future of telebusiness

As to the future of telebusiness, I believe that it will be in increasingly common use in a widening variety of business ventures. Like every other product of the revolution in information technology, telebusiness systems will become simultaneously more sophisticated and simpler to use, as well as cheaper to buy and more widely available. Progress is doing more with less.

Already many companies have their telephone departments linked to their distribution system. The moment an item request is keyed in, it is automatically sent to the distribution department and the item is sent out that night. Soon database and script package will include background data, allowing calls to be automatically diaried forward to a particular time, based on past analysis, receipt of stock, discounted prices, etc.

As geodemographics and other modelling software becomes more widely available, we shall be able to get the systems to alter the scripts and improve prompts to telebusiness users. Businesses in the financial sector will have calls triggered automatically by customer behaviour. When the customer does something, such as buying some shares or going overdrawn, the system will place them in a queue for the telebusiness person, complete with the appropriate call guide.

Figures are deplorably scarce, but the most recent survey indicates

that in 1992 the telebusiness spend in UK companies with over 100
employees stood at £10.4 billion (Henley Centre Telebusiness
Survey, 1994). As impressive as this figure is, I would suggest that if
companies continue to develop telebusiness creatively, the increase
in its use will be dramatic. After all, telebusiness has the potential to
reach out to even more of the adult population.

I am a committed advocate of professional telebusiness because I
have seen just how effective it can be. Frankly, a lot of current
practice is terribly mediocre. You do not have to make vast
adjustments to see a tremendous improvement. In today's
competitive world, where many companies are often distinguishable
from their competitors only through their reputation for quality of
service, telebusiness should be giving your marketing mix the edge
that will allow you to capture and keep your competitor's
customers.

Checklist

Telemarketing, or telebusiness as Wendy Aldiss urges us to call it, is
big business worldwide and getting bigger by the minute. Is this
rational? Or is it, perhaps, a symptom of everyone jumping on the
latest bandwagon, all else in marketing communications having
(presumably) failed?

The forensic marketer will have no ambiguity about telebusiness. It
is the embodiment of so much that we aspire to—micro-
segmentation down to the individual unit, fully interactive,
measurable, data and information rich, controllable, and susceptible
to very precise behavioural analysis.

Of course it has had a mixed press: invasive, insensitive,
inappropriate and incompetently done, to name but four generic
criticisms. But these relate to execution not concept. Similarly, the
medium has been abused by get-rich-quick operators of dubious
chatlines. These problems are likely to be with us for all time, but as
the professional exploitation of the medium grows, they will
diminish in importance. For the present they put a serious distortion
upon the image of telebusiness.

In Chapter 12 we shall look at the impact of technology innovation
upon marketing communications, but it is worth repeating here
Wendy Aldiss's observation that telebusiness is migrating fast

towards a state in which any communication via telephone media will be included in the term—whether digital data, voice or video content. Telebusiness will be seen as a branch of the multi-media industry—one that is forecast to grow at an exponential rate over the next 20 years. Thus, in thinking about the particular attributes of voice telephony within telebusiness, we should not lose sight of the fact that the key learning points will apply generically to multi-media as well. If you are a reluctant telebusiness user or aspirant today, ask yourself whether you are missing the opportunity to gain valuable experience now in a young technology, thereby establishing a competence level for the bigger things, just around the corner.

Earlier in the book I referred to the dilemma for direct marketers represented in the achievement of, say, a 5 per cent response from a mailing campaign. I stressed that another way of looking at the result is a 95 per cent non-response or failure. The worst thing that can happen to a forensic marketer is not knowing why something has, or has not, happened. It is surely an axiom of good marketing that if you can understand why a customer buys you can get them (and others) to do it again. That is the concept, but until telebusiness techniques became widely available, it has been difficult to put into practice cost effectively. Telebusiness has changed in so far as we are now able to ask buyers and non-buyers alike the whys and wherefores of their decision.

I rather doubt whether the market research techniques needed for this are yet refined enough to release the full potential of this approach, but the progress is encouraging. What is more restrictive is the psychological barrier to be overcome by many marketers wanting to explore why prospects did not buy: it means peering into the entrails of failure. I would argue that there is a full spectrum between the few customers who would have bought at any price and the few prospects who would never have bought at any price— different gradations of positivism or negativism. Bart Kosko (1994), in his insightful book *Fuzzy thinking*, reminds us that most things in life are not simple yes or no choices. Between yes and no are unlimited possibilities. These, familiar to the direct marketeer, constitute the clusters of significant variables found in regression analysis.

Where many marketers have been limited in their ability to improve performance is in the realm of moving from yes/no analysis to establishing the fuzzy continuum between those points. I believe that telebusiness offers, besides a potent tool for achieving direct sales, the best hope for detailed pre-facto, de facto and post-facto analysis of markets so that the continuum can, at the very least, be divided into meaningful clusters of positivism or negativism, opening the way for structured single variable tests of offers in pursuit of incremental effectiveness.

That might be seen as the ultimate rationale for the medium. On the way lie many benefits, enumerated by Wendy Aldiss, and too tempting I believe to ignore. Telebusiness, coupled with the cluster analysis techniques of geodemographics (see Chapter 10), allow for structured mass market testing. The knowledge gained has durable value and can be extrapolated to provide beneficial national profiles—the leverage of the two techniques is immense.

Even though I may seem only to be exhorting consumer-oriented marketers to seize the telephone, the principles apply in equal measure to the business-to-business marketer. It is true, regrettably, that reliable information on commercial clients, including their behaviour under various stimuli, is conspicuous by its absence. Generally there is too much reliance on transactional data, which may well mask the reasons why a buy decision was made. Forensic marketers understand customer and client behaviours. Telebusiness is the key to that competence.

Questions to consider

11.1 What part in the marketing mix does telebusiness play now?
11.2 What else could telebusiness do to enhance the value of each element of the marketing mix?
11.3 What do we know about our customers?
11.4 What would we like to know?
11.5 What are the principal bands with the fuzzy decision continuum that we wish to define?
11.6 What do we know about non-buying prospects?
11.7 What would we like to know?
11.8 How large is the market that nearly bought?
11.9 How large is the market that nearly did not buy?
11.10 What systems have to capture both buyer and non-buyer information?
11.11 What competences do we need to make full use of telebusiness?
11.12 What uses of telebusiness can we make in serving other stakeholder communications?
11.13 What communications do we currently undertake that could be better canalized through telebusiness?

11.14 What is the connection between effective relationship marketing and telebusiness?

11.15 What is the competitive utilization of telebusiness and what is it likely to be over time?

11.16 What use of tele-response mechanisms do we design into above-the-line advertising and what use ought we to make of them?

11.17 What do we know about the likely technology developments in telebusiness, such as Integrated Services Digital Network (ISDN), interactive non-voice telephony, telephone-based payment systems and voice recognition developments?

11.18 Where does telebusiness fit within our market research programme?

11.19 Where ought it to be?

11.20 What are the legal implications of telebusiness?

11.21 What are the economics of telebusiness, both absolute cost and as cost of sale?

11.22 What lessons can we learn from the growth in UK telebanking against the relative failure (to date) of TV and phone-based home-shopping systems?

11.23 What is our ethical position on telebusiness to home- based consumers?

11.24 How accessible are we as a business? Could telebusiness enhance our accessibility?

11.25 What do we know about telebusiness support systems, from hardware and software vendors, including the telecomms industry?

Wendy Aldiss draws out a number of important points about the interpersonal skills that lie at the core of effective verbal telebusiness. The power of the technology is likely to be realized by those organizations that have a firm grip, if that is the word, on the softer skills of marketing. Telebusiness is a rare amalgam of highly measurable activities and often intuitive interpersonal skills. It is a young technology in relative terms and many marketers, particularly those who accept the rigour of the forensic approach, will want to make fast progress in the field. You cannot start telebusiness too soon.

12

New technologies

Anticipating their impact

Monica E. Seeley (Mesmo Consultancy)

Introduction by Gavin Barrett

Chapters 4–11 have in the main addressed the communications mix in terms of the here and now—reviewing techniques and arguments likely to be familiar to a significant proportion of readers. In this chapter I have asked Monica Seeley to review the emergent technologies that are likely to impact the roles and resources of marketers. Some of these technologies, like interactive multi-media, are already being used to good effect by marketers, for example in the leisure fields of music and travel, as well as automotive, financial services and real estate sectors.

Multi-media is a young technology, with much written about it, much claimed, and, as yet, only a little delivered. It is, however, likely to be one of the significant technologies available and relevant to almost all marketers.

Other technologies are still in the laboratory stage, pending the solution to major problems of mass application. Central to this group is the concept of image compression which will allow high-quality video digital data to be distributed at low cost and high speed through established telecomms networks, combined with interactive facilities. At the moment image compression is some way off that definition, albeit the compression ratios achieved in the laboratories of the major players already represent 90 per cent of the battle objectives.

Another factor that will undoubtedly change the face of marketing is the so-called concept of the Negroponte Switch, developed at the Massachusetts Institute of Technology (MIT), which demonstrates that whereas television has been a mainly broadcast technology, with modern enhancements through multinational satellite broadcasting systems, it is likely in future to be a mainly terrestrial technology, distributed to consumers via land-based systems of copper wire or fibre optics. Meanwhile telephony, which has been primarily a terrestrial system for the mass market, will become a broadcast technology, building on the formidable pioneering work in cellular networks.

The technology ins and outs of the Negroponte Switch need not concern us over much, although Monica Seeley provides more detail later in the chapter for readers who will see applications for their sector sooner rather than later. What the forensic marketer will need to think about are the implications of these twin phenomena.

The main implication will, I believe, lie in the precision with which marketers can reach markets, with unprecedented interactivity. Mass marketing has generally been a blunt instrument because of the technical limitations of the media available (television, radio and national media, for example). Now that will change: telephone numbers will become personal to the subscriber, rather than specific to a geographic location and will allow contact wherever and whenever desired. With the advent of digital telephone systems, these broadcast networks will support mobile fax, computing, and, when the image compression technology catches up, video transmission—and all with interactivity.

Similarly, with television becoming a terrestrially based technology, the ability to establish interactive links with the viewer become relatively straightforward. The cable TV operators are already well advanced in home shopping, home banking, security systems and information access facilities. As cable penetrates markets, or is supplemented with the same range of options via the telecomms networks, the influence on traditional views of television advertising, for example, will be massive. Of course, the debate rages in the advertising world that consumers will not want either the choices implicit in this new frontier technology or the interactive capability that goes with it. I find that too simplistic: some consumers will not change from passive viewers to active information and decision-taking correspondents, but a significant proportion will. Over time that proportion will grow to a point at which, with 30 per cent conversion to active behaviours, the economics become highly favourable. As with the penetration of PCs it has become a question of which generation are you talking about? The interactive scenario that I am painting is already familiar territory to millions of teenagers worldwide.

France has shown some of the potential with its Minitel information and transaction system, provided at low cost to any telephone subscriber who wants it and capable of providing vast amounts of data. Its limitations are mainly its unfriendliness to the user and the necessary precondition that subscribers know how to mine through data to find the information they want. None the less, it is a national system, effective, cheap and profitable. Minitel is a mass consumer decision-support system and is a powerful example of what will become commonplace: what will change for most of us will be the quality of service and ease-of-use of these systems.

Naturally, all these changes to established communications media bring threats as well as opportunities. Printed media are concerned about the current lack of interactivity to most of their advertising, but they are experimenting with telephone response support systems as I write. The advertiser now knows that within a short timespan it will be possible to target, with unitary precision, the homes and phones of highly segmented markets and obtain a response. On the other hand, tens of millions of people commuting to work each day will still, presumably, value their daily digest of news and features in a traditional newspaper. Or will they?

One scenario gaining ground is that consumers will specify what their interests are for news, current affairs, lifestyle and advertising and receive a highly tailored *newspaper-on-demand* via their domestic, office or mobile PC—allowing them to print out only the bits they want. These newspapers-on-demand will be continuously updated: one commmentator (Chronis, 1994) speaks of the 'hourly edition'. What is being transferred to the consumer is the power of editorial choice and, to some degree, the ability to side-step the blandishments of advertisers. Over time, publics will become more sophisticated in their ability to choose what they see, hear, read or do and it is this changing balance in the relationship between the *done-to* and the historic *doers* that marketers will need to come to terms with.

While much of this scenario painting has addressed mass consumer markets, the potential for new technologies to transform the way in which business-to-business marketing is conducted is equally dramatic. E-mail (electronic mail) and its derivatives are commonplace in linking organizations and their trading stakeholders together. Electronic data interchange (EDI) is well established in many industrial processes allowing the automatic placing of orders and payments between customers and suppliers—dramatically illustrated in the chemical sector where continuous process plant electronically senses the need for more material, places a direct order on the supplier's computer system, including all special requirements, and logs delivery allowing automatic payment transfer. No paperwork, no delay, and little room for error.

Integrated Services Digital Network (ISDN) has been around for some time, but is now beginning to be taken up. Its clever combination of simultaneous voice, video and digital transmission from one PC to another is transforming knowledge transfer and decision processes in many industries. As the users at either end (or station on a network) have identical information on their screens and any change made by one is immediately visible to the other, it becomes possible to draft contracts, literature, advertising copy and so on in real time, regardless of distance. Given that voice and video are part of the ISDN system, interpersonal communication is as well supported as the digital components.

Overarching all of the new technologies is the dramatic change in the way information is made available. It has become easier, by an order of magnitude, to become well informed about so much more than we used to. It is likely that we can take better decisions quicker as a result. We shall have more choice because we shall know more. Solutions offered to us will become more sophisticated because we shall be more sophisticated. Our expectations of information from suppliers will increase sharply. The amount of knowledge we shall be able to gain about our customers will, equally, increase on a massive scale. Just as it is commonplace for the food industry to have continuous real-time information from supermarket checkouts on what is bought and where, allowing extreme behavioural monitoring, so that will be normal in mass consumer transactions of every type.

This is a new world for marketers, whether a brave new world in the Aldous Huxley sense, or something more friendly, only time will tell. In the meantime, I am certain that forensic marketers will need to address these changes, become well informed about them and think through the consequences as they will apply to the marketing proposition between them and their customers, their use of the communications mix and, in the full sense of Hamel and Prahalad's (1991) expeditionary marketing, what new markets can be established, consolidated and exploited as a result, before the competition has woken up to the new reality.

Thus, while Monica Seeley's chapter is theoretically ahead of the context of this book, it seems to me to be wise to take a forward look. The rate of change is so fast and significant that many of the

points we have described as coming may well have become
established within a year or two. Others will never happen, and
concepts we have not been able to imagine will be seen as obvious
by the end of the nineties. The forensic marketer is unlikely to be
complacent about his or her present reality.

Introduction by Monica E. Seeley

As Gavin Barrett indicates, there is a growing range of new
technologies which offer the forensic marketer an opportunity to
gain a competitive edge, by either enhancing the response from a
campaign or simply doing things better than the competition. While
none of these new technologies directly replaces the media outlined
in the earlier chapters each, as we shall see, can add considerable
value to existing marketing activities as well as support the ability
to be *well informed*. We shall undoubtedly see a shift in marketing
spend from traditional forms of advertising towards more emphasis
on the use of the newer cable and interactive television media.
Indeed these technologies will lead to a complete rethink about the
criteria for determining when to advertise, because there will no
longer be peak viewing times. Other factors such as duration of
advertisements and response mechanisms to them will need
rethinking.

From the bagatelle of new technology, here are the ten which at the
time of writing look the most promising and the most likely to
influence the basis upon which marketing is undertaken:

- Image compression and fibre optics
- Multi-media
- Integrated Services Digital Network (ISDN)
- Cable and interactive television
- Mobile telephony
- Groupware
- Internet
- Personal digital assistants (PDAs)
- Virtual reality (VR)
- Neural networks.

These technologies create an *information paradox* for the marketer.
On the one hand, technologies such as Internet and PDAs enable us
to generate a torrent of information, in the face of which some may
feel overwhelmed. On the other hand, technologies such as
groupware and neural networks provide us with the tools to

process, analyse, and share huge volumes of information at speeds and with accuracy which were undreamt of, until the mid-nineties.

Broadly speaking there are five ways in which the emerging technologies can help us as marketeers. They are outlined below and summarized in Table 12.1:

- Communicating our message more effectively and efficiently
- Improving the quality of information available and our ability to share it with others involved in the decision-making process
- Bringing new services and products to market more quickly
- Changing the basis upon which we do business
- Improving our personal effectiveness as marketers.

Table 12.1 Potential impact of different technologies on the marketing process

	Communicating the message effectively	Improved information processing	Bringing new services and products to market faster	Changing the basis for business	Improving personal productivity
Image compression	√		√	√	
Multi-media	√		√		√
ISDN	√	√	√	√	√
Cable and interactive TV	√	√	√	√	
Mobile telephony	√	√	√	√	√
Groupware		√			√
Internet	√	√		√	√
PDAs	√	√			√
Virtual reality		√	√		
Neural networks		√	√		

Image compression and fibre optics

Underlying many of the new forms of technology and especially interactive television and multi-media and the information highway are developments in the fields of image compression and fibre optics (*Business Week*, 13 June 1994). Image compression enables information (in any format, audio, text and image) to be converted from traditional analogue format into digital format which can then be compressed for transmission and storage in a fraction of the space previously required. Developments in fibre optics mean that vastly increased band-widths are available to transmit information. For example ten television channels can now be transmitted across a band-width which in the late eighties could transmit only one.

Neither technology is new: both have been around for decades. What is new is the meeting of the minds of technology and media giants such as AT&T and Time-Warner to exploit the combination of the two technologies to create brave new worlds which enable us to create interactive communications in ways and speeds hitherto unknown. It will be possible to transmit a multi-media presentation faster than the fastest fax and, of course, in colour. The developments in image compression and fibre optics underpin the developments in cable and interactive television, ISDN and multi-media.

Multi-media

Multi-media is the word used to describe a computer-based presentation which incorporates text, graphics, digital sound, computer output, and video all on one storage medium. To date the main uses for multi-media have been within training, as a method of delivering highly interactive distance learning materials, point-of-sale activities, and within the leisure industry for home entertainment (Latchem *et al.*, 1993). However, there are five areas (*Business Week*, 12 July 1993) within marketing where multi-media will be used to enhance the communications process and provide business benefits:

- Development of presentations
- Design of promotional materials
- Development of corporate image
- Strengthening customer loyalty
- Video conferencing.

Before we look at each use, let us consider what is known about how we absorb and remember information. For most people information retention increases directly with the number of different information processing channels being utilized, and the level of interactivity. That is to say we are more likely to remember and understand a message if we can engage and use both our audio and visual channels of processing rather then just visual. Similarly we shall remember more if we interact with the presentation, for example by answering questions rather than sitting passively.

Multi-media technology provides the opportunity to capitalize on both these well-proven theories of human information processing, and hence communicate our message far more effectively and efficiently than if we rely on one, and at best two media, such as traditional video.

Development of presentations

The time we have to create a favourable impression and gain customers' or prospects' attention is very short. Think back over the last few times when you have been on the receiving end of a marketing or sales presentation. How quickly did you start to form an impression of whether or not you wanted to deal with that person or organization? On what did you base your judgement? I can assert that a key factor was the quality of the visual aids. Multi-media can help provide sales and marketing presentations which

- Are of the highest quality and make an immediate impact
- Utilize a wide variety of communications channels and hence optimize the chances of prospects and customers remembering your message
- Can be made interactive and not passive, so again improve the chances of the message being remembered
- Bring life to the presentation and convey a high level of reality
- Provide structural continuity within the presentation while incorporating a range of media sources.

A handful of organizations are already using multi-media techniques to good effect and finding benefits such as a significant decrease in the sales time needed to sell complex products. I suggest that multi-media based presentations will become the norm over the next few years to a point at which any salesperson and marketer who does not use this technology is certain to be at a disadvantage. Moreover, the interactive nature of multi-media provides an as yet untapped source of data about your clients and prospects.

Design of promotional materials

Desk-top publishing revolutionized the production of paper-based monochrome promotional materials. However, the production of colour materials, especially those with plenty of graphics, is still primarily the domain of the specialist design house. Multi-media offers the potential for significantly improving what can still be a costly and time-consuming task. Multi-media helps the planning and design of the creative approach and the final artwork. How many times do we make last-minute changes to the creative elements or the artwork? The cost goes up and so does the production time. Multi-media eliminates some of the problems because we can see the end product immediately. If those needing to approve the artwork are geographically dispersed then consider an ISDN link (see below), instead of the conventional courier, for distributing the materials.

Development of corporate image

There are a number of areas surrounding the development and communication of the corporate image where multi-media offers significant advantages. Take a situation wherein your product offerings are complex and promotion of them would benefit from the client seeing a realistic simulation of what the future will be like after the acquisition of the product. Typical examples would be a motor car, a new piece of technology, or a drug. Multi-media can help provide just such a simulation presentation, conveying a realistic image of the product and, thereby, shorten the sales cycle.

If you are running a television media campaign, consider the impact on the client of a sales presentation which reinforces the television campaign by incorporating the same visual material. This is largely only possible with multi-media, which can incorporate video images.

Strengthening client loyalty

The more ways in which it is made easy for customers to buy, the more likely they are to stay. Conversely you are seeking to make it more difficult for them to switch out of the relationship. A powerful way to do this is to put buying aids *on the customer's* desk. Examples include your catalogue, a link to your order entry systems—via electronic data interchange (EDI)—estimating and forecasting tools. For example, this might mean the components your client needs either to manufacture products or to provide other services. But before customers can order from you they must work out quantities and precise specifications. Relationship marketers provide clients with the tools to make their life easier.

Increasingly corporations from financial services to component manufacturers are already exploiting multi-media within the marketing context in the ways outlined here and gaining distinct business and competitive benefits.

Video conferencing

Until the advent of multi-media and ISDN, video conferencing had been the prerogative of the very largest organizations and took place only in a specially equipped studio. However, it is becoming possible to run a desk-based video conference using the technologies of multi-media and ISDN at quite low costs. Such ideas have already found a home in the thinking of leading players in the financial services sector in the USA and UK. Boeing found that it could cut back some project times by 90 per cent by using video conferencing linked to groupware. While the automated teller machine (ATM) can be used to provide more and more services, there will always be a need for some human interface to deal with questions and provide personal and expert advice. This can be done by video conferencing, even though the customer and the banker are separated geographically. Think too of the potential for running focus research groups. Video conferencing looks set to take off again and this time be accessible to all.

Integrated Services Digital Network (ISDN)

Integrated Services Digital Network is the telecommunications technology which allows the transmission of text, audio and images between personal computers. The main distinction between this and video conferencing is that with ISDN at its present stage of development one cannot simultaneously see the person with whom one is communicating. However, if that is not a mandatory prerequisite, then ISDN offers some exciting potential. To do both requires a combination of ISDN and video conferencing using technology like BT's PC videophone.

Cable and interactive television

Much has already been written about these increasingly familiar forms of television. With interactive TV consumers can provide specific information about their needs; in response, material is transmitted to meet these needs, including advertisements, information, or programmes. Users include the Ford Motor Company and General Motors in the USA. Conversely the buyer (consumer and business) can browse though catalogues and order directly, interacting only with the television set. Such technology is being used extensively in the USA and in limited ways in the UK, especially in clothing and consumer electronics.

There is no doubt that cable and interactive TV will take off. The breakthrough is likely when digital TV becomes the norm, which is some time ahead. Meanwhile, there is plenty to be gained from exploring the potential of these media and being ready to exploit.

Mobile telephony

Phone numbers will become personal numbers, and remain so for life. Thus, if consumers can escape from the conventional television advertisement there may be scope to recapture them through the telephone. Moreover, there can never be any excuse for us, as marketers, being out of reach.

Groupware

How often have you tried to prepare a marketing brief and involve all who need to be involved, only to find them either reading from different versions of the copy, or unavailable to read the copy and provide a timely input. Groupware is software which allows organizations to share information on a PC network, regardless of location and time. However, unlike ISDN, only text and images are shared on the screen. But the information that is shared is the same for everyone and, as updates are made, so they are shared with everyone immediately.

Currently groupware is being exploited for creating shared database for sales account management, customer service, document management, and new product development in which many people need access to the same information, at every stage. The principal benefits come from reduced error rates and lower usage of time and thus cost. Organizations finding these benefits include Reebok, Texaco, British Airways, Price Waterhouse and Lotus, the latter being the leading supplier of groupware software (called Notes).

Internet

The Internet (or network of networks, as it is sometimes known) is a global network which allows you to access, communicate and share information regardless of time and location. Unlike ISDN or interactive and cable television, the Internet is a text-based only system. However, it is relatively inexpensive and thus accessible by organizations and consumers. As a result many are already on-line. Upwards of 20 million are estimated to be on Internet. Current uses include gathering and analysing competitor intelligence, creating *bulletin boards* about your products and services, providing public reports, recruitment searches, and patent searches, and decision support. The Internet is a little like an on-line encyclopedia. If you need information you will undoubtedly find it on the Internet. Conversely it offers one of the fastest ways of communicating messages to other users on Internet. Through Internet you can log in to your own organization's e-mail from anywhere in the world.

Personal digital assistants (PDAs)

A PDA is a hand-held computer with the capacity of a very powerful workstation. A PDA allows you to enter data using conventional handwriting or freehand drawings. In the case of the latter it will then automatically tidy up your sketch and leave you with a near-perfect graphic on the screen. A PDA has diary management, contact and database management, fax facilities, and common software applications such as word processing and spreadsheets. Data can be exchanged between the PDA and main computer systems. Leading players in this market include AT&T and Apple computers with their Newton.

PDAs and, in particular, the Newton offer the potential to

- Overcome the socially unacceptable side of the laptop, especially within the sales situation
- Convert the esoteric into reality
- Cut down on the paperwork involved in agreeing or confirming a sale
- Improve communications externally
- Improve the flow of information around the organization
- Capture broader-based information about your customers.

Virtual reality (VR)

Virtual reality (VR) is a computer-based system which allows one to model the real world on a PC, while providing visual, audio, and tactile reality in response to body movements. Such body movements are detected and analysed electronically. To date, the major uses of VR have been as highly sophisticated high-reality simulations for training (Rheingold, 1991) and the larger market of arcade games.

However, there does seem to be some potential in it for the marketing function in terms of market research on new products, which may as yet be little more than an idea on the drawing board. Virtual reality affords the opportunity to test new products and ideas before incurring major production costs such as shop layouts. Indeed the textile industry is starting to exploit the technology via the creation of a *virtual catwalk* on which new designs for garments can be market tested before a cut is made in the cloth. Link this to video conferencing, and focus group research starts to take on a new dimension.

Neural networks

Neural computing, and hence networks, originate from the world of artificial intelligence. Neural networks simulate the way our biological brains work. They can deal with fuzzy and incomplete data to produce a model or approximation (Beale and Jackson, 1994). They gain their intelligence from being 'trained' on real data, usually historic in the first place. However, a neural network is the epitome of the well-informed individual as it goes on learning, updating the basis upon which it makes decisions and as it receives new data.

Some companies (including Thomas Cook and several financial service organizations) are starting to use neural networks to help them plan and analyse their direct marketing. Neural computing can take an incomplete database and provide buyer profiles, many of which are beyond the profiling systems based on current conventional statistical methods, such as regression and cluster analysis.

One of the major problems facing any airline is how accurately to predict seat occupancy and the level of overbooking. Neural networks are providing some of the answers. The Airline Marketing Tactician has been found to predict resource allocation far more efficiently and effectively.

Within the financial services sector a neural network-based system to assess loan and default rating was found to be more accurate than the human decision-making process so that a 7 per cent increase in profits could be achieved. The use of neural networks is already quite extensive within the financial sector.

The limiting factors

As every marketer knows, there is no such thing as a free lunch, and none of the above technologies is without its drawbacks. First, there are the hardware and software issues. For all these technologies to truly revolutionize the way we do business, whether on a business-to-consumer or business-to-business market-place they must be operable and accessible from the desk-top PC, whether that means that the desk-top is fixed or mobile, or a home TV, whatever shape that will take in future. These technologies all need significant levels of processing power and special circuit boards and CD-ROMs. Such PCs are still not readily found on most desks or in most homes. This will become less of a problem as more powerful PCs become available at cheaper prices; but when the optimized cross-over will happen between cost and power for mass market penetration is another matter.

Second, there is the competition within the technology industry itself, with each manufacturer striving to establish its system as the de facto standard. This is particularly marked around the multi-media and interactive TV technologies as the big players fight to provide the dominant viewing device, the PC or the television screen.

Third, there is the gap between the capability of the technology and our own competence to use it. This gap will undoubtedly be eroded in time as more acquire the necessary technical skills and knowledge to use these technologies to their full potential.

Fourth, and perhaps more fundamentally, there is a generally negative attitude among managers to be innovative. Innovation means taking risks and being able to think and solve problems inductively. There are skills and attributes that many lack. We are far too steeped in the traditional deductive approaches to problem-solving whereby we either wait for a problem to arise and then seek out the technology, or we wait for someone else to burn their fingers. Have no doubt that the innovators will gain the high ground in terms of information management and all the advantages that will bring. (Davenport, 1993, and Hammer and Champy, 1993.)

Fifth, there are the socially acceptable standards. For some (clients and suppliers) technology is a total anathema, while others may shun you and your organization if you are not using technology to communicate and provide services (Mitroff and Linstone, 1993). You will undoubtedly need to test-market your use of technology and may even need to do some old-fashioned segmentation, as to who and how you make your offer using new technology.

Sixth, there is cost. None of these technologies is currently cheap and, adding in the cost of change necessary for success, you are looking at a significant investment. While the underlying base costs of PCs and telecommunications are falling, you will need to weigh up the price that you are prepared to pay for relative competitive leadership against the lower cost of being a follower.

Last, but by no means least, is obsolescence. Technology is changing so fast that what is state of the art now may be old hat tomorrow. Obsolescence means new ways of accounting for and valuing the technology investment. What is also important is to maintain a *balanced* technology portfolio of the tried and tested and the innovative.

Keeping well informed about technological developments

Do not wait to read about such developments in the marketing press. By then the information will be second-hand, based on a deductive opinion, and be stripped of its real significance. Attend the trade show and read for yourself the computer press (such as *Computing, Computer Weekly*, etc.). Talk to the professional technologist in your IT department. Above all, make your own first-hand well-informed judgement about the value and potential of these (and other) technological developments to you and your organization.

Checklist

It is easy to forget just how much development in technology there has been in the few years since Sir Clive Sinclair launched his first LED (light-emitting diode) calculator at £100 in the early eighties. That same calculator specification, now housed in a credit card format, costs less than £0.50. It is forecast that within a decade the processing power of the PC will have increased by a factor of 40 at a cost which will have declined in real terms by a factor of 10 (Printing Industry Research Association 1991). Indeed, the rate of innovation is such that the marketer must find ways and means of understanding the underlying technologies rather than specific products, as these latter will have very transient lives. The race by the likes of Xerox Corporation, IBM, Microsoft, Apple, AT&T, Time-Warner, and Cable and Wireless, as well as telecomms operators worldwide, to master the technologies of image compression so that high-resolution video images can be transmitted via telecomms networks on demand is likely to be resolved well before the millennium. The pilot initiatives in the USA by Time-Warner allow some 500 *channels* to be distributed in parallel throughout large parts of Florida, giving the consumer unimaginable choice. This formidable capability, coupled with interactive systems, will perhaps revolutionize not only the entertainment industry, but also personal financial management, home security and information retrieval, let alone home shopping.

The challenge for the marketer is not only to understand the basis of the technologies but also to develop the imagination to harness them within the marketing mix. It has been asserted by leading media owners that it will be the ability to supply information on demand and in customer specific formats that will differentiate the high performance companies of the next 20 years, rather than cost revenue productivity management. Imagination will be the most valued competence. Monica Seeley, in her tour d'horizon, has concentrated on the immediately available technologies and, in particular, multi-media. Already well established in high-ticket retail merchandising, especially the motor industry, its applications are increasingly visible in business-to-business marketing. Special applications in the fields of education, travel and management information have changed the outlook of whole sectors.

Questions to consider

12.1   What are the technologies currently available for our business area?

12.2   How well do we understand these existing technologies?

12.3   What new technologies are anticipated which have application to our business?

12.4   What mechanisms have we for monitoring technology innovation?

12.5   What mechanisms have we for evaluating technology innovations?

12.6   What use are we making of information systems to enhance our marketing decisions?

12.7   What account of technology change have we taken in developing our marketing strategy?

12.8 Which technologies would enhance our data-gathering effectiveness?

12.9 How well integrated are our data sources, allowing us to take well-informed decisions?

12.10 What technology-based communications would enhance our relationships with business-to-business customers, or intermediate stages in the distribution chain?

12.11 What are the creative skills needed to ensure that new technologies do not become mere gimmicks in our marketing mix?

12.12 What impact will cable-based systems have on consumer viewing and buying behaviours?

12.13 What impact will cable-based systems have on the advertising industry?

12.14 What impact do we expect technology to have on general levels of literacy?

12.15 What impact do we expect technology to have on time to market for new product development?

12.16 What scope do the new technologies offer for increasing personal customization of products and services in our sector?

12.17 Which technologies do we expect to see having a major impact on retail selling?

12.18 Which technologies will have a major impact on face-to-face selling?

12.19 What are the potential uses of automatic teller machines?

12.20 Should we lead or follow in the introduction of technology-based marketing?

12.21 What are the critical success factors for achieving the optimum benefits from technology innovation in our business?

12.22 What are our priorities for technology overall?

12.23 Where are we going to acquire the new skills to optimize the potential of new technologies?

12.24 Who are the bench-mark organizations for technology application that we could network with?

12.25 How well informed do we need to be to survive and prosper?

Rather a challenging set of questions perhaps, but illustrative of the dilemma facing marketing professionals. There have been too many expensively embraced innovations in recent years for marketers not to remember the pain and the scars—the long trench-war between the VHS, Betamax and VCC formats in video, for example—and to have developed some degree of technophobia. However, ostrich-like behaviour is highly risky given the sledge-hammer blows that some technologies will deliver to mature, seemingly well-founded businesses, such as newspapers, banking, education, legal services, telecomms and inter-company trading in general.

We shall all, no doubt, back some losers, but I believe that if we concentrate on the access to, added value to and distribution of information as the critical focus, we shall not be far wrong. To do nothing about new technologies is not an option.

13

Common ground, valuable differences

Making sense of the choices

Chapters 4 to 12 graphically illustrate the marketer's dilemma—too many choices, too little budget. In reality, however, most marketers make a judgement about the two or three techniques within the communications mix that they intend to use, conducting their 'beauty parades' accordingly. The choice is between suppliers of the marketer's predetermined solutions rather than an evaluation of which techniques best could meet the need and in what combination. Believing this to be a less than ideal approach I have sought to challenge it by providing a wider-than-usual range of choices, articulated by powerful professional advocates, so that readers may see the potential in general and of new and original combinations of communications techniques in particular. It is certainly a wider choice than many of us draw upon. It can also be wider still: I have not included the role of the salesforce nor the full panoply of sales promotion techniques, for example. The nine options provided in these chapters do, however, represent the lion's share of bought-in expenditure for most marketers.

At the end of each chapter I have proposed a short checklist questionnaire which will help determine the appropriateness, or otherwise, of each individual technique in meeting the particular marketing need. Since marketers ought to be rigorous about finding the problem before the solution, I am hopeful that readers will empathize with the challenge implicit in the checklists: 'Am I making the right use of this or that approach?' The enemy is, of course, precedent—if it worked before then it will work again. Fair enough at one level—risk avoidance—since trying out new ways of meeting the objective is always risky. Not to try out new ways is riskier still. Less easy to justify is the unvarying use of fixed combinations of communications tools, based on precedent, wherein the added value of each is not known, nor the particular attributes that work well in combination, but not necessarily so in isolation.

Consider the communications options in a government privatization programme. First, the target audiences are complex and diverse, ranging from political lobbies who need to be persuaded, to investment institutions, individual investors, existing customers, existing suppliers, existing staff, future potential customers, competitors, future employees, regulatory authorities and individual local communities. I could go further and break each of these segments into more precisely defined groupings, each with their own agenda. I certainly need to be able to define them with some precision if they are to be addressed on their own specific agenda, rather than some turkey-shoot catch-all platform.

Second, the three generic questions: 'What do we want them to know?' 'What do we want them to feel?' and 'What do we want them to do?' In each case very different answers will be found.

Third, what tools are available? Direct mail, public relations, above-the-line advertising, telemarketing, briefings or seminars and exhibitions come easily to mind. But which is right for which segment? Readers will have widely differing views, as will their professional suppliers. Yet I am fairly sure that consensus would emerge that above-the-line would be important, public relations (in the fullest sense) equally so, and direct marketing tools where specific individual actions are required—sending for the issue prospectus, for example.

Fourth, while the success of the privatization is the goal of government, it is merely the beginning for many other stakeholders, facing different futures and elements of real uncertainty. What should the communications strategy be to create the conditions for durable success beyond the first milestone of privatization? Here the question of corporate image looms large—it is the focus of the strategic positioning of the enterprise both prior to, and beyond, the historical moment of change. Furthermore, the question arises as to how far the new management will want their hands tied by pre-privatization image building, let alone explicit commitments made. How can they possibly know before they take charge?

We could go on exploring the ever-widening circles of dilemma facing our hypothetical privatization enterprise, but it must be obvious, even within this brief exploration, that the deployment of the full range of communications tools is more a question of an integrated plan than of the valuation of the individual merits of each one. No one communications task can be divorced from another—because the cross-over effect may be unknown. This is a statement of the obvious as far as the run-up to our privatization is concerned. It is less obviously so for life after 'P-day'. A maxim for all those engaged in this sort of activity might well look like this: 'Be sure you know where you want to end up before you start the journey'.

Translating this challenge to the more straightforward everyday communications tasks faced by marketers in commerce and industry, the lesson is clear. Each objective is only a milestone. Consequently, marketers have, I believe, to face the real discomfort of the discipline of playing the long game. Every marketing action has a past and a future.

This is what gives this book its particular orientation in helping the marketer view the task of marketing communications in as objective a light as possible, because to do the other, succumbing too easily to the individual blandishments of one technique versus another is to miss the point entirely. It is the guardianship of an integrated and continuous communications strategy that must precondition almost all tactical decisions.

The aphorism that there are no second chances at first impressions is cautionary enough for those contemplating a new market. It is as nothing in terror terms when compared with the notion that once you have started you must continue. By this I mean that every communication to a segment (right down to the individual level) is inevitably linked to what preceded it and what succeeds it. At least that ought to be the case. Those members of the UK clearing bank community basking in the full glow of dynamic market growth in the late eighties paid, it would seem, scant regard to their future potential in pursuing a relentless product-driven scatter-gun communications strategy, often ill-segmented and always super-tactical. The British Chancellor of the Exchequer, in his 1990 Budget Statement, rightly admonished the sector for the 'indiscriminate promotion of credit, especially to those who could ill-afford to take it'. He might well have gone on to chastise the same people for having destroyed, in a few ill-conceived tactical campaigns, their brand values built up over centuries, betokening financial rectitude and good sense.

Like it or not, there is a continuum to marketing communications which should be recognized and respected. In evaluating the choices available to the marketer, as represented in Chapters 4 to 12, it is important, I believe, to be able to test each for its fit within this continuum—does each lend itself to the long game as well as the short? Since this continuum is often expressed in terms of core brand values, it might be as well to think of it thus.

I argue the point about the continuity of marketing communications because it seems clear that markets, in the reality of the purchase decision, value confidence in the product or service (and its supplier) higher than choice. If the reverse were true then we could all live happily ever after in a tactical free-for-all. But it is not—most of us are concerned with gaining and retaining markets, securing growth however we can and believing that trysting in a warm bed is much to be preferred to cold encounters of any kind. We cannot, therefore, put tactics first.

Assuming that you accept the premise that the goal comes before the getting, it is useful to have a checklist of questions that fix the backdrop against which the play will be made.

Journey's end checklist

13.1   What are our core brand values?
13.2   How do we know they are?
13.3   What should our core brand values be, and in whose opinion?
13.4   How much flexibility do we want from our brand values?
13.5   How much clarity does our statement of purpose (mission) provide for defining our communications strategy?
13.6   How clear are the milestones in brand development that will guide us towards our internal vision?
13.7   How well have we defined our core stakeholders (e.g. investors, customers, suppliers, employees, bankers)?
13.8   How well have we defined our relationship strategy with each?
13.9   How clearly have we resolved the strategic tension between adding to shareholder value and customer service quality? Do we see any tension?
13.10 How necessary is it for us to have sustainable relationships with the stakeholders?
13.11 What is the long-term basis of our competitive advantage—from differentiation to cost?
13.12 What ought to be the long-term basis of our competitive

advantage, what are our core competences that we must be valued for by our stakeholders?

13.13 What have we learned from monitoring our competitors' long-term behaviours in communication terms?

13.14 What have we learned from analysing our own past communications behaviours?

13.15 How well does our business planning process take account of the need to develop and implement a consistent communications strategy?

13.16 How precisely have we defined our values and beliefs that will inform our communications plan? The things we will always say and those that we will never say?

13.17 How much do we know about the barriers to sustainable relationships with our stakeholders?

13.18 How willing are we to accept the discipline of a communications strategy?

13.19 How do we avoid the perils of a five-year plan, with rigor mortis already set in, without living the high-risk life of just-in-time strategy formulation?

13.20 What proportion of our revenue are we prepared to budget for strategic relationship development with our core stakeholders?

This checklist may look obvious, but just pause and ask yourself the question 'If I can answer all these questions, will my colleagues also come to the same conclusions?' After all, a communications strategy is no more and no less than an expression of the tenets that bind an organization together. If it is not the 'will of you all' will it be deliverable?

I have emphasized the need to develop this backdrop since, without it, the use of communications techniques from the kaleidoscope available will perhaps too easily represent the end rather than the means. In Chapter 1, I referred to the natural and important factor of ego-driven marketing—the feel and flair for great marketing ideas. I would not suppress that drive for a moment. All I do plead is that the ego-powered energy of marketers is canalized through a strategic process, rather than tactical enthusiasms.

Sadly, it is immensely difficult to maintain a strategically consistent course. I have already mentioned the trap of the 'fourth quarter fire fight' when strategy is tipped overboard just as readily as the women and children. Even so it must be striven for.

A major breakthrough will be achieved when the suppliers of professional marketing services either offer an integrated portfolio of techniques that serves the strategic communications agenda or are willing to work in open collaboration with their fellow suppliers in agreeing the givens by which all will abide. The former is, increasingly, on offer—whether it is a reality is another question, but as with all heterodox organizations, getting any sort of cross-party consistency (let alone conformity) is a tall order. We, as clients, should be very demanding in this respect, if only to help the one-stoppers achieve deliverable internal alignment as the basic condition of contract. The latter solution is very much down to the client to make it possible for diverse suppliers to work together. Whether this means a primus inter pares or, more simply, a joint briefing process is a matter for individual circumstance. One of the purposes of this book is to help suppliers in one field of the communications mix to see what their counterparts elsewhere think and say—I hope that they will understand better the origins of so many needless turf issues.

Clients cause turf issues by tolerating them on the one hand and being ambiguous on the other. Lack of clarity in the briefing process when dealing with any professional supplier is serious when just one supplier is involved. It is a capital crime when dealing with a pack of them. It is this question of integrating supplier talents that next colours our evaluation process of each of the siren calls made in Chapters 4 to 12. How do they fit together to achieve a seamless join?

The supplier jigsaw

Jigsaw puzzles do not, of course, start life in pieces. No more should the communications plan. I stress should.

The overall picture must be visualized clearly since it is something we are going to have to look at and like for a long time to come. Then it can be divided up into interesting pieces—interesting to the supplier and the client. Implementation of the communications plan is the putting together of the jigsaw itself.

Each of us, no doubt, has a preferred approach to jigsaws. I tend to find the four corner pieces, followed by the edge pieces—that at least dimensions the task. The same applies to the communications plan—what are the corner pieces? How do we dimension the whole?

I have argued that the 20 point checklist earlier in the chapter will provide the main architectural framework, defining many of the outer pieces of our jigsaw. Other pieces in the puzzle come from having a number of tactical tasks—product launches, call cycles or follow-through campaigns, annual reports, half-time and full-year results, life-cycle modifications and the like. But because this is a jigsaw, each of these tactical pieces must fit with the others around them.

The same metaphor applies to the suppliers, who are also pieces in our jigsaw. Which fits with which? Extending the image a little way, we might allocate above-the-line and PR to the sky pieces, whereas relationship marketing and geodemographics belong to the detailed foreground. Given the cases put forward in Chapters 4 to 12 you can judge where they each see the natural links between them.

It goes without saying that it is far easier to complete the puzzle if a copy of the final picture is always to hand. Only when the picture is complete must we drop this metaphor, because it is at the very moment of triumphant completion that the puzzler may succumb to the temptation to break it all up and start again. If the picture is worth completing it is worth keeping.

There are no rules, I believe, for saying that one technique must always be used in this or that combination with others. What is at issue is which technique is best for which stage in the continuum? It is clear that corporate image is always the key to providing the backdrop: without a well-developed sense of image throughout all functional areas of the organization there can be no consistency of communication to all stakeholders. Yet it is a constant surprise that either it is not addressed at all or it is changed at will. Corporate image, as Wally Olins has stated, is the core set of perspectives from which corporate opportunities are viewed. It would be difficult to argue that corporate image comes anywhere but everywhere in the continuum.

That said, the rest of the communications tool-set is less obviously positioned. It depends very much on what the continuum actually is. So before moving on let us consider in a little more detail what I mean by the communications continuum.

The communications continuum

Unless your organization is brand new, it has a past and, since you have joined it, hopefully a future. It has relationships with its stakeholders in varying degrees of maturity. It has goals and a sense of purpose—the latter which it probably wants to communicate to all stakeholders. It has past customers, now lapsed, present customers and it has potential customers yet to be found or won. It has past products or services, current offerings and a belief that it can create more in future. It has retired staff, current employees and children that are yet unborn as potential employees.

In the midst of these continua are the old favourites of product life cycle, Boston Consulting Group's (1971) *Stars, Queries, Cash Cows and Dogs*, Hamel and Prahalad's (1991) *Core Competences model,* Porter's (1985) *Value-Chain* and new models of lifestage and lifetime value definition.

It is on to and off these continuous escalators that we marketers must step adroitly with our interventions. Not in the Shakespearian sense of strutting and fretting our hour upon the stage and then being heard no more, but conscious of the need to add value to each moment as well as the momentum of corporate growth and success.

The question in determining how to make use of the powerful tools available for communications is more to do with 'Where will it lead?' than with 'What will it do now?' The latter, however, is where we too often get stuck, since it is what we, as marketers, are paid to deliver.

Another way of putting 'Where will it lead?' is 'What will it leave behind?' I have already touched upon the notion of organizations viewing marketing as the resource which pushes out the frontiers of experience so that it becomes wiser through experience. In the Forensic mnemonic *I* stands for *inertia* (see Chapter 3) and betokens the constant challenge to marketers to understand why things happen or why they do not. It is critical that organizations value discovery of better ways of doing things. For this purpose the scientific principles I have advanced for the Forensic approach become vital. Similarly, only some of the communications tools lend themselves readily to scientific analysis. I stress readily because it is possible to determine measurable impacts of all aspects of the communications mix if you set out to do so. Whether it is worth doing so is a matter for judgement.

However, there can be no progress without learning from experience and if there is one macro lesson from considering the continuum approach to marketing communications it is the responsibility of marketers to try and test new approaches to old problems from which learning can be achieved. It is not the task of marketers to reinvent the wheel. It is, however, a major duty for all marketing-minded people to recognize that there is always a better way and hence the supreme value in using communications suppliers to challenge both the status quo and the lessons of history: the professional marketer simply ensures that this does not mean reinventing the wheel.

Finally, I subscribe to the view that it is through close interaction with professional suppliers in marketing communications that we stand the best chance of finding the hidden markets—the people who nearly buy—the markets that nearly happened. This is surely the last frontier for marketers—tapping the key to why the sale did not happen.

We have thus considered the mind of the marketer in evaluating what our siren chorus has had to say. We think long and we think hard and we think consequences. But is that it?

The answer is not quite: there is the small matter, as I mentioned in the opening chapters of the book, of selling your enlightened view of the communications task to your boss. This will be the burden of the final chapter.

14

Back to the start-line?

Selling it to your boss

Thus far we have explored the relationship between top management's business strategy agenda, the role of marketing professionals in interacting with the client environment, thereby developing a relevant marketing strategy and the harnessing of powerful external resources in a coherent fashion, supported by the FORENSIC technique, to achieve outstanding implementation of both the high-level business and marketing strategies (see Fig. 14.1, which is Fig. 1.2 repeated here for easy reference).

In Chapter 13 I argued that it is the strategic view of the stakeholder relationship continua that must inform the marketer's actions, rather than solely concentrating upon tactical campaigning aimed at near-term objectives. That, at any rate, is the logical model. I am confident that you are nodding in agreement at this point. But how realistic is this concept? The answer, like so many in business, is a function of what is meant by realistic. I mean 'Can it be achieved?' At one level of rationality it is entirely possible to set a strategic framework for marketing communications and work within it.

Business life, however, is seldom rational and we shall need to take account of political realities in securing corporate-wide agreement to the serious discipline of working within a strategic framework. In every business there are a host of myths and legends which form the political milieu: finance functions are infallible: salespeople see the world through rose-tinted spectacles; operations do not care about customers; marketing is one big 'jolly'; general management is out of touch; customers are a nuisance and disrupt the smooth running of the organization. You could go on and on and get more and more depressed. Yet against this stereotypic backdrop of prejudice and assumption, the forensic marketer must seek to make

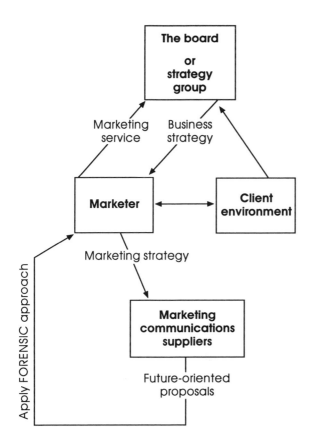

Figure 14.1 Applying the FORENSIC model to the decision-making processes of the marketing function

progress and deliver sustainable competitive advantage. In this final chapter we shall examine what can be done to install the better way.

The start-line is the business strategy. I have always felt that organizations would do better to adopt a retrospective approach to strategy formulation rather than a prospective one. By this I mean working backwards from, say, a 10 years into the future milestone, towards a 5 year view and then a 1 year view, whereas the commonplace is to adopt a 1-5-10 approach (see Fig. 14.2).

I see a 10-5-1 method (and it could easily be 12-5-2 or a similar range) as providing a completely different perspective from the 1-5-10. First, we are exhorted by Hamel and Prahalad (1991), in their exemplary *Harvard Business Review* article, 'Corporate imagination

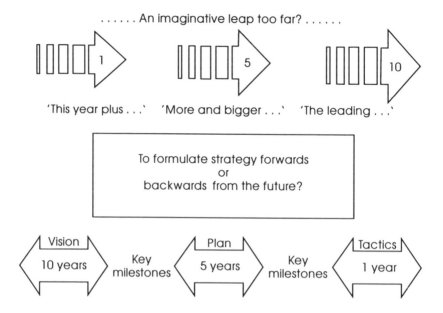

Figure 14.2 A balanced forwards and backwards view of strategic options is likely to be more reliable than a single direction approach

and expeditionary marketing', to make sure that we view the future uninhibited by today's products and markets relationship. They warn that if the future is seen as an extension of the present it will, in most cases, lead to disaster because competitors can and will get to the same point as well—the competitive ruck will be unprofitable and resource intensive. Central to their thesis on corporate imagination is the need for organizations to drop the products/markets linkage and think instead of needs and solutions. Only when durable needs are identified and generic solutions evolved is it safe to move to more detailed levels of product specification and market segmentation. I endorse their argument unreservedly provided organizations can be convinced that the only way to adopt the needs/solutions approach is to work to a 10-5-1 strategic framework. I do not think it credible to have forward-looking strategy decoupled from current products and markets thinking: they are simply too attractive as anchors when sailing into future unchartered waters.

Another attraction of the 10-5-1 view is that once the organization has achieved a level of comfort in defining what business to be in, and what it will be like, in 10 years' time through highly facilitated creation of the virtual organization of the twenty-first century, it becomes quite straightforward to look back to the present and define the milestones needed to reach the virtual goal. I generally find that organizations make a good job of the strategic path definition process once they get through the pain barrier of creating their virtual future. The enemy of all strategic thinking is uncertainty. The 10-5-1 approach provides large measures of virtual certainty because it is designed to define fundamentals not details: 'What will people still need in 10 years' time?' is a vastly simpler question than 'What features should this or that product have?'

Similarly, once the future has some clarity to its shape, it becomes relatively easy to assess current assets and capabilities for their suitability for the future of the organization. In the opening chapters of the book I argued that SWOT Analysis undertaken in that logical sequence will lead to tears. The analysis must be OTSW based, so that we only put into our strategic plan the development of assets that will be valuable in seizing the opportunities we see at a profit, and best of all, ahead of the competition. Snapshots of current strengths are, in this view of the world, largely meaningless unless tested with great rigour for their core competence value. Again Hamel and Prahalad have performed a signal service in defining three tests to apply to current strengths. I paraphrase:

- Does each provide wide access to identified current and future opportunities?
- Does each deliver real and significant benefit to clients, in their perception?
- Is each difficult, if not impossible, to imitate?

Of course, all three tests must be satisfied for a current asset or capability to be designated a core competence. However, once these core competences have been identified they take on a radical significance to the business strategist and the marketer in that they represent the prime focus of strategy and management: these are the things that we shall develop and play to. Interestingly, if you find core competences in your organization you should be able to satisfy yourself that they are not vulnerable to short-term environmental problems: rather like a gyro compass they help the organization maintain its attitude regardless of the storms howling outside.

I have stressed this strategic framework point, and especially the 10-5-1 view, since analysis has shown time and again that it is often in the quality of brand management and customer relationship systems

that the real core competences of organizations are to be found.
Take, for example, the *Reader's Digest* organization. I do not think
that their products are their core competence, although some might
argue that the *Reader's Digest* magazine is. Rather, I believe it is their
customer database technologies which allow them to analyse
customer behaviours with incredible sophistication so that the
critical variables that make for the difference between propensity to
buy or not buy are isolated and, in subsequent campaigns,
eliminated. Admittedly, *Reader's Digest* have had 70 years to get the
system right, but they have had no ambiguity for decades about
what they must get right—a system that allows them to understand
why customers do what they do so that they can get them (and
more) to do it again and again. Put another way, *Reader's Digest* are
a business for the twenty-first century, because they are likely to
have exceptional advantages in lifestyle and lifestage analysis
techniques, allowing them to meet the needs of the day, with the
solutions of the day—their competences are their marketing tools
and techniques.

Acceptance of this strategic premise by senior management will
define the things that are valuable, even critical, to long-term
success. If durable opportunities are in view they demand durable
strengths. Durable opportunities attract growing competition.
Therefore, strategy must deliver a competitively bench-marked
growth in core strengths. I believe that there is no more vital
strength to build and play to than quality of relationships with the
key stakeholders in the organization's future—with particular
emphasis on customers and shareholders (in that order).

Now the conditions are improved for a mature debate about the
imperatives of marketing and, especially, the policy framework for
marketing communications. Here I need to return to the myths and
legends and see whether there is a way of integrating the virtues of
this book's arguments with the political realities that you may be
faced with. I believe that marketers need to improve their
accountability and willingness to offer proof of effectiveness. Since
the numerative side of management thinking tends to be viewed
with favour, it is surely good sense to play by those rules. Why so
much of the marketing communications mix should be considered
non-susceptible to numerative analysis defeats me. It is a weakness
that undermines the credibility of the function and its professional
suppliers.

I have no need to argue the case for measurement of telemarketing,
geodemographic systems, electronic systems and direct marketing

as they are all intrinsically measurable. Whether the fact is understood in non-marketing circles is something else.

But other tools and techniques are a numerative challenge: public relations, corporate image, above-the-line advertising, corporate literature and market research all sound useful, but are difficult to prove in purely numerative terms. Hence reading and noting scores, awareness studies, pre- and post-differential analysis, retention, market share and equally malleable measures. Those of you who find the FORENSIC approach attractive will see that it offers a different view of performance effectiveness. Since its whole premise is to be disciplined, structured, even scientific, then it should be helpful in demonstrating to general management and other functions that marketing is not black or white magic, but a process which is fully accountable.

Where many marketers get into difficulties is in their relative inability to explain what each element in the marketing communications mix, being deployed in this or that campaign, is contributing to the whole. I sometimes wonder if marketers know themselves.

Yet this is the critical confidence question. Marketing budgets can be large, the stakes high and the need for accountability real. So why are campaigns designed in such a way that it is difficult to measure the whole effect and, more often than not, impossible to measure the individual contribution of each element? This is less adequate than it might be.

Designing-in measurement is realistic, smart and central to the premise of marketing people being the leaders of learning from experience—the seekers of the better way. While this view may be much more prevalent today in supporting television and large-scale media campaigns, it is almost invisible in below-the-line work outside of direct marketing.

The following checklist should provide a basis for approaching the measurement question.

How-will-we-know checklist

14.1   What customer behaviours are we seeking to change?
14.2   What are the current behaviours?
14.3   What do we expect the post-facto situation to be?
14.4   What can we measure before and after?

14.5   What do we need to do to set up the measurement(s)?

14.6   What are the easily defined metrics of each communications tool we plan to use?

14.7   Which communications tools are the most measurable?

14.8   Have we designed-in aspects to the campaign that will increase our facility in measuring change (i.e. response coupons in press advertisements)?

14.9   What do we know about the techniques of market research that will help us measure behavioural change?

14.10 What other functional areas of the organization can provide hard data in support of marketing?

14.11 What do we have to do to get these data from other functions?

14.12 What are the fundamental measures of business that are directly linked to marketing activity (even if through other functions such as sales or operations)?

14.13 How well do we integrate sales performance data with related marketing activity?

14.14 How well do we use the full range of transactional data held in the accounting systems?

14.15 How able are we to extrapolate from transactional data information of value to marketing, such as underlying trends, regression analysis, forecasts, comparative time series analysis?

14.16 What computer resources and skills do we have to provide quality marketing information?

14.17 How averse are we to making the marketing function numeratively accountable?

14.18 How well do we design head-to-head tests in our campaigns allowing single variable impact analysis?

14.19 What are the bench-mark standards in our sector for marketing measurements and who set them?

14.20 How seriously does our general management want marketing to be numeratively accountable?

14.21 What responsibility for measurable outcomes do we assign to our suppliers?

14.22 What use are we making of other data that may be available in the organization and do we know where they are?

14.23 What are the measurements we need to have to optimize our long-term relationships with each stakeholder?

14.24 Who in the organization can define success for each stakeholder relationship?

14.25 What are the standards of performance we should be working to in marketing accountability?

By now it will be apparent that it is a question of mind-set that has the greatest impact on the success or otherwise of marketing accountability. The analytically curious will have little problem with my exhortation to get measuring. They know that there is already a large amount of data available within the organization that can be put to good use: they need only to track it down. One example might serve to make the point. A major commercial lighting company created a state-of-the-art lighting theatre in order to be able to demonstrate every lighting condition, from open-plan offices with large numbers of computer terminals, to the best way to light Granny Smith apples in a supermarket. The aim was to show designers, architects, merchandisers and developers what could be done with the lighting medium. In fact it is a powerful tool for influencing the key decision-makers.

Visitors to the theatre were asked for their business card. Each was given appropriate literature on departure. Few follow-up discussions were arranged. Infrequent checks were made that everyone had, in fact, left a business card. The theatre generated a lot of heat, even with air conditioning, and the remedy of those who suffered was to prop the door open with a shoebox full of the very same business cards—one description of asset management.

This cautionary tale, now well remedied under new management, reminds us that if you do not know the value of your data and their potential uses you are likely to permit the same sort of thing. Again I subscribe to the view that a premium value must be placed upon those in marketing who are curious and seeking to take well-informed decisions rather than upon those who are characterized by originality and flair. Science first, art second: this must also be true of suppliers, whether in isolation or in combination. I warm to suppliers who want to know 'where will this campaign take you and what are we seeking to learn together from it?'

I am not going to open a debate on performance-related pay for marketing suppliers (and marketers themselves), but it might just be worth considering. Certainly the impact on other functions' perceptions of the marketing resource would be profound. The key would be to define the standards and performance measures—the incentive would be clear.

The ultimate business case for marketing communications

Readers who have reached this point in the book will have had the opportunity to travel through a 360 degree scan of many of the issues in marketing communications and the Forensic approach—whether you are a marketing professional within a client organization, a supplier or a general manager seeking to make sense of the arguments. A number of key themes have been introduced: the need for all marketing activity to be co-ordinated within a strategic framework; the treatment of marketing as primarily a science subject to rigorous analytical techniques; the dangers of assumptiveness; the ability to identify and rationalize the individual and collective merits of the various tools available within marketing communications and, last but not least, the concept that all marketing activity takes place within a series of continua. Marketers must make their optimal impact conscious of the alpha and the omega of their relationships with all the stakeholders of the business.

So what more need be said? One final challenge remains—to establish the business case for investment in the integrated marketing communications plan that is the prime vehicle for delivering Forensic advantage.

Marketing as a function, according to Nigel Piercy of Cardiff Business School, is not universally deemed necessary or valuable. In his authoritative studies (Piercy, 1991) of the issue he has found that significant numbers of organizations have no marketing function *per se*, but rely on everyone to think and behave in a customer-focused way. In other organizations marketing may be an ancillary function to sales, producing materials for their consumption. Yet others have sales reporting to marketing, and, less frequently, every function reporting to marketing! Nigel Piercy analyses the size of department versus its influence and concludes that it is the positioning of the marketing function among the strategic power-brokers of the business that determines its scope and influence.

In those instances where marketing is a comparatively weak function there must be the question of who is taking responsibility for the long view and the full range of relationships with stakeholders that will determine the durable success of the organization? I suspect that these critical marketing issues are neglected in the belief that they belong to the chief executive or company secretary's empire. This seems a short-sighted, high-risk approach.

The business case for the centrality of marketing comes from the following set of principles for the Forensic Marketing Organization:

1 Marketing is the custodian of all stakeholder relationships.
2 Marketing will be fully accountable for what it does.
3 Suppliers of marketing communications will be valued for their ability to realize the aims of the brief they are given.
4 Marketing will brief its suppliers on the business outcomes that must be delivered and the measurements that will determine success or failure.
5 Marketing will determine a strategic framework for its activities that is derived from the business strategy and will explicitly relate to the milestones within the strategic plan.
6 Marketing will value a scientific approach that will drive a relentless, but structured, search for performance improvement.
7 Marketing will value creativity and entrepreneurship in service of activity that will yield explicit and measurable results.
8 Marketing will always seek to validate its assumptions.
9 All functions will recognize the imperative of a co-ordinated policy for relationship management.
10 Organizations will encourage and enable the Forensic approach.

These somewhat didactic principles are designed to help marketers to demonstrate to general management that unity of purpose may come only through unity of control. The issues that have been raised in the book and which lie behind the ten principles are too important for sustainable business advantage to be left uncoordinated and unallocated in terms of responsibility. If marketing is about championing the interests of all external stakeholders within the citadel of the organization then it must be given the teeth to deliver the right actions. I am sure that any marketer would accept the awesome accountability that that level of permission implies. Furthermore, the best suppliers would flock to work for organizations who place such emphasis on the management of communications strategy as well as tactical activity in support of the goals of the moment. Those, too, we cannot ignore.

Bibliography and further reading

Ansoff, H.I. (1968) Corporate Strategy, Harmondsworth, Penguin.

Baker, K. and Bermingham, J. (1979) Paper given to the Annual Conference of UK Market Research Society, Brighton.

Bangs, D.H. (1992) *Creating customers*, London, Piatkus.

Beale, R. and Jackson, T. (1994) *Neural computing: an introduction*, Bristol, Institute of Physics Publishing.

Bird, D. (1982) *Commonsense direct marketing*, London, The Printed Shop.

Business Week (1993) 'Media mania', *Business Week*, 12 July 1993, pp. 94–101.

Business Week (1994) 'The information revolution', *Business Week*, 13 June 1994, pp. 35–59.

Chappell, R.T. and Read, W.L. (1984) *Business communications*, London, Pitman.

Chaston, I. (1993) *Customer-focused marketing*, London, McGraw-Hill.

Chronis, T. (1994) Private paper to a UK national newspaper board of directors.

Collins, A. (1992) *Competitive retail marketing*, London, McGraw-Hill.

Coulson-Thomas, C. (1983) *Marketing communications*, Oxford, Butterworth Heinemann.

Davenport, T.H. (1993) *Process innovation: re-engineering work through information technology*, Cambridge, Mass: Harvard Business School Press.

EDMA/NTC Research (1993) *Direct marketing in Europe: an examination of the statistics*, Marlow, NTC.

Ehrenburg, A. (1988) *Repeat buying*, Oxford, Oxford University Press.

ESOMAR (1993) *European Society for Opinion and Marketing Research Annual Market Study on Market Statistics 1992*, ESOMAR, September.

Fletcher, W. (1990) *Creative people: how to manage them and maximise their creativity*, London, Hutchinson.

Forsyth, P. (1993) *Marketing for non-marketing managers*, London, Pitman.

Hamel, G. and Prahalad, C. K. (1990) 'The core competence of the corporation', *Harvard Business Review*, 1990 (3), pp 79–91.

Hamel, G. and Prahalad, C.K. (1991) Corporate imagination and expeditionary marketing, *Harvard Business Review*, July–August 1991, pp. 81–92.

Hammer, M. and Champy, J.C. (1993) *Re-engineering the corporation*, New York, Harper Business.

Henley Centre (1994) *Teleculture 2000*, The Henley Centre Telebusiness Survey, London, The Henley Centre.

Hutton, P.F. and White, G. (1993) 'Research and the realization of dreams in local government: the case of Colchester Borough Council', AMSO Second Annual Market Research Effectiveness Awards, London, AMSO.

International Journal of Advertising (1984).

International Water Supply Association (1992) A talk given by Peter Hutton of MORI to the International Water Supply Association PR workshop, 2 June 1992.

Kosko, B. (1994) *Fuzzy thinking*, London, Harper-Collins.

Latchem, C., Williamson, J. and Henderson-Lancett, L. (eds) (1993) *Interactive multimedia: practices and promises*, London, Kogan Page.

Levitt, T. (1983) *The marketing imagination*, New York, Free Press.

Libfried, K.H.J. and McNair, C.J. (1992) *Benchmarking*, New York, Harper Business.

Llewellyn, D.T. (1985) *Evolution of the British financial system*, London, Institute of Bankers.

Llewellyn, D.T. (1989a) *The banking structure in major countries* (ed) G. G. Kaufman, Federal Reserve Bank of Chicago, USA.

Llewellyn, D.T. (1989b) 'Structural change in the British financial system' in C. Green and D.T. Llewellyn (eds) *Surveys in monetary economics*, vol. 2, Oxford, Blackwell.

McDonald, M.H.B. (1984) *Marketing plans*, Oxford, Heinemann.

McKenna, R. (1992) *Relationship marketing: successful strategies for the age of the customer*, Reading, MA, Addison-Wesley Publishing.

Mitroff, I.I. and Linstone, H.A. (1993) *The unbounded mind*, New York, Oxford University Press.

MORI (1987) *Residents' attitude survey*, August–September 1987. Research study conducted for Solihull Metropolitan Council.

MORI (1988) *Residents' attitude survey*, January–February 1988. Research study conducted by MORI for the London Borough of Richmond-upon-Thames.

Nilson, T.H. (1993) *Value-added marketing*, London, McGraw-Hill.

Peters, T. (1987) *Thriving on chaos*, New York, Knopf.

Piercy, N. (1991) *Market-led strategic change*, London, Thorsons (Harper-Collins).

Porter, M. (1980) *Competitive strategy*, New York, Free Press.

Porter, M. (1985) *Competitive advantage*, New York, Free Press.

Price Waterhouse (1993) *The 1993 market and customer management review*, London, Price Waterhouse.

Printing Industry Research Association (1991) *Ten Year Forecast, 1992–2002*, London, PIRA.

Reichfeld, F. (1993) *Loyalty based management*, a presentation to the Marketing Association Conference, London, Spring 1993, DMA.

Reid, T. (1993) 'They know what you are trying to do', Tim Reid Partnership.

Rheingold, H. (1991) *Virtual reality*, London, Secker & Warburg.

Stewart, R. (1982) *Choices for the manager*

TARP (1988) *800 numbers for customer service, a 1988 profile*, Society of Consumer Affairs Professionals in Business in conjunction with Technical Assistance Research Programmes (TARP), USA.

Toffler, A. (1980) *The third wave*, New York, Bantam.

Wilson, A. (1993) *Marketing audit checklists*, London, McGraw-Hill.

Index

Sight

Also by Jessie Greengrass

An Account of the Decline of the Great Auk,
According to One Who Saw It

Sight

Jessie Greengrass

JOHN MURRAY

First published in Great Britain in 2018 by John Murray (Publishers)
An Hachette UK Company

2

A CIP catalogue record for this title is available from the British Library

ISBN 978-1-47365-237-8
Ebook ISBN 978-1-47365-238-5

Typeset in Minion Pro by Hewer Text UK Ltd, Edinburgh
Printed and bound by CPI Group (UK) Ltd, Croydon, CR0 4YY

John Murray policy is to use papers that are natural, renewable and
recyclable products and made from wood grown in sustainable
forests. The logging and manufacturing processes are expected to
conform to the environmental regulations of the country of origin.

John Murray (Publishers)
Carmelite House
50 Victoria Embankment
London EC4Y 0DZ

www.johnmurray.co.uk

For Ada, who made this hard, and made it possible

I

The start of another summer, the weather uncertain but no longer sharply edged, and I am pregnant again. In front of me is all the ordinary and useful disarrangement of my desk and beyond it the rain-smudged window with a view across our garden to where my daughter plays, watched over by Johannes. She has begun to lose, lately, the tumbling immediacy of toddlerhood. I notice it when we walk together, our strides separate, or when we sit face to face across a table – how she is taller now and straighter, and inflects her actions with intent. Once her thoughts broke like weather across her face, but that readable plasticity is gone and she is not so transparent: complexity has brought concealment. The weight of her body when I lift her takes me by surprise, its unfamiliarity a reiteration of the distance between us. She used to clamber over me, her legs around my waist, her arms around my neck, as though I were furniture or an extension of herself, unthought-of or intimately known. Now she stands apart and I must reach for her, on each occasion a little further until it

seems her progress towards adulthood is a kind of disappearing and that I know her less and less the more that she becomes herself. This is how things ought to be, her going away while I remain, but still I think that if I could then I might reach across to where she stands, outlined against the violent yellow mass of a forsythia bush, and pull her back to me, to keep her always in my sight so that she might be nothing more than the sum of what I know of her.

On 28 December 1895 at the Salon Indien du Grand Café in Paris the Lumière brothers, Auguste and Louis, presented to the public for the first time a screening of a selection of their cinematographic films. All that afternoon along the Boulevard des Capucines a line of people waited, their breath rising through the freezing air, in expectation of a wonder. Later, sat in rows on slat-backed chairs, they saw it: the flickering black-and-white image of Auguste holding his baby daughter up to a fishbowl, balancing the child on her feet so that she might look down at the water inside, the tumbling elision of the film's frames making manifest inside the winter darkness a months-old summer afternoon – and at the same time, 600 miles away in the Bavarian city of Wurzburg, Wilhelm Conrad Röntgen, chair of physics, ran through the streets to hand over a paper to the president of the university's Physical Medical Society, a first description of the X-ray. For weeks, while the Lumière brothers had prepared their films, Röntgen, alone in his laboratory, its windows draped with heavy cloth to keep the winter's weakened sunlight out, had seen all that

had been solid grow towards transparency. Opaque materials – wood, stone, his own flesh – had been reduced for him to shadowed outline, leaving the image of a substrate world spread out across a photographic plate, a catalogue of metal and bone and all that would not rot to set against cinema's preservation of surface—

There was a point, some years ago, when this concatenation of dates preoccupied me. I was trying to decide whether to have a child. For months, all through a wet spring and an early, lightless summer, Johannes and I sat side by side in the evenings on the sofa or in the garden and we talked about it, or we didn't talk about it, but it seemed that we never talked of anything else, all our words mere surtext to my inability to find a way out of the bind in which I had placed myself. I wanted a child fiercely but couldn't imagine myself pregnant, or a mother, seeing only how I was now or how I thought I was: singular, centreless, afraid. I was terrified of the irrevocability of birth and what came after it, how the raising of a child, that unduckable responsibility, might turn each of my actions into weighted accidents, moulding another life without intention into unpropitious shapes, and caught between these two poles – my desire, my fear – I was miserable and made Johannes miserable, too. Minute by minute I would be sure that a decision had been reached but they wouldn't stick: I felt that I was staring at a fissure to be leapt across, and each time, making my feint at its nearer bank, I would run out, and over and over again that year I knelt on the floor in front of Johannes and said

—I don't know what to do, what should I do?

until he could only hold my head in his hands and say

—I love you

because he had exhausted all argument. For him the answer was obvious: we would have a child, and the rest would follow. He didn't fear himself to be inadequate, insufficient to the task of making someone whole, nor see how afterwards, when it was too late, the ground might give beneath our feet to let us fall, the child that we had wanted tumbling through the air between us; and although he was never less than kind he didn't know what to say to me and I began to catch, at times, a hastily suppressed frustration in his voice. During the day, instead of working, I sat at my desk with its view across the garden, empty then, and watched the 42-second-long *La Pêche aux poissons rouges*, the Lumière brothers' film. This is what we cling to at such times: the illusion that in the world there is a solution, if only we can find it, and it seemed to me that into that infant's face, turned towards the curiosity the camera made on a hundred-years-ago Lyon afternoon, a whole childhood had been distilled, and that if I looked hard enough, absorbing into my own body each detail of the way Auguste's hands held his daughter, of her responding smile as she reached down to pat the surface of the water, then I might understand what it would be like to be either of them. I had no idea how it might function, Johannes and me and a child inside the same house. My own father had slipped out halfway through my childhood, leaving little of himself behind, and my mother had died when I was in my early twenties, her

4

death so desolating that for months afterwards I had been unable to recognise my unhappiness, mistaking the joyless pall I wore for adulthood's final arrival: the understanding, come at last, that the world was nothing but what it appeared to be, a hard surface in a cold light. To fill the space that even grief refused to occupy I had read, at first indiscriminately and widely and then, as I began at last to reconstruct myself, building piecemeal on the foundations of all that had been demolished by my mother's death, on Wilhelm Röntgen and the early history of the X-ray. Now, happening on the coincidence of that single darkening afternoon at the end of the nineteenth century, I began to believe that if I could see how these two events fitted together, the way that simultaneity tied them, then perhaps I might see also through their lens the frame on which my own life had been constructed, its underlying principle, or how it was that I should find myself considering motherhood when it seemed that I had barely altered from unhappy adolescence. Perhaps, too, I might find the guarantee I wanted that in the future I would not fail or fall – but after all there was nothing to it. What I had mistaken for significance was mere concurrence – the burghers of Paris waiting in the street while elsewhere Röntgen ran through an empty university – and so as each long afternoon bled towards its close, as the cat began its plaintive cry for food and as Johannes, working in the room above, began to shift and stir, the floorboards creaking out their sympathetic indication of his winding down towards the evening, I remained as I was, *La Pêche aux poissons rouges* playing over and over on my

computer screen, the image of the child and her father, a key which failed to fit a lock.

As a child in the Netherlands, where his family had moved from their native Germany when he had just turned three, Wilhelm Conrad Röntgen showed no particular academic talent. He was marked out, if at all, by little more than a precocious skill with machinery, an imagination articulated from cogs and levers, and a manual dexterity that he would later use to make his own laboratory equipment, believing that it was with this intimacy of construction that insight might be bought. Beyond this he was an ordinary child without particular aptitude for lessons, easily distracted, although possessing a kind of outdoorsy curiosity, an interest in the natural world which in a less solid boy might have been called dreaminess. At the age of seventeen, for refusing to divulge the authorship of a caricature of one of the masters, he was expelled from his technical school in Utrecht without the necessary qualifications for university admittance, becoming instead a student of mechanical engineering at the polytechnic in Zurich, where entrance was by examination rather than qualification; but even after he had moved from there to the university and gained his PhD, coming under the influence and patronage of Professor August Kundt, his lack of a school certificate was a stumbling block, so that it was some years before he could secure an academic position in his own right, moving instead between Würzburg and Strasbourg as Kundt's assistant. By then, though, he had learned the habit of application, an

unfaltering dedication which appeared imagination's opposite, and he tackled these obstacles with the same solid determination with which he approached all aspects of his life – his marriage, friendships, interests, his work: a steady, undeflected, incremental progress towards a goal, each step taken cautiously, tested and retested so that at the end he could be sure that what he had made was sound. He retained the meticulousness which as a child he had used to make mechanical devices, developing an interest in photography and in player pianos alongside his scientific work, buying a Welte-Mignon for the drawing room to demonstrate to guests. He also kept his love of the outdoors, a fondness for snow and winter sports, spending his autumns in the Engadin mountains and his springs at Lake Como where he took his wife, Bertha, whose health was not always good, on excursions in a horse and cart. By the winter of 1895, six months past his fiftieth birthday, it seemed that his life had attained a kind of coasting form, the satisfactory shape of one of his own mechanisms: something soundly made and set upon a steady course, well-tended, gently oiled. His position in the university was assured and his career was an ordinarily distinguished one. He was respected in his field and his name would be remembered, if not in chapters, then in footnotes and appendices: those places clarity inhabits, the carefully worked-through detail in which a subject's virtue lies; and afterwards, after the few short weeks that he spent working on X-rays before returning to his previous work, after he had written the three papers which were all that he could find in himself to say on the subject, he seemed

to look back on this smaller renown as something lost, its sudden overturning an act to be regretted.

My mother fell ill shortly after my twenty-first birthday and for a long time, despite the fact that I became responsible, by increments, for her care, I tried to carry on as if nothing was happening, living in the shared flat behind the Elephant and Castle roundabout that I had moved to after leaving university and travelling each morning out to my mother's house, an unprepossessing mid-60s' villa set back behind a driveway deep in the eliding sprawl that seeps for miles beyond the city's boundaries, small towns running into one another under a canopy of trees. This was the house I had lived in all my life but I felt little affection for it, and nor I think did my mother. Our place in it had been built not on choice or fondness but on circumstance, a constant provisionality defined by our wish to leave if only those things which kept us there – work, school, a habit of thought or of routine, the convenient proximity to the city which we valued in principle but rarely took advantage of – could be evaded. Leaving for university three years earlier I had thought myself to have escaped from it at last, the process of growing up an inevitable upward curve, exponential and away – but then my mother became ill and once more I was pulled back. I gave up my attempts to find a job and instead each morning I sat in an empty outbound train to make this journey backwards, watching through the scratched window-pane the full carriages run past in the opposite direction, heavy with their complements of lives. The unfairness of this

forced return angered me, but I felt too the impossibility of my anger, the imperviousness of events towards it; and sometimes as I struggled in the morning to force my way to the ticket barrier against the suited tide I felt again the disempowerment of childhood, that awareness of injustice and the futility of its protest. Then, in the evenings, after the hospital appointments and the hours on drips, after the loads of washing done and the twin plates drying in the empty kitchen, after the silent afternoons, the long gap between lunch and tea filled with nothing but the anxious, empty tedium of the ends of lives, I would travel back the other way; or, more often than not, some minor crisis would keep me where I was so that instead of going back to the city I would lie awake in my childhood bedroom listening to the sounds from the garden, the bark of foxes and the hoot of owls where the roundabout's traffic roar should be, and feel that the world was turning elsewhere while I lay, still and confined, rerouted from that easy future which I had assumed would be my right.

By degrees, over the course of the months after her initial collapse, caused by a sudden burst of blood into the soft substance of her brain which, while stemmed, could not be stopped, my mother's illness stripped her of strength and agency. Her muscles were unsprung, her joints unlocked. The medication which she took to keep the worst at bay caused her body to swell, doubling in size to a facsimile of health, her face plump and ruddy. For a while, with a diagnosis made and treatment-regime established, with radiotherapy a fortnightly inconvenience, she had seemed almost well, until that first

week during which she had lain pale as paper in a hospital bed became a memory that left us giddy with relief for all it had marked an end to unchecked time. She was tired, perhaps, a little unsteady on her feet, and down one side of her skull, surrounded by a fur of regrowing hair, a scar ran that was the length of my hand and pink and smooth, but although she was not what she had been, neither had she become what I had feared she might, as I had sat amongst the tangle of tubes and monitors, the drips and beeps, and waited for what was left of her to surface from the surgeon's work. Those first weeks, when it still seemed to us that we might pick up our old lives again somehow, had the stolen air of holidays and our sorrow was exultant, a pouring forth of hope and love, because we had not yet felt the truth of it: that there would be no afterwards from which we might look back and count ourselves lucky to have escaped. My mother needed help at first only with domestic chores, with cooking and cleaning and trips to the supermarket, and someone to accompany her on hospital visits, to sit next to her in hot rooms and stare out of windows as bad news was delivered and explained; but as time went on these solid remains of her health began to erode and more and more things became impossible for her. She started to need help moving about the house, climbing steps and manoeuvring herself in and out of chairs and, when her left arm began to weaken, with cutting up her food and washing her face; and so our lives began to fold in around one another, tangling, contracting, her need for me forcing into reverse that inevitable process of separation which was the work of adolescence.

We both felt it. As I sponged her head with water to get out the last of the soap from what was left of her hair or as I helped her dress I tried to be kind but for me to be so, for me to try to comfort or to shield her, to be more gentle with her than was necessary for the completion of the immediate task at hand, would have been only to more brutally invert our natural roles, and that itself would have been a kind of violence towards this woman who had always sought to protect me, to soften the impact of the world and keep me safe. We were often silent with one another. It began to seem that the only solution to our physical closeness was an emotional distance – we hid from one another, we shrank apart, until all affection was leached from our touch and only pragmatism, necessity, was left. We allowed practicality to stand in for compassion and my nominal residence elsewhere acted as a boundary line, a point of principled separation, until one morning I arrived at the house to find her curled up on the bathroom floor, asleep, a child's steroidal plumpness at her elbows and her wrists. For weeks, since that part of her brain which governed spatial awareness had begun to fail, she had been unable to dress herself, her knickers having come to represent a geometrical puzzle that she couldn't solve, but now she had lost the ability to navigate from one room to another, becoming confused in doorways, turning herself in odd directions. Although she still recognised the house, although she said that nothing really looked any different to her, and although she still knew that, for example, the kitchen was on the left of the living room and the bathroom at the top of the stairs, when she tried to

translate this knowledge into action it confounded her. That mental construct which she had of the house we had lived in for the entirety of my life – the two of us echoing backwards through the sheltering closeness of its rooms, our arguments, our gestures of anger and our reconciliations, our particular celebrations and our daily grinding still present in the marks across the walls and floors, the ghost stains on the carpets, the wonky handle to the study door – this no longer bore any relation to the space through which she moved, the fact of it unparsable even while her memory of it remained clear and detailed. Her body, too, had become strange to her, its shape no longer matching the map she had of it, so that her idea of where she was in space floundered and was unreliable and any movement was a conscious effort of attention, a matter of watching, pushing her body about as though it were mere mechanism while elsewhere, on an empty plane, its mental analogue moved freely through a steady silence. The following day I packed up my room in the Elephant and Castle flat and moved home, stuffing my belongings into a holdall and, when that was full, into plastic carrier bags. I took a taxi to the station and then at last I found myself going in the same direction as everyone else, sat as the evening rush hour began in the corner of a commuter train on top of my unwieldy pile of things. Changing at Clapham Junction one of my bags split, sending a cascade of jumbled paperbacks and underwear slithering down into the gap between the train and the platform to settle on the tracks. I stood in the crowd of homing workers, my dirty jeans and high-tops squalid amongst the multitude of

suits and brogues, the remaining bags slouched about my legs, and I watched the trains run again and again across my things—

and if, afterwards, I was unable to see quite how deeply grief ran, if I felt I had no right to my unhappiness, then in part I think it was because I was ashamed that this last journey home was one that I had made, not out of love, nor even from compassion, but only from expediency, because it was necessary and because there was no one else to do it.

In 1890 in the physics department of the University of Pennsylvania, five years before Wilhelm Röntgen made his observations on the effect of a new kind of rays, Arthur Goodspeed placed an unexposed photographic plate beneath a pile of coins on a table next to a Crookes tube, the same piece of equipment that would lead Röntgen to his discovery. Later, when the plate was developed, Goodspeed found on it in place of the image he was expecting a series of small, round shadows, speckled blotches, as though it were the jacket of a book left lying on a window sill for months, its ink bleached by the sun to leave a sharp outline of what had sat on top of it. He kept the plate, because it was a curiosity or a puzzle – and five years later, after he had read Röntgen's paper and seen the pictures which accompanied it, X-rays of weights inside a box or bones inside a hand, Goodspeed repeated the work that he had done before, and found, as he had suspected, that the image was the result of the plate's exposure to X-rays. This picture, reproduced, appears both old and accidental, like liver spots on skin or something spilled, the two circles left by the

coins distinct but not entire, their edges collapsing on one side, the blackness of their shadows bleeding into grey, and seeing it I find myself constructing an image of Doctor Arthur Willis Goodspeed, stood in his laboratory with its view across the campus gardens to the Schuylkill river, as he performed with good grace those experiments which would prove that he, unlike Röntgen, had suffered a failure, not of understanding, nor quite of luck, but of something in between – a felicity which is both attention and timing.

Shortly after I first met Johannes we spent an afternoon together at the Victoria and Albert museum. It was a Saturday and I walked to the museum from Marble Arch station, across Hyde Park to the Albert Memorial, skirting the edge of the Serpentine. That week had brought a false spring, a parting of winter's drapes to let through light and air into the early part of March, an unexpectedly warm sun still low enough in the sky that its illumination mimicked that of late summer, September's heavy gold across the bare branches of the trees, the only colour in the flowerbeds from the purple petals of the banked-up Hellebore. By the next weekend drear grey would confine us again to our coats and scarves and we would stay that way for another month or more, but for now there was an impression of unexpected possibility. I was nervous. This outing had been my idea and I was worried about how it might go, that I might have a bad time or that Johannes might, so that one or the other of us would have to stutter our excuses after an hour and leave, the slow disappointed deflation of a

hoped-for connection come to nothing. We had, until this point, hardly ever been alone together, meeting only accidentally and in company, through mutual friends, and I was afraid that this alteration in the balance of our relationship would bring with it an awkwardness, or that we would find out that we had, after all, little to say to one another.

Entering through the wide doors that lead in from Cromwell Gardens and walking across the wide atrium of the museum's central lobby, we turned without any particular intent to the right, passing through an arch into the mediaeval galleries, those long corridors with their rood screens and panel paintings, their carvings and assorted armoury, relics of a past which feels at once unimaginable and ordinary, its strangeness quotidian, like a different answer to a familiar question. For a long time we stood in front of an altarpiece, a peculiar, hallucinatory work made in Hamburg towards the end of the twelfth century, two wooden leaves sat either side of a central panel, the whole divided into forty-four smaller squares on which scenes from the Book of Revelation were painted, a meticulous rendering of the coming of the apocalypse. Image by image we were walked through the end of the world: the seven seals opened, the seven trumpets sounded, cracks appeared in the earth. Brimstone fell like black hail and through the narrowing streets of a mediaeval market town, bright rivers of blood carried drowning horses past the burghers leaning out from upper-storey windows: a world at its unmaking. Standing next to Johannes, the footsteps of other visitors cracking through the silence about us, I tried to

imagine how it would be to go about one's daily life with this picture hung above it, freshly painted – how it might fade into the background until its horrors would be taken for granted, drifting each day further from notice as they failed to come about. Instead I felt only what enormous coincidence existence consists of that it should have brought that picture here, and us – and how easily, how unwittingly we might break each possible future in favour of another and how, looking back, in place of what had been possible we would see only that thin contingent line, what happened, rising through the vast and empty darkness of what did not.

Afterwards, we wandered through the rest of the museum, the statues and ceramics fading into a grey expanse of time and place, and our conversation was a carefully trivial list of observations until, sitting in the cafe later on, Johannes started to tell me about his family, the unremarkable but intimate details of a variably happy childhood, his absconding English father forgiven, his mother resilient, a tall woman in a tall house with a view across the sea at Harwich, that grey stretch of water somewhere on the other side of which was the place she had been born. These facts, ordinary in themselves, were offered as a gift, a gesture of trust or intimacy made across the table, and searching about for something to show in return I could think only of my own mother, of how her death had seemed like a sudden event slowed down, a single shocking moment that went on for months. All through the summer that came after it, as I slid into grief's silent central eye, falling asleep like a cat in sunny patches, on the corners of settees or

curled on rugs, I dreamed that she wasn't dead at all, and had only gone away without telling me; and now she had come back, forcing herself into the shadow-space of her absence – but she no longer fitted. Even in so short a time I had grown and changed – her house was gone and there was no bed for her in the flat I had replaced it with, no extra cup and saucer, no clothes. These dreams were horrible and waking from them I would find my hands clutching at my chest so hard that the nails left crescent indentations in the skin above my breasts. For minutes I would lie, paralysed, until at last the silence of my empty flat began to reassert the truth: that what had happened was immutable and that my grief was earned, awful but particular, a possession whose ownership could not be rescinded.

—My mother died

I said to Johannes, and across the emptiness my words made I extended my hands towards him.

At last, even with me always present, the work of caring for my mother at home became too much. One morning, struggling from her bed to the bathroom, pushing a walking frame in front of her, she stumbled and fell, sitting down heavily on the carpet. She was unhurt but she no longer had the strength to stand back up again and although for a while I tried to right her, tugging her this way and that, bringing various items of furniture to use as props or levers, I was unable to lift her weight. I had to call an ambulance and because she wasn't a priority we sat for hours, side by side on the bedroom floor,

waiting for it to arrive. I made us lunch, sandwiches to eat on our knees, the sort of indoor picnic she had made me sometimes as a child on rainy Saturdays, and the fragile cast of this memory brought a kind of complicity between us, a resurgence of the intimacy that we had once possessed, so that for a while it was almost as though we were happy.

When at last the ambulance came the two paramedics between them managed to get her back on her feet. We refused their offer to take us to the hospital and they didn't push, believing, I think, that we were right to do so; but the next day the district nurse came and said that a bed had been made available for my mother at the hospice. I packed a bag for her, a rucksack with spare clothes, her phone and charger, and the book she had been pretending to read for weeks, too proud to tell me that her sight was failing: such a paltry collection of things but after all what else would she need that could be taken from this house. The hospice sent an ambulance of their own to collect us and we tried to give the journey a jaunty air, sucking boiled sweets to keep us from travel sickness in the lurching, windowless interior, and joking with the driver, but the sweets tasted dusty and our jokes fell flat, having the dull clang of cracked bells. Arriving we were shown to a tiny private room and I unpacked my mother's things, plugged in the radio I had brought for us to listen to, went to find the cafe and came back with half-stale pastries. Beyond the rooms for consultations, for art therapy or massage, which made up the ground floor of the building, there was a walled garden, a surprisingly beautiful area of

paths and overflowing flowerbeds, jasmine-hung arches and patches of sunny grass, and I said

—We could ask for a wheelchair and I could take you to sit outside. They have a pond—

but she refused, and that was that. A decision had been made, somewhere in the closing corridors of her mind: that she would no longer try to reach beyond herself, nor put aside the business of dying in favour of an experience she had no way of holding on to. She could have been generous. I might have liked to have, later on, this memory of sitting with her watching sunlight fall on water, a last fragment of accord, but she had nothing left to give me now, not even this. Her room became all there was to us, its grubby cream paintwork and its window with a view across the road, its smell of must and disinfectant. For a fortnight she lay on the bed and shrank into herself. Each morning I made this new journey, taking the bus and arriving early to sit beside her bed in the burgundy reclinable armchair that she refused to try and use. I brought her fruit she wouldn't eat, grapes and mangoes, watermelon, and I read to her until she drifted into sleep and then I went and found the nurses or the ambulance drivers drinking tea on their break and told them how important it was that I be able to take my mother home again, my tearful fervour the result of a denial, not of how close my mother was to death, how it shivered about us, a long boundary to be crossed, but of how I wished it would be done because I was exhausted and because there was nothing I could do now but sit and watch, and even that was too much.

I had expected her death to be a radical change, a moment of perceptive clarity after which all would be altered, all rearranged, and so I was unprepared for what came instead: the long descending rallentando of these last few weeks – an extension, by slight degrees, of the gap between my mother's thoughts, her words, her breaths, until at last I was able to stop waiting for the next to come. It was the middle of the night. I had stopped going home some days before and one of the nurses had brought me a blanket so that I might doze, off and on, in the chair by the bed, waking at intervals to see my mother's eyes open or closed, to check the rise and fall of her chest. I thought of nothing and we were quite still; for the first time since her illness had begun I did not wish myself elsewhere. There was nothing to be done or said and nothing to be felt, and I sat and stared out of the window or slept; and on this last night I didn't even sleep but only held my mother's hand, leant forward with my head against her belly as I had lain sometimes in childhood when ill or needing comfort. And then, when I was sure, I pressed the button that hung down on a wire over her bed, and a nurse came, and everything was as it had been except that my mother was gone.

The work that Röntgen began late in 1895 he had been meaning to undertake for the best part of a year but it was only now, as the winter brought about its annual deceleration, returning students, technicians, professors to their homes, that he found the time. It was, to him, a matter of curiosity. He liked to repeat experiments others had already performed, not so much to

check the veracity of their results as because this careful reconstruction, the slow rhythm of test and repeat, brought with it
that particular quality of understanding which is got only by
having seen for oneself: a grasp which is something like illumination, the reframing of proposition to fact so that the truth
of it is felt, immediate. At such times, holidays of sorts when
Röntgen could set aside the strictures of his academic interests
in favour of a kind of happy tinkering, the boundary between
work and hobby blurred, and alone in his laboratory that
winter he began to repeat investigations into cathode rays
which had earlier been performed by two others – by Heinrich
Hertz, who had died on the first day of the previous year at the
age of thirty-six, leaving behind him two small children and a
proof of the existence of electromagnetic rays, and by Philipp
Lenard, whose modifications to the Crookes cathode-ray tube
had included a small, aluminium-covered window, preserving
the pressure inside the tube but allowing the possibility of
escape for the rays whose nature was, through such a process
of deliberate tinkering, slowly being unravelled. Röntgen had
been busy for a week already when on 8 November he noticed
something glowing across the room from which all light had
been excluded, and, walking towards the faint light, he found
discarded on a workbench a sheet of paper which had been
treated with barium platinocyanide, a chemical already recognised as useful because, in the presence of radiation, it would
fluoresce.

Afterwards, Röntgen would become reticent on the subject
of the work he had performed during those weeks. In addition

to the paper in which he described his discovery he would give only a single interview, to an American journalist who happened to be passing through Wurzburg during that brief period between the publication of *Über Eine Neue Art von Strahlen* and Röntgen's return to that more ordinary research which constituted, to him, his life's work. This interview was conducted across three languages – German and French, of which the journalist possessed only a partial understanding, and English, which Röntgen spoke as a language of conferences and equipment specifications, a technical dialect sufficient to explain only a sequence of events: the observation of light, the approach towards it – and it seems that the two spoke at cross purposes, their intentions unclear to one another. Röntgen appears to have been baffled by the journalist's interest, his persistent attempts to force Röntgen towards an account, not of the work that he had done, its procedures and its progress, but of the way it had felt to do it. What, the journalist asked, did you think when you saw the faint glow across the laboratory? To which Röntgen answered, 'I didn't think; I investigated—'

but still I can't believe it was so simple, the facts so baldly uninflected by that extra thing that meaning is, the part of truth which is the work of memory and mind, our own felt contribution to the way things are, and so I imagine it like this: the few short steps to bring Röntgen to a halt before the glowing paper as at a reliquary, and then the sudden rush of understanding – an opening up, the world reframed. This is what we cannot help but feel: that surely this was nothing less than

gnosis, the penetration of mystery to show the nap of things, a pattern comprehended – and if we could understand these moments and the weeks that followed them when Röntgen, alone, placed object after object in front of his machine and saw them all transformed, then we too might know what it is to have the hidden made manifest: the components of ourselves, the world, the space between.

The effect he had observed could only, Röntgen noted, have been caused by the presence of light but he was certain of his blackout, of the heavy drapes which covered the doors and windows, thickening the darkness. He began to move the piece of paper by increments further and further away from the cathode-ray tube, and then to place what objects were near at hand between the tube and the paper so that he might get an idea both of range and penetration. Within a few minutes it was, he said, clear to him that the source of the glow could only be the tube, that it could not be light escaping because of the shield, and that neither could the phenomenon be the result of cathode rays, whose range was too short and penetration too limited to reach through a sheet of cardboard and across the room – that what he saw was, in short, the activity of a new sort of ray; and over the next seven and a half weeks he would continue his investigations, testing the limits of what, in honour of its unknown quality, he dubbed the X-ray.

Later there would be a persistent discomfort even amongst Röntgen's supporters about the ease of his discovery, the way it came from nowhere like an unexpected present, and perhaps it is true to say that this knowledge was something waiting to

be found, hardly even buried. He was not even the first – as well as Arthur Goodspeed there was Philipp Lenard who, while pursuing those investigations earlier that year which Röntgen was repeating, had observed the same fluorescence but had failed to recognise the significance of it, this softly glowing indicator of the presence of something new. Unlike Goodspeed, who would take with such grace his understanding of what he had almost seen, Lenard held this failure against Röntgen for the rest of his life. His own oversight had been, he considered, a matter of ill luck, his failure to explore or to document what he had observed a function not of decision but of circumstance; and so how could Röntgen's success have been anything but the opposite. Had it not been him it would have been someone else that winter, or early the next spring, any of those who that year set up their electrodes and their tubes and ran their currents through to see what they might find, and if that was the case then perhaps Rontgen's experience was little more than treasure trove; but we cannot deal so easily in counterfactuals. To say that something other might have been is not to diminish the value of what was, the marvel of it or its solidity, besides which it is not the fact of Wilhelm Röntgen's discovery which fascinates but rather it is those days and nights through which he worked alone, bringing to this mystery's unravelling all of his slow, systematic persistence until he possessed not just the sight of something but that extra thing that knowledge, understanding, is – not the mere serendipity of discovery but the moment of its tipping into insight which draws our lonely curiosity. We are unsatisfied.

24

Revelation is by definition isolate, it can neither be communicated nor transferred, and trying to comprehend it we feel only the chill of our exclusion.

For months my purpose had been imposed by circumstance, the structures of my life externally defined so that I had been like a creature inside an exoskeleton, soft and pulpy, held to shape by a rigidity which was not my own, and I had resented it. I had felt that control of my life had been taken from me to be housed elsewhere, amongst the articles of chance, the lottery tickets and the slot machines, the hopes for better weather – but waking on the morning after my mother's death to a house that felt as empty as the body in the half-lit hospice room, having for the first time in months slept as long as I had wanted and feeling sickened that my initial experience of this redrawn world was relief at being rested, I lay in bed waiting for a call to drag me from it, the pressing urgency of someone else's need, and when none came I was stranded, and could only lie and wait as around me the shadows moved slowly across the walls of my outgrown room. I had felt the first shock of this abrupt redundancy the previous night. In answer to my pressing of the bell a nurse had come and as she began to move quietly about my mother's bed, checking and re-checking, ordering, I stood awkwardly by and watched her, my expulsion from a world that I had occupied for months abrupt, my role as carer curtailed by the absence of anyone to be cared for. After a few minutes I began to gather up the belongings that over the past few weeks had been spread about the room, a

scarf and hat, the book I had been reading, my house keys left on the table by the door, and it was as though I were packing up a hotel room after a night's residency, erasing all traces of myself to return it to the anonymous state in which I had found it, ready for its next inhabitant.

Eventually, the private ritual of her immediate tasks completed, the nurse turned her attention towards me

—This way, my love,

and I could have cried at the endearment, its tacit acknowledgement that I was not quite an adult yet and all this was more than I could find my place within; but I didn't, my dry eyes a first indicator of the silence which would fill my skin to bursting for the best part of a year. She led me to another room, a softly lighted space with seascapes on its walls and, on the small tables that sat at intervals between the furniture, glossy plants whose leaves concealed a multitude of tissue boxes. I suppose it must have been used for this purpose only, that small and quiet room: as a place for the recently bereaved to sit, to contain them while the necessary procedures were put in place, and everything about it was designed to fade into the background, a physical iteration of the noise the nurses' shoes made on the building's carpets – a gentle, hardly audible shush-shush which was somehow less noticeable than nothing would have been. I waited. I didn't want to return to the room my mother's body was in, had nothing more to say nor any need to add to the store of memories I had, the majority of them shadowed already into near-invisibility by the details of her dying face, her chilly hands, but when the nurse returned

to take me back to the room that neither my mother nor I could occupy any longer I lacked the energy to refuse and instead followed her to where my mother's body lay. The lights had been dimmed now, and someone, out of a kindness that was sharp as pity, had taken one of the yellow stargazer lilies from a vase by the bed and folded my mother's hands around it, evening out at the same time the position of her body, smoothing the sheets so that whereas before, rumpled and lined, she might have looked asleep, now she was incontrovertibly dead. It was not a comfort to me to see her this way, as though she had been dressed for the occasion. It didn't make any more acceptable those other things, all the accumulated worry of the days and nights before, the unbreeched sadness, the things unsaid, the white foam which had filled and refilled her mouth during the last evening, rising upwards from her failing lungs, or the absenting, her slow withdrawal from me which was so much like being left behind – but still it was something: the transformation of this specific, immediate instance of dying into a standard form. The folded hands, the flower, the sheet were all conventions, recognisable from a thousand paintings, pictures, pointing my path as buoys do at sea away from dangerous currents and into a mapped channel, custom stepping in where my own map had failed. It was a ritualisation, and with it came an offer of entrenchment into a prescribed routine which, accepted, would carry me forwards, allowing me a tiny insulating distance from the cold reality of things, and it was this which saved me the next morning, too, the need to start passing on the news forcing me

27

out of bed, and it kept me going through the days that followed, the business of mourning setting me a course to follow so that my thoughts might rise away from me to nothing – the funeral to be arranged, condolence cards to read and answer, visitors to be fielded or received until everything that needed to be done had happened and, elsewhere, normality had commenced its slow return. Beyond the walls of my mother's house, things again began to move as they had before, I could hear them hum, but there was no place for me – I had no past life, no extant position to step back into; the world was a sum to which I was remainder – and I was adrift, a near-ghost, insubstantial. Those tasks which had previously filled every hour of the day – the shopping and the cooking, the cleaning, the washing up – were now discharged in minutes, with the time left over aching out around me. Even the house disowned me. My mother's belongings lay where she had left them, her shoes in the lobby, her scarf knotted round the banister, and in a drawer spare glasses, unused stamps, these objects enacting a mourning within which I was not made welcome. I spent an afternoon trying without success to pay an electricity bill but my mother's name was still on the account and no one at the electricity company would talk to me. Finding myself cold, the wind worrying at the doors and stripping the leaves from the trees, I tried to bleed the radiators but only ended up with foul-smelling water on the bedroom floors. I didn't know how to replace the salt in the dishwasher or reset the boiler. A bulb blew in the porch light but the shade needed a key to open it which I couldn't find and so darkness pooled,

accusatory, around the front door. All these things reproached me, my tiny failures accumulating in drifts about the corners of the rooms – all this arcana of ownership which my mother hadn't thought to tell me and which it hadn't ever seemed the right time to ask about, and now was lost, so that I could never be more than interloper here, my feet treading unwelcome grooves across the carpets—

This is where grief is found, in these suddenly unfilled cracks, these responsibilities – minute, habitual – which have lain elsewhere for years and which, having failed amongst grief's greater broil to be reapportioned, are overlooked in favour of the more dramatic, until even the ordinary starts to crumble. If I thought, all through those freezing months I spent alone in a house whose owner had abandoned us, that I did not grieve, then it was because I had been expecting something else – something both larger and lesser, a monument or a mountain, simple, scaleable, and not this seeping in of space to undermine the smooth continuance of things. I had thought that loss would be dramatic, that it would be a kind of exercise, when instead it was the emptiness of everything going on as before and nothing working as it ought.

Having nowhere else to go all winter I stayed there, in my mother's house that I had never wanted to return to, narrowing myself down until I lived between my bedroom and the kitchen while the rest of it lay empty about me, the disorderly, reproachful quiet of its closed rooms undisturbed, until at last, as the crocuses began to flower in the muddy garden borders, the house was sold. Then I was faced with the problem of what

to do with all my mother's things. I felt that I was expected, somehow, to keep them, to make myself curator, but the thought of storing this detritus of an ended lifetime, of dragging it behind me like a deadened limb, turning myself into little more than a conduit for memory, was horrifying; and so in the end I gave away what I could to anyone who wanted it and hired a skip for the weekend to deal with the rest. Across the augmented stillness of an Easter weekend its yellow maw sat in the driveway and I fed things into it, books and photographs, letters, odds and ends of furniture and boxes of knick-knacks, jewellery, clothes – from Friday to Monday I carried things out to it in armfuls through a steady, penetrating rain whose ruinous action spared me from need for second thoughts, and instead of sadness I felt a kind of soaring joy, as though each armload lightened me, and at times I felt that I could hardly contain it but that it must bubble out as laughter to mix with the sound of the rain – except that for the four nights during which the skip sat outside the house, before a lorry came in the early hours of Tuesday morning to drive it away, I found myself unable in the evenings to draw the curtains on it and so I sat, darkness flowing inwards, keeping a kind of vigil, until at last the house was empty and so was I.

Over dinner in a restaurant sometime during that year when I was trying to find the courage to have a child Johannes said, searching for a subject that would have the magnitude to eclipse, however partially, the one we wished to avoid
—You never talk about your mother,

30

and I was surprised, because it seemed to me that her death had been the defining event in my life and that I talked about it endlessly, a muttered thrum beneath all other conversation. Trying to describe her, though – to lay out on the sanded wooden tabletop between the sea bream and the steak those things which had made her singular – I found myself able to name only her physical characteristics, the least order of things, and even these were cut not directly from memory but from photographs – the black-and-white strip of passport pictures which had fluttered out one day from between the pages of a copy of Elizabeth Bishop's letters, my mother's unsmiling expression set above the square neck of a cotton frock, or the picture of her standing on a beach, bent over to examine something half-buried in the sand, her bobbed hair tucked back behind her ears. These static faces were as far from hers as a shape is from its mathematical description – they conveyed nothing of her but were all that remained to me to describe. It was not that I had forgotten – I could feel quite clearly how it had been, as a child, to hold her hand, what surety of comfort it had brought me and how, the first time I had been sent to my grandmother's alone in the summer holidays, I had cried every morning, waking to a house which reverberated with her absence, and spent the days in listless moping until at last she came to fetch me; and I could remember how it was to listen to a telephone ringing in the certainty that she would answer it, and the particular tilt her head made as she read – but these things were obdurate of explanation. My memory of her, what remained, was like a memory of

distance or the cold, intangible, unsymbolic, not sight nor sound, not touch, not taste, and my attempts at a description of it floundered like the description of music does in words, conveying nothing of its sound or substance. Instead, sat opposite Johannes in the restaurant, searching for something to say, it was the image of the skip that came to mind – the shadow that it made in the light cast out by the living room windows, the rain slanting down towards it; and I thought, although I didn't say it, that the truth was that my mother's death, coming as it did so exactly at that turning spot between adolescence and adulthood, had fractured my life, breaking it into two parts, the second one a product not only of the first but of the first plus its curtailing, built to fill the space its end had made – and so it was hard to think about my mother, to speak about her, without acknowledging that it was impossible to wish she hadn't died, because without her death I would have been undone.

After we had finished eating Johannes and I walked for a while along the Embankment, past Blackfriars Bridge towards St Paul's, the cathedral's floodlit bulk against the glass and metal towers of the city a reassurance like the promise of continuity, the persistence of things. It was a relief to be walking like this, side by side, my hand burrowed into the crook of Johannes' arm, feeling the familiar scratch of his coat's tweed against my skin. Like this, freed by the rhythm of our steps from the need to fill silence with speech, I felt the scurrying rat-wheel of my thoughts begin to still, and I could almost believe that I had come to a decision; except that as soon as we

stopped walking I knew that the whole thing would start up again. We had taken to spending evenings out like this, in restaurants or in bars, at concerts or talks in which we had only the most cursory interest, as though to make a pass at happiness or because it gave us something else to talk about, the whole city and all the people in it a distraction from ourselves and from the space that spread between us, a membrane's thickness but so wide – and from all the other choices which we couldn't make until this one was settled, from every part of our lives which was made provisional by my indecision, and from the way I rattled to the touch. Often, afterwards, we would walk home instead of taking the Tube, spinning the evening out, deferring the moment when we would arrive at our house and be confronted by all that we had left inside. Walking bought us the right to easy silence and I found that all evening I would look forward to it, the brief and quiet concord which came with the recollection of how things had been when the question of children was still in the future, its distance lending me the certainty of hypothesis: that Johannes and I would have a child, but not yet. As we neared the steps which led upwards to the wide flank of London Bridge I turned my head to look at him, this man I loved or thought I loved, not knowing always what it meant to do so beyond the sharing of bills and preferences, the ordinary ways our lives grew to synchronise and intertwine. We climbed up towards the road and I watched the way the shadows fell across his cheeks, the way his forehead creased, the hooding of his eyes by heavy eyelids, these features as familiar to me as my

own skin but his mind elsewhere, a place I could not gain admittance to, and I wondered what I would remember of Johannes, if he were no longer there – which of his particulars I could list that would convey the least measure of how it felt to walk with him like this, the easy placidity of his company, the salve it was and the certainty spreading out beneath our feet like the solid city pavement that what engulfed us now was temporary, that it would be resolved and that we would survive its aftermath – and for a moment, despite the fold of his coat caught between my finger and thumb, he seemed impossibly distant from me, not only unreachable but unfamiliar, a singular instance of the whole he made, both precious and strange, his likeness uncatchable by anything other than himself; and I moved closer to him, holding more tightly to his arm, as though in doing so I might reach across the gulf which kept us separate, that unmeasurable gap between subject and object, and catch hold of all he was and I was not, and keep it safe.

After my mother's house was sold I moved to a flat in the East End of London, somewhere in Hackney's most unlovely parts, close to the canal. The flat was on the first floor of a solid concrete block, a place of extraordinary ugliness, and I think that this was partly why I chose it – because I didn't want to feel that I had benefitted from my mother's death, that her loss had been instrumental in purchasing even the small happiness that a pleasant place to live would have constituted. This flat's rooms were boxy, its ceilings low, and both kitchen and bathroom were floored with the same peeling, nicotine-yellow

lino. Through the thin walls my neighbours' lives filtered –
their conversations and their television programmes, their
cooking smells. Damp rose. The furniture, an ill-assorted
collection of chairs and tables, refused to cohere into anything
approaching comfort, and as weeks passed I continued to feel
that I was waiting for something to happen, a final marker of
my residence which would make me feel welcome here,
banishing the persistent impression that, even when I was in
it, the flat remained unoccupied. My days drifted. It seemed
that I existed in a kind of hinterland, lost between an end and
a beginning, my life ruptured in a way I couldn't resolve. Those
friends whom I had seen often before my mother's illness I felt
unable to contact, the necessary explanations being too
weighty to bear thinking of. I was lonely but I couldn't see that
I was, except at particular times, waking from dreams of
company or hearing laughter come through the walls from the
flat next door, when I felt it acutely, a sudden awareness of
constriction. It was as though I had been ousted from myself,
my flat and featureless mind an unfamiliar landscape to which
I had only partial access. I couldn't concentrate. I had no appetite, for food or for anything else, and I had almost no energy.
No matter how much I slept I still felt the need for more, my
limbs heavy and my eyelids sluggish – the sort of all-consum-
ing, intractable tiredness which I have since felt only in the
early months of pregnancy. I had nothing to do, no job, no
interests particularly, but I felt that to succumb to inactivity
would be to welcome that spectre of my own emergent failure,
ill-defined but insistent, which haunted the space around me,

so each morning at half past nine when the Tube fare tipped over to off-peak I took the train into central London and walked down the Euston Road to the library at the Wellcome Collection. There I would leave my bag in the cloakroom and, scanning my reader's card at the library's turnstile, make my way to a small room at the back where there was a window that could be opened a few inches to let in the heavy, traffic-sodden summer breeze, and then for a while I pottered about, laying my belongings on one of the desks, my handful of unlidded pens set square beside the dog-eared notebook I always carried, my jumper folded neatly down, my phone silenced and sat on top of it. That done I would wander through the library in search of something to read, running my hands along the shelves until I found a subject that caught my attention. I read not with any particular object in mind, nor really with the intention of retaining any information about the subjects that I chose, but rather because the act of reading was a habit, and because it was soothing and, perhaps, from a lifetime's inculcated faith in the explanatory power of books, the half-held belief that somewhere in those hectares upon hectares of printed pages I might find that fact which would make sense of my growing unhappiness, allowing me to peel back the obscurant layers of myself and lay bare at last the solid structure underneath.

All morning in the library I would sit at my desk, flicking through contents pages and indexes, appendices, photo captions, chapter headings, following this lead or that a little way until I became distracted or until it was time for lunch, a

slice of quiche or tart and a salad in the library cafe, and then often in the afternoons I would give up even that pretence of activity, setting a book to lie open in front of me, the pages rustling softly in the breeze from the open window, and allow myself to drift through the brackish backwaters of the after-noon, the roar of traffic from the road outside a lulling constancy. I stayed each day until the library was almost closed, until the assistant librarians came round with their trolleys to pick up that day's cast-off texts and until the sound of a hoover started up in a distant corridor; and then at the last possible moment, dragging my feet, I would dawdle back out into the street – and although at the time the sound of pages turning seemed to grind against me until I worried that I might be worn away by it to nothing, now I recall that long summer as though it had been spent within the papery confines of a cocoon. I had been reduced to nothing, and now I sought amongst so many books a way to understand myself by analogy, a pattern recognised in other lives which might be drawn across my own to give it shape and, given shape, to give it impetus, direction. The things which I learned without noticing all through that year recur to me still, those images from medical textbooks, the bodies dissected or described, the case notes and the cabinets and all the many ways there are to see inside ourselves, and still I feel that, correctly understood, they might constitute a key—

Each evening when the library shut I walked home, an hour's steady, thoughtless progress through the evening streets with their clots of drinkers outside pubs, their newspaper

sellers and fruit stalls, skirting north through the decaying
Georgian streets above King's Cross towards the gentility of
Islington's garden squares and then down onto the towpath to
walk along the canal into Hackney. On one side of me, small
brown fish darted between drowned carrier bags and bicycle
wheels lay submerged in three feet and six inches of slow
water, and on the other, beyond a tangle of vegetation, clumps
of catmint mixed with goosegrass, lavender with dandelions, a
peculiar combination of intention and neglect, rose the solid,
damp Victorian brick wall that sheltered the canal, in its
sunken bed, from the city beyond. It was cooler down there,
with the water and the shade, than it was above, where the city
had spent all day absorbing heat and now let it go, the pavements shimmering slightly in the dusk. In that narrow passage-
way left over from an older iteration of the familiar city I felt
that I could breathe again, and as Haggerston gave onto
London Fields and the sharp striations of gentility and grime
above the towpath began to meld into a kind of uniform grub-
biness, when darkness was beginning to spread through the
evening air like ink, I felt at last a brief alleviation of my discon-
nection from myself and for a quarter of an hour, before I
reached the steps which led back up to road level and the
entrance to my building, everything else fell away, and for that
short stretch I felt only what I was: young, adrift, bereft.

At Johannes' suggestion I spent a weekend by myself, staying
in a tiny stone-walled cottage in a valley near Hay-on-Wye. It
might, he said, help me to think. Perhaps without him there I

might feel less pressure to articulate what was on my mind and might instead be able to concentrate, and so might find myself able at last to come to a decision. He kissed my cheek and said

—Whatever you decide will be all right,

and I tried not to append my own clauses: that he wished only that I might decide, one way or the other, because he had begun to find my indecision intolerable; but Johannes was not so unkind. It was only I who felt the pressure – the pronged implement which caught me was wholly of my own devising. Sometimes, when I saw a woman in a cafe pick up a baby from a pram, I felt a weight in my own arms, a heaviness where nothing was, and the force of my longing for a child was such that I had to turn away but still I could only feel how impossible it was that I should ever manage such uncomplicated love. I took the train to Hereford and then the bus to Hay and from there I walked, my rucksack heavy with provisions, the few miles further into Wales to where the cottage was, its windows facing down the long corrugation of the valley. There was a tiny garden with a bench, a handkerchief of lawn, an apple tree, a single bedroom with a sloping ceiling and an iron bedstead. Arriving, putting cheese on toast under the grill and pouring myself a glass of wine, I thought that in such a place, so simplified, I couldn't fail to find a way to think, but thinking without context is a near impossible activity. I tried to focus my mind, sitting down at the kitchen table half-drunk to write a list of pros and cons, but the effort was ludicrous and I only felt ashamed; instead I drank more and read my way along the shelf of detective novels that sat beside the bed. I missed

Johannes desperately. While at home I often felt that my love for him was intangible, out of reach, an emergent quality that I struggled to locate amongst the objects which filled our lives, the dirty dishes and the small change for the window cleaner, the arrangements for visits to his mother's house, the constant flow of words on minute variations of domestic trivia; but without him I could feel nothing else, love filling the space his absence made, and I wished I could go home, leave the green serenity that I had longed for and return to our dishevelled, smog-blackened house – wished, even, that I could return to the complicated discontent the last six months had been, if only it would mean his hands, his voice; but he had sent me here and how could I return without reaching a conclusion – and anyway I would walk back through the door and all this certainty of love would fade behind the unwashed windows and the unbought milk to the usual chafing familiarity with one another. I sat the week out, unhappy, and went home to tell him with defiance that I wouldn't have a child; but two days later I cried and said that after all I might, because still I could feel nothing but how much I wanted to.

As August failed into September the year after my mother died I began to suffer from headaches, near-migraines which were unlike anything I have experienced either before or since. For months I had drifted further and further away from myself. The faces of strangers caught sight of in the street, or on the opposite escalator as each morning I descended into the station to make my journey to the library, appeared familiar,

rising suddenly out of the jumble like friends I had forgotten, their likenesses caught and lost again. The line between recognisable and unrecognisable blurred and the world appeared fragile, glassy and flat, so that I felt that it might shatter if I touched it, falling to my feet in shards to reveal whatever solidity was hidden underneath. Sounds – the grind of traffic, the voice of a man calling from a doorway, a radio spilling outwards from a windowsill – were both muted and precise, as if they were passing through some medium more viscous than air, but the pain of my headaches was something different again. I was incapacitated by it for days at a time, prostrate on my bed with the blinds pulled down and the curtains drawn across them, pain turning the passing of days and nights into the ticks of an excruciating clock, indefatigable and cruel. I felt as though there was something swelling inside my skull, an abscess filling slowly with whatever stuff unhappiness is made of, its edges pressing against the bone like mud against stone, extruding into my sinuses, my eye-sockets, squeezing through my tear ducts and down my throat. Sometimes, at night, when exhaustion would briefly overcome pain and I would pass into a fitful doze at last, then I would dream that my mouth was filled with something like wet sand, a claggy, white substance which regenerated as fast as I could spit it out or excavate it with my fingers from the space between my gum and cheek; and waking I would have the taste of it still, the lingering memory of something like rotten milk catching in my throat.

Afterwards, as the pain receded, I would feel weak and new, a beach scoured clean and still unmarked, and I would lie on

sheets stiffened with sweat and watch the dust motes fall slowly through the light which slanted down between a gap in the curtains, feeling the tiny chill of each indrawn breath, and I would wait until I had the strength to totter to the kitchen and pour a glass of water from the tap, lifting it with both hands to my mouth to feel it run into me, and it would be as though I had been reduced to almost nothing, my skin a fragile membrane parting light and liquid. Beforehand, though, in the days leading up to an attack, I would feel glorified. For twenty-four hours I seemed to glow, my body's radiance reflected back to me from every surface of the world to be reabsorbed and retransmitted, a refiner's fire which sharpened as it grew, and I was ecstatic. I teetered on the brink of visions. Revelation pended, the veil between myself and understanding was in a constant state of almost-rending, and I thought I could see shadows through it, the outlines of an as-yet uncomprehended truth, until all at once the mania crested and what came out of it, in place of elucidation, was agony, my head pinned in a vice, my body hanging limp below it, a disarticulated sack of bones and blood around which my limbs curled, stiff and liable to snap. Still, though, for almost two months I did nothing. After each attack the memory of pain was erased, but I could recall clearly how it had felt to be so enraptured and how the aftermath had been, that hollow peace that was so much like resurrection, and I wondered if it might be worth it. At other times, as the pain began and brought with it the certainty that nothing could be recompense for this, I was afraid, sure now that that there was something really wrong

42

with me and not wanting to know what it was, so that it wasn't until the period of these cycles had shortened to leave barely space between them to restock the fridge and wash and dry the bed sheets in preparation for the next headache, that I finally made an appointment to see a doctor.

Bertha Röntgen was used to lost hours, to her husband's absorption in his work which kept him away from home or returned him only in part, his mind elsewhere across the dinner table or as they sat with the fire between them in the drawing room where the piano was; still, though, even she began to worry as, by mid-November 1895, he had taken to sleeping in his laboratory, to taking his meals there, returning to the house only to wash and change his clothes while Bertha watched him, trying hard to keep both concern and curiosity in check. Later, Röntgen would try to diminish what these weeks had been. He would seem to feel keenly Philipp Lenard's attempts to discredit him, the rumours muttered from the sides of mouths that his achievement had been nothing but an accumulation of serendipity. Even the speed with which his friends came to support him was felt as accusation – the suggestion left open by their quick defence that there were charges to be answered. 'It is almost,' he would write some years later, 'as though I had to apologise for discovering the rays' – and by late spring he would have done all the work on X-rays that he would ever undertake, publishing three papers and giving a single lecture. Such was his determination to avoid the subject that when, in 1901, he was awarded the

inaugural Nobel Prize for Physics he declined to speak; but, whatever he might have come to feel afterwards, on the subject of those few weeks his own words betray him. The account of his work that he gives in *Über Eine Neue Art von Strahlen*, written hastily through the scrag-end of December to meet the Physical Medical Society's deadline, is a description cried aloud while still in flight, an account of actions performed while hours slipped past like river water, while the world remade itself in front of him, its solid surfaces dissolved to offer up their innards to his gaze; and the speed with which he wrote it, his figure running through the frozen Würzburg streets, is an indicator of his awareness of how fragile was his claim to priority and how much, reflexively perhaps but certainly, he wanted it. While Bertha sat in an empty house and tried to keep her worries to herself, Röntgen in his laboratory reached for whatever was to hand, to hold it up in front of his machine. 'I have,' he wrote, 'observed and photographed many . . . shadow pictures. Thus, I have the outline of a door covered with lead paint; the image was produced by placing the discharge tube on one side of the door, and the sensitive plate on the other. I have also a shadow of the bones of the hand; of a wire upon a bobbin; of a set of weights in a box; of a compass card and needle completely enclosed in a metal case; of a piece of metal where the X-rays show the want of homogeneity . . '. For seven weeks and three days Röntgen existed in a private world transformed for him and him alone, and perhaps this too was a part of his later bitterness: that despite this experience of revelation, the conferral on him of a

44

scientific grace, afterward nothing was different at all, and although he had seen through metal and seen through flesh to what was hidden, and although he had known, or thought that he had known, its nature, what had been left afterwards was only so much quibbling at the bill.

At last, on 22 December 1895, Röntgen broke his run of solitude. Returning home he found Bertha, who for weeks had been his placeholder, moving through the routine business of their lives to keep the edges of it taut on his behalf, and he asked her to come with him. Without questioning she put on her coat and gloves, and together they walked through the winter streets and then through the university, their footsteps echoing in its empty corridors, until at last they reached the door of his laboratory, and Röntgen opened it and pushed her through. For a few minutes, while Bertha stood, uncomfortable in this space which belonged to a version of her husband she knew only by reputation, he moved about, making sure of his equipment; and then without flourish he turned out the light and laid his wife's hand on a photographic plate. Bertha stayed still, doing as he asked of her, while he prepped the Crookes tube and shot the current across it, her hand an object sat between them in the darkness. It took ten minutes for Röntgen to develop the picture, the only sounds his footsteps and the ticking of the regulator clock which hung on the wall above them, and then it was done and, the lights on again, they looked at it, this picture which has become Bertha's enduring image: her skeletal hand, open, fingers curved above the convex length of her palm. Across the lower phalange of her

fourth finger Bertha's wedding ring is an uncompromising mark, its blackness against the shadow of her bones a marker of the metal's immutability. Röntgen, who for weeks had been alone in his newly understood world, had sought with this image Bertha's admittance to it, the making of the picture a gesture of both initiation and affection: the tenderness of her bones made visible to them both, confirmation of the life which had formed such extraordinary structures; but these things are a matter of interpretation. To Bertha, whose hands were solid, whose body unitary, who had not doubted those things that constituted her – her skin, her thoughts; the single object that was flesh housing mind – nor sought to understand them, it had the chilly, soily smell of tombs.

—It is,

she said

—like seeing my own death—

and she turned away, and refused to look again.

After I returned from Hay, Johannes and I clung to one another. Something had changed between us: Johannes no longer reassured me that things would be all right and I no longer tried to talk about my fears because to do so seemed to wound him and I wanted above all that he should not look so sad. There was a breaking distance in the way we were so careful with one another. Although we were in contact with one another always, a hand on a shoulder, a leg slung across a knee, our fingers reaching out to twine about the other's, it was not for comfort but rather because it felt that to let go would

be to risk a loss that would be absolute. At night we lay awake, our arms around one another, and although in the silence we pressed ourselves together, trying to reach one another, between our naked bellies there was a barrier that we couldn't break and we remained apart. Once from nowhere Johannes cried

—I can't bear it,

but I could offer no comfort, not even that which comes from conjoint suffering.

In the end it was nothing at all which brought resolution. We went away, together this time, walking for ten days in Cornwall along the coast path from Falmouth round the Lizard to Land's End as though in this steady progress west-ward we might outdistance ourselves. We walked until my mouth filled with the taste of salt and iron, scrambling from sea to cliff-crest and back again with the turn of each cove, hours of arduous labour lost in the traversal of a few straight miles. Once, pausing for breath, looking out from the edge of the cliff at the sea five hundred feet below, we saw a peregrine falcon hovering barely an arm-span away from us and almost on a level, watchful and still, its spotted grey wings barely moving in the updraft, and I felt myself touched by something – privilege perhaps, or luck – that came, after so many months, like a sight of the first green growth through winter earth. We carried a tent, split between our two packs. At the end of each day's walking my skin was covered in a rime of salt, half sweat and half evaporated surf, so that rubbing my fingers on my face it came away in grubby curls, and after dinner in one pub

or another we crawled into our tent before dark and in the gentle, subaquatic murk the canvas made of the evening sun, we slept. We barely spoke to one another. At first it was because we had nothing to say that had not been said already but by the middle of the week I felt that it was because we had been emptied out, poured into the rough path, our thoughts nothing more than surface, as routine and repetitive as the passage of the summer breakers up the beaches. In our matched strides we had found a mute accord which had been lacking for months, our only current concerns the cresting of each rise and the need to reach a campsite in time to pitch a tent before the pubs stopped serving dinner. The weather for most of the week was uniformly clear and hot and in the middle of each day we scrambled down off the path to the sea and ate our packed lunches side by side, facing out across the North Atlantic, bread and cheese and packets of crisps after which I swam, the water so clear that I could see shoals of tiny blue fish in it; but on the last day it rained, a thick and heavy summer storm, the clouds descended down low so that air and water merged into a heavy, directionless grey spume and when we reached Land's End at last we couldn't even see as far as the edge of the point. We waited in line with all the other thwarted sightseers to have our picture taken by the signpost to John O'Groats and felt a sense of disjunction, after the solitary days, to be surrounded by such crowds of people, all of them looking askance at our dirty faces and the soaking, mud-splattered clothes we'd been wearing all week. Sitting on the bus back to Penzance we said how funny it was to have been striving so

hard to reach a place so completely lacking in any kind of peace or beauty, so forbidding of contemplation, as though we had undertaken a pilgrimage to a supermarket, and we laughed. At the station we booked ourselves onto that night's sleeper and spent the balance of the afternoon and early evening drinking in the station bar, our wet things steaming on a radiator, and I realised, standing on the chipped tiles of the pub toilet looking in the mirror at my half-burned face, that at some point in the week I had outdistanced my anxiety. After all, my decision had been made months ago. I knew that I wanted a child and it was only the point of crossing from the abstract to the particular which was at issue, that gap I saw between myself and the people who were mothers already, my fear of being found wanting, but I was not alone – there was Johannes, strong where I was not, and after all we were only people and a part of us was made for this, I wouldn't fail any further than others did; but most of all I had exhausted myself with indecision and was too tired for any more of it. I wanted to think about something else. I wanted the whole thing to be over and done, and the only way for that to happen was for me to do that thing which I had wanted from the start.

Reading Röntgen's paper for the first time one sunny afternoon at my desk in the library I had been able to follow the thread of it with comparative ease; and surely this was the last time that such a feat was possible: the framing of a radical scientific discovery in ordinary language, the ability to impart understanding without first having to construct a language in

which to do so. Röntgen's description of his work comes like the unravelling of a magician's illusion which, explained, quickens rather than diminishing, the understanding of its working conferring the illusion of complicity – the impression that we, too, might be so deft, so sure; and within weeks of the paper's publication interest in it, both academic and popular, had exploded. During 1896, forty-nine books and 1,044 scientific papers were published on the subject of X-rays, as well as newspaper reports and editorials, magazine articles, cartoons and sketches. Into the tail end of a repressive century it came like the promise of a change in the weather, that unsettling notion that far from the troublesome corporeality of bodies being obscured by their enfolding layers of lawn and calico they might themselves become transparent, giving up their secrets to a gaze. By the summer of 1896 there were slot machines in Chicago that would X-ray your hand, and at that year's Electrical Exhibition in New York there was a tent in which the boxes stood one beside another in rows and people queued up to use them, the lines stretching backwards to the door. Afterwards, congregating in groups, talking in whispers as one might do in church, their eyes shone with the wonder of conversion and they said that during those few moments when they had seen their hands dissected on a screen they had received confirmation of their place among the living; or else they saw what Bertha Röntgen had done and in the peculiar repetitivity of the images, each skeleton so like the last, they found the unindividuated mass of bones that we will all become. All through that year and the next, the enthralling

mystery X-rays represented, their apparent promise, the sense they brought of a future already overtaken and inhabited, was such that when in Cedar Rapids, Ohio, a man claimed to have used X-rays to transmute base metal into gold, finding the philosopher's stone in a cathode-ray tube, for a while he was almost believed; and why not, since if a solid body might become transparent – if one might step inside a fairground booth and see the bones of one's own hand – if one might pay a dime and see one's life or death – then what after all might not be possible, what understood – and surely this is what brought them, all that summer, running to the fairground booths: the promise of the simplifying power of explanation, sight: that knowing the constitution of their bodies they might be granted understanding of their minds.

Ten days after seeing my GP about my headaches, I went to the local hospital for an MRI scan. This hospital, tucked behind a busy road and hedged with bus stops, was nothing like the one I had so often visited with my mother, where well-tended gardens functioned as a euphemism does, to cushion and obscure, but was instead a vast and sprawling complex of concrete and peeling paint, its central portion grown incrementally outwards, extended and tacked on to as though it were trying to reproduce itself, scaffolding poles like aerial roots hanging from its walls and squat, shrub-like Portakabins sprouting from its car parks and what might once have been its lawns. Anxiety made me hurry as I walked into the main building's busy foyer but it took so long to find

the right place that I was barely punctual by the time I presented myself at the MRI unit's reception desk. There I was given a sheaf of forms to fill in and directed to a corridor where half a dozen others sat already on plastic chairs lined up against both walls, each trying to keep as far from the others as they could. After a slight hesitation I picked a seat at the far end of the left-hand row next to a large man with a face which was badly swollen around its right eye, the skin about the socket stretched smooth, his eyebrow a muddled burr across a discoloured patch the size of a tangerine. Sitting down beside him, maintaining polite separation in this public space, I wished for a moment that instead of this withdrawal I might have the nerve to catch his gaze – but to do so would have been to pretend to a solidarity with him which I wasn't entitled to, because, after all, I was unlikely to be seriously ill, whereas he already had a slightly rotten look, his skin the flat, yellowish-white of sheep's cheese. We sat for nearly an hour, the pair of us, side by side, and all that time he remained unmoving apart from his thumbs, which he tapped gently and soundlessly against one another in a complicated rhythm I couldn't find the knack of, and I wondered if perhaps he was reciting some list or prayer in his head, a strengthening psalm or an accounting of all that stood to be lost; but when at last a nurse came and called him he stood up straight and square and greeted her with friendly courtesy, and so perhaps after all it had only been the waiting which had bothered him and my anxiously examined pity, my assumption that I must have what he did not – health, strength – and could therefore

confer upon him with my glance some warmth of comfort, was only another form of conceit.

When my own turn came the same nurse led me further into the building, down corridors which smelled of linoleum and disinfectant and through a door into a tiny, white-walled cubicle where, left alone, I stripped off my clothes and put on instead a blue serge hospital gown, stiff from the laundry, its hemmed edges scratchy against the nape of my neck. My own things – my trousers and T-shirt, my shoes, the silver bracelet I wore all that year and my earrings and glasses – I placed in a locker; and so, stripped and blinded, it was as though I had been divested of all those complicated trappings which made me into myself, leaving nothing beyond them but the feature-less core; and I felt that I was approaching, not a routine medi-cal examination, but some ritual of passage, a proof at last of all that constituted me. Another nurse came and took me into the room where the scanner was and I lay down on its waiting pallet, my head enclosed inside a frame, my knees raised on a cushion. Things were explained to me but without my glasses I found it hard to concentrate, the technician's words emerging indistinctly from a haze of colour. I was given a button to press in case claustrophobia should cause me to panic but without my glasses myopia had already enclosed me, cutting the comprehensible world down to a few inches of recognisable space, and I had no choice but to surrender, which was itself a relief after the months in which I had fought to keep myself in motion: here at last I was taken care of and might rest. Despite the headphones I had been given the volume of the machine's

working was almost overwhelming, a roar of turning metal which occupied my skull, replacing thought with sound. I lost my sense of time and it began to feel as though I might have been fixed in that position, my head held in its cage, my knees on their pillow, for some elastic version of forever, and that I had reached at last a sort of crisis, a crux or an apotheosis after the months of anxious emptiness: that caught there, stuck inside an enormous white box, helpless and bare, I had become a pivot on which my life might turn; but afterwards, sat in the consultant's office with a picture of my brain spread out against a lightbox, I felt nothing. This was not how I had imagined it. I had thought that, seeing the illuminated image of that part of myself which was the keeper of the rest pinned up against a screen, the details of its operation picked out in nebulae of colour, I might know at last that I was solid, sure, and that I was well-made; and I had thought that I would recognise it, this invisible part of myself where consciousness resided, that I would know it was mine as an infant knows its mother, and that at last the understanding buried deep inside it would be made accessible, but this could have been a picture of anyone and I felt only a sort of dull surprise that what I saw should be a part of me at all. It told me nothing. I sat in my chair and listened patiently while the consultant explained that there was nothing obviously wrong with me – the scan was clear. I would be referred, she said, to a headache clinic, but there was a waiting list and in the interim I should continue with my routine of pain killers, avoid alcohol, try and sleep regularly; then, early the next year when the letter came with the time of

my appointment, my headaches had gone. I had met Johannes. A shift had occurred and my mother's death was no longer present but past, its recalling an understanding of pattern instead of a wound, something woven into me, a part of that composite I had become which was a fraction of what I might have been; and this feat had been achieved not through understanding but only by familiarity of occupation, and by the passage of time.

II

II

When at last the long bell of my mother's death had ceased to sound, after the obliteration of her belongings in the skip and the scouring that my illness had been, after I had met Johannes, I felt for a long time that the past mattered very little. I lacked curiosity as much as I lacked material for it. My mother had been all that was left of my family and to accept the absolute nature of her loss, its insusceptibility to reconstruction through the careful husbanding of facts or objects, was almost a badge of honour. On those occasions when I thought about it at all, I considered myself to have done well in avoiding the temptation to become curator, the embalmer of my mother's memory. Even after my daughter was born – even after she had reached an age at which she showed interest when my mother's name was mentioned or when I saw how shadowy to her was the figure of this other grandmother, as distinct from Johannes' mother who was so pointedly alive, with her trips to the zoo and the national gallery, or to the Dutch church at Austin Friars – even then I felt little more

than inconvenienced by the need to traverse with my child such difficult territory as inherited grief. Trying to articulate it once to Johannes, explaining during one of those evenings in the first years of our daughter's life when she slept spread-eagled in her cot as though unconsciousness had assaulted her, knocking her out, while we lay next to one another on the sofa like the survivors of some localised disaster, I told him that the past is as prosaic as the future and the facts about it only so much stuff. To pick through dusty boxes, to sift through memories which fray and tear like ageing paper in an effort to find out who we are, is to avoid the responsibility of choice, since when it comes to it we have only ourselves, now, and the ever-narrowing cone of what we might enact. Growing up, I said, is a solitary process of disentanglement from those who made us and the reality of it cannot be avoided but only, perhaps, deferred – and my discarding of the physical mani-festation of the past, the emptying of my mother's house piece by piece into a rain-filled skip, had been a statement of intent and with it I had let myself be unencumbered—

—But you aren't,

Johannes said.

—You are not unencumbered.

My mother was an only child and my grandmother a psycho-analyst known to everyone, myself included, as Doctor K. This name didn't strike me as strange. It was to me only another part of the landscape of my childhood and I regarded it with solipsistic insularity, the assumption by one whose age is still

in single figures that the world was what I saw of it and everything familiar was also ordinary, so that I was almost into my teens before I thought to ask her about it. We stood in her kitchen, the table between us and on it the knife that she had been using to chop vegetables, she having set this task aside so that she might offer my question the attention she believed that it deserved. This was a trick of hers: to treat conversation as an activity which should be given full attention, weighed against the virtue of silence, so that talking to her one might never have anywhere to hide one's face.

—Names,

she said

—are symbols. Particularly those we allocate to ourselves, and not knowing what to say in response I said nothing, but only stood and felt myself grow hot under her gaze until at last, satisfied, she picked up her knife again and went on with chopping carrots.

About my grandfather I know almost nothing. He was gone before my mother was born and left behind him little sense of absence, no space or lack, no mark to show how he might have fitted with us. On those occasions in childhood that I asked my mother about him, empty Saturday afternoons when I drifted bored about the house looking for threads to pull, she claimed to know only that he had worked at one of the journals that my grandmother contributed to and, if pressed, she would go to the large bookcase in the hall on which we kept our good books, the hardbacks and the row of old Penguins with their yellow spines, the classics in translation and the

poetry, and she would take down a copy of the collected Kipling between whose fragile pages she kept a photograph of a man sat on a beach, a stretch of runnelled sand beyond which squat, grass-topped dunes rose to an indifferent sky. I don't know if the Kipling was a joke but

—There he is,

and she would pass the glossy sheet to me and go back to whatever she had been doing before my question interrupted her, leaving the book on the hall table to be refilled and replaced when I was done.

Calling this picture to mind now I place the man somewhere on the east coast, Thorpeness or Cromer, Snape – one of those long, flat beaches that separate the marshes of East Anglia from the uncompromising sea, places that Johannes and I go to sometimes, early in the autumn when the ground is warm but the air has a chill to it and when, in the late afternoons, the moon hangs like its own ghost in the sky and the reed-beds cast long shadows and everything is dusty, gold, and both of us are pierced, slightly and not unpleasantly, with a nostalgia for something that we have never seen but know, instinctively, that we have lost. The man in the photograph wore a pale-coloured shirt, open at the neck but awkwardly so, as though his tie had been discarded in a gesture of intentional carelessness and his trousers were rolled up to show an inch of pale skin above gartered socks and laced brogues. His hair, disordered by the wind, framed a face that was little more than a smile and a squint, eyes screwed up against the sun, his features so indistinguishably

ordinary that they seemed to me to approach disguise. Across the bottom of the picture the shadow of the photographer fell, clear and dark, and it is a peculiarity of the image as I remember it that there was more apparent character in this shadow – the body's black outline stretched across the sand, straight legs set apart, elbows raised like a first growth of sharply angled wings – than there was in the photograph's ostensible subject, the man who was my grandfather. This photo I lost years ago – abandoned, presumably, with the Kipling, cast off to become someone else's curiosity, the sort of thing that turns up from time to time in books bought second-hand, but I remember how at the time I studied it with absolute attention, gazing at it with my nose inches from its surface. Picking at its details, I tried to find anything in it that might prove its connection to myself; but he could have been anybody's grandfather, that man, and I wonder now if in fact the photograph had anything to do with us at all or if, rather, it came as it went, sandwiched between the verses of 'Gunga Din'. It seems unlikely that my mother knew as little about her father as she claimed. Doctor K's honesty was scrupulous, her determination that one must not hide from facts nor shirk the task of interpreting them verging, at times, on aggression. In response my mother had become pragmatic. She prioritised outcome over fact and she was not above lying, feeling, I think, that by doing so she was protect-ing both her own privacy and mine, the right I had to under-stand the world as I chose. It seems so obvious now that I wonder how I hadn't seen it before: that my mother's

professed ignorance on the subject of her father was her own invention. Such an equivocation would have seemed to her no more than expedient, this judicious husbanding of complicated trivia a way of shielding me from something which she thought unimportant; and after all what difference is there between an honestly told untruth and a lie: our understanding of a past we didn't inhabit will always be a fiction. To say that I might have had a right to truth would have seemed, to my mother, absurd, so that even if I had recognised this fabrication before her death and found a way to ask about it, the question rising through those empty tracts of space that filled the house as illness abraded her, then still I don't think she would have seen any reason to answer.

In the afternoons Johannes takes our daughter out and I lie with my feet up on a cushion and try to rest, my body an uncomfortable object to inhabit. My hips ache. The baby kicks. My fingers thicken and are unwieldy; the doing or undoing of buttons is a chore. At such times, wishing the lot of them gone – Johannes, the children both inside me and out – I wonder what they will keep of me, later; what off-cut memories will remain to be re-stitched, their resemblance to myself a matter of perspective. I want only what I think we all must want: to come off as better than I ought, more generous, more sure – kinder than I know myself to be; but I want also to be known, to be counted and to be excused. I can't have both. The thought of it makes me surly and resentful and

when the baby knees me in the ribs I snap at it through the intermediary layers of my flesh; and later, guilty, I hold my daughter close and sing to her as though I might with such tendernesses obliterate her recollection of all the times I haven't come quite up to scratch.

My grandmother lived on the upper floors of a large house in Hampstead, the heath rising like a city's dream of English countryside beyond the end of its long garden. She had bought the house, dilapidated then, the year that she turned thirty, shortly after qualifying as a psychoanalyst, and since then she had slowly reworked it, fitting its rooms around herself, until she seemed to sit within it like a stone inside its setting. Except in the attic, which had been her childhood bedroom, there was no trace of my mother: no photographs, no mementos. Such things had no place in those high-ceilinged rooms from which emotion had been smoothed to leave reason, the salve, behind. The house's basement had been converted, shortly after my mother had left home, into a separate flat, a source of income which insulated Doctor K from the fear of growing old, and for as long as I could remember it was occupied by a former patient, a very upright ex-schoolteacher who wore tweed suits smelling of peppermint and camphor, and seemed to live in a perpetual state of just-held-back decay. Often during the month-long holiday that I spent there each summer, while Doctor K saw clients, I would go and sit with him on the stone terrace that ran along the back of the house, separating it from the garden, and

which was his to use, French windows opening onto it from his living room. These are a child's memories perfected by adulthood's glaze and in them the days were always hot, the sky blue, and the garden stretched out, private, perfect in the dappled light which fell through the leaves of the over-hanging apple tree. The tenant made me cups of sweetened tea and we were companionable. He told me how my grand-mother had cured him, years earlier, of a form of compulsive self-harm which had driven him, over the course of several years, to pull out all the hair on his head and face by the roots. Now he spent his days growing roses, and I would watch him, his fingers deep amongst the leaves, checking for greenfly. Often he would stop what he was doing and stand for minutes on end staring at nothing, his arms loose at his sides and his head bowed down towards the ground, as though he had been momentarily uncoupled from himself, and at such times I would feel pity for him and this feeling, hot and uncomfort-able, would send me running back towards the house.

In the same way that it was always hot and the garden always very green, in my memories of the summers that I spent there my grandmother's house was always cool and always very quiet, a muted and a peaceful place where one might sit in comfort between the bookcases and feel that an escape had been effected. It was not a house that welcomed children. Its rooms had the same authoritative calm that university librar-ies possess – knowledge both offered and assumed, with learn-ing the price for further learning – and it conferred on me, for the duration of my stay, a sort of precocious adulthood. I

enjoyed it, the graceful shapes my body made in the armchairs, the way I walked along the corridors with steady steps, the free rein I had amongst the books. My grandmother granted me autonomy. Staying there I might do as I liked, going out alone to watch the kite fliers on Parliament Hill or swim in the bathing ponds, taking a picnic with me that I had made myself, and I was responsible for brushing my own hair and teeth, for choosing appropriate shoes and taking a coat or not, and if I got wet then it was my own fault; but I was a child still and when I came home shivering my grandmother wouldn't run a bath as my mother would have done, or wrap me in a blanket to warm me through, making disapproval of a piece with care, and when I fell and grazed my knees it was my own hands that peeled the plaster from its plastic backing and stuck it, bloody, to my skin.

In the morning when our daughter wakes, Johannes goes to her and opens up her bedroom blinds. He takes her to the bathroom, sits her on the toilet, makes her wash her hands. He finds breakfast, bowls of porridge or slices of toast which the two of them eat together at the table. When it is time for Johannes to work I dress and go downstairs and I do the washing up while my daughter nags at me to read her a story. I fold laundry. I think about what to have for lunch. When we go out I make sure that my daughter's shoes are on the right feet, I check the bag for water and spare pants. I take her hand. We go to the park or we sit on the upper decks of buses and travel to the places that she likes: the library where she can pretend

to work at the computers, the museum with a rocking horse on which she can take turns. We do the shopping. She chooses her own fruit, apples or nectarines, and is allowed to eat some of it on the way home, juice smeared across her face and down her neck. In the evenings, after Johannes has come down from his office, we sit together, all three of us, and talk about the days we've had and sometimes we are happy and sometimes we are tired and cross and each minute is an effort of patience. We make dinner. We put our child to bed. This is what routine is like, or love.

Each year on the first Saturday of August my mother and I would walk past the post office and the pub, past the primary school and the supermarket to the station and, leaving suburbia behind, would take the train into London and, changing at Waterloo, the Tube to Hampstead, whose broad streets sat above the city, looking down. As we came in sight of my grandmother's house we would see her waiting for us, standing at the kitchen window dressed in evening clothes, a long, full skirt with a narrow waist and a high-necked blouse, a cameo brooch pinned to her throat, her hair in its tight wave and, walking in and out of the shadows that the plane trees cast across the pavement, I would feel my mother's fingers tighten round my own, as though she were afraid that I might run away from her and that I would be lost.

By the time we reached the steps which led from the small front garden with its clay-tiled path up to my grandmother's front door she would be there to welcome us and,

stepping forward, would take us each in turn by the shoulders and would kiss us twice, two evenly placed markers, one on either cheek; and then I would be sent upstairs with my suitcase to the small room Doctor K kept for me through the eleven months that elapsed between each of my visits. This room was in the attic, reached by a staircase whose narrow steps, rising awkwardly away from the rest of the house, were tucked in behind a brass-handled door opposite Doctor K's bedroom. It smelled differently to the rooms on the lower floors, a musty scent like long-stored wool, and often, closing the staircase door behind me, I felt that as though I were leaving the house altogether and entering a space that was both separate and my own, and each evening this came as a relief, tension leeching away from me with every ascended step. This room lacked the restrained beauty which made the rest of the house seem so much like a stage. The furniture was tatty, old: an iron bedstead, very high off the ground, its mattress covered in a patchwork quilt; an armchair upholstered in velvet, much faded and scratched; a chest of drawers with a cracked walnut veneer. Around a two-paned dormer window looking out across the roof and the garden towards the heath, the room's whitewashed ceiling sloped towards a floor whose boards were covered in overlapping rugs, many of them with their naps worn through to leave bare patches of pale-coloured warp. I loved this room very much and still, at times, I wish that I could go back to it, to feel myself both above and alone. Before I was born it had been my mother's, and the white-painted bookshelf which leaned fifteen degrees west of true

was still filled with books which had once been hers. Sometimes, opening them, I would disturb loose sheets of paper that fluttered downwards, drifting to the floor to settle gently amongst the swirling patterns of the rugs, disjointed lists of words, phone numbers or addresses or single pages cut from longer letters, descriptions of nameless places, congratulations on achievements since forgotten. I would pick them up and hold them and, trying to connect their recipient with my mother, so uncompromisingly grown up, so firm and sure, I would catch from the corner of my eye the outline of my own inescapable adulthood flicker against the yellowed walls, a long shadow cast by a low sun.

After I had unpacked, putting my own books alongside my mother's on the shelf, filling the chest of drawers with my clothes, laying out my pyjamas on the pillow, I would go back downstairs to find Doctor K trimming runner beans at the kitchen table while, in the living room, my mother sat quite upright in an armchair, a gin and tonic and a bowl of crisps on the little table beside her.

—Have you unpacked?

she would ask, and

—Have you washed your hands?

and when I said that I had done both she would tell me to go and find my grandmother and ask her if she needed help but, trailing into the kitchen to do as I was told, my grandmother would tell me not to get under her feet, and often during those first evenings, uncertain of my place, I would sit outside in the hall, folded up across the span of the staircase's

bottom step, listening to the murmur of the radio spill out with the scent of garlic through the kitchen door.

For three days we remained in such uneasy equilibrium. Each morning I would come down to the kitchen where Doctor K stood, arranging my mother's breakfast on a tray, fresh croissants from the bakery split and spread with jam, and next to them a small pot of coffee and a jug of milk. I was not allowed to visit my mother in her room. My own breakfast was eaten in the kitchen and Doctor K insisted that I stayed downstairs until my mother had dressed, and then, during the morning, Doctor K would give me chores, laying out newspaper on the kitchen table and setting me to clean candlesticks, the damp wadding from a can of Brasso turning my fingers black while outside in the garden my mother lay on a rug, reading, and after lunch my mother was sent back to her room to rest while I was turned out onto the heath. At the time I regarded these separations as an unnecessary affront and I thought my grandmother excessive, my mother frail for giving in, because I took for granted that she resented them as much as I did. It is only now that I can see these few days for what they were: my grandmother's only way of taking care, my mother's only way of being cared for, this exchange effected silently while we all pretended to be occupied elsewhere. I did what I could to undermine them. Given the opportunity I would escape my grandmother's planned occupations and run into the garden to lie next to my mother on the rug, pulling up grass by the roots and knowing that now I had won through

I would be allowed to stay with my mother for the rest of the day. Doctor K would come out into the garden, hands smoothing out the creases in her skirt, and she would tell me that I must go indoors but

—Let her stay,

my mother said, and wrapped her arms around me. With a child's unhesitating cruelty I made my mother choose and, as if to emphasise the strength of her decision, on those reclaimed afternoons we would go out, up to the brightly painted shops in Hampstead Village, and she would buy me things – lawn cotton dresses or handwash-only cardigans, brightly coloured sandals, kites of Japanese paper stretched across a bamboo frame or soft-haired dolls too delicate for play – things to be coveted rather than owned; and afterwards I would clutch the loaded bags to my chest and we would sit and drink lemonade in front of one of the pavement cafes. This was the closest that I ever felt to her, I think; but I felt too as though in the winning of proximity something had been dismantled which had kept me sheltered. Love, for my mother, was not distinct from action. For years she had been putting into practice the contention that we exist, not as icebergs do, nine-tenths hidden and the visible portion no more than a poor clue to the greater, deeper bulk below, but at the surface, spread out along our planes of intersection; and now for an afternoon we had replaced this solid surety of position with something else and, perched above London with our parcels, I felt the lack of it.

*

Throughout the early stages of her illness I assumed that at some point in her dying the barrier between my mother and myself would be breached, no longer being necessary, and that through it some manner of truth would spill, coming as a trickle or a flood to engulf us and to wash us clean. I assumed that I would be granted access at last to those parts of her life which, throughout my childhood, had been kept meticulously separate from me, their presence felt but unmentioned, surrounding me as though I were a visitor to a house with half its rooms unseen, and that at last I would be able to walk through them, these stores for all the private tat and trivia of thought which makes a person both fragile and themselves. I assumed, then, that in the end I would take ownership of this as I would of all the rest of it, the house, the garden – a matter of legality, a process of inheritance in which preference had no part. Through those last long months, though, the physical intimacy which her illness demanded of us left no space for any more metaphorical form of contact – the present was too onerous to allow any intrusion by the past, and the work of being kind, against the urge to hurt which comes as vulnerability's unwelcome companion, left no energy for confession. The only times that we ever hovered close to revelation were on those afternoons in Hampstead. Then my mother would talk about herself as if she were someone else, a person whose life was meat for speculation, and she would talk about Doctor K, so that at times I could glimpse an otherwise unapprehended truth: that they were not what I had taken adults to be, each a finished entity, but rather were still in progress, and that

they too were a mother and a daughter, tied to one another. Once, after we had drunk our lemonade and paid the bill, as we walked slowly back towards Doctor K's house carrying the purchases whose extravagance already shamed us, my mother told me how, each morning during childhood, she would sit at the scrubbed table in the Hampstead kitchen, surrounded by the toast crumbs and the jam pots, the teacups' dregs, while my grandmother asked her about her dreams, questioning her in detail about their content; and that because of this, by the time my mother was five or six years old, she had stopped dreaming entirely. Afterwards I wished she hadn't told me. The thought of my mother as a child, her dreams jettisoned as though they were no more than empty wrappers, chilled me. All through the evening I avoided talking and at dinner I hunched over my plate as though it were a penance until my grandmother said I must be coming down with something, and sent me up to bed, where I lay, miserable, all through the fading evening, a jumper over my nightdress, an extra blanket from the bottom of the chest of drawers wrapped round my shoulders, wondering how often knowledge comes like this: a casually effected violence which throws the world just west of true.

After three days my mother left, returning to that quiet analogue of her life in which I was absent, trying in the earlier years to repair her relationship with my father and later to recover from it, and then I would feel the guilty lightening of relief like an unacknowledgeable weight removed.

Released from the entangling strictures of a relationship I didn't understand I felt as though I had run a swift course into open water and, alone for the remainder of the month with Doctor K, left largely to my own devices, I felt myself free. During the greater part of every day my grandmother worked; I learned to keep doors closed, to leave no personal possessions in the hallway that led past the kitchen and the study to her consulting room – learned, too, to retreat to some deeper portion of the house between five to and five past every hour, those ten minutes during which one client left and another arrived, sitting round the bend in the stairs so that I could listen to the sound that two shadows made sliding past one another and trying to imagine from the sound their footsteps made on the hallway's wooden boards the details of these incomprehensibly other lives. On hot days when the windows were open and voices carried clearly through the still air, the walls of the house responding like a sounding board, I would find myself occasionally startled by the noise of weeping or by a shout, its echoes deadened by the still air of the summer garden.

At the start of each day – after the breakfast things had been cleared and the floor swept, the papers straightened on the hall table, the mirror that hung above it wiped; those minutiae which, attended to, transformed the lower floor of the flat from habitation to a refuge for paying strangers – Doctor K hung a laminated sign on the door of her consulting room on which the words *Analysis in Progress* were written in heavy-inked, formal lettering. This, said Doctor K, when I complained

that it was unnecessary given that I knew better than to interrupt, was not for my benefit, being used even when, as was more usual, there was no one else in the flat. Rather it was a part of the ritual of analysis, a formal acknowledgement of the pact that she made to be available as absolutely as she was able for the time that she had allotted to those who came to visit her, climbing with what combination of anticipation and anxiety I could not imagine five or six times a week up the stairs from the street. Doctor K was always ready to explain to me the mechanics of her profession, taking my questions more seriously than I ever intended them to be. At such times she would treat me as a sort of proto-adult, stopping what she was doing to speak, and, flattered, I would try hard to concentrate, although lack of comprehension made it difficult, her words slipping past while I squinted to catch the shape of them. I didn't doubt the truth of what she said. I assumed, then, that knowledge was synonymous with fact – that understanding must bring with it certainty so that, knowing, one would know for sure; and such surety I looked forward to, taking it to be a part of adulthood which would come, at last, when I had earned it.

Left to my own devices for the greater part of each day, I spent most of my time reading and I was happy, if this is what happiness is, this tendency to be engrossed, an enthusiasm for the drowning out of thought with words; and then each evening, when Doctor K's last client had left, she would come and find me. This was the only time that I was allowed into her consulting room: when, for half an hour each evening

before dinner, we would sit in there together, in a pair of facing armchairs set beneath the window. The room was large and its windows looked, as those of the living room did, out across the garden. It seemed always to be cool, even when hot days stretched on for hours, and it had that kind of heavy, impenetrable quiet which I have since come to associate with National Trust properties: the peace of things that are not used, that are curated, precisely placed, unmoved and untouched by those who pass through. The floor was lime-washed wood, pale and clean, covered for the most part by a large red-and-purple Persian carpet, and besides the two chairs on which Doctor K and I sat, and the bookcases that lined three walls of the room from the floor to a foot off the ceiling, and which housed all Doctor K's psychoanalytic books, the only furniture was a bureau and a couch, a long, low ottoman upholstered in velvet faded to the washed-out brownish green of a shadowed pond. This couch, low-backed and piled with cushions at one end, I was not allowed to sit on, it being imbued, or so I inferred from the way that Doctor K spoke about it, with some power of compulsion, a mysterious tendency to induce in its occupants a time-consuming and uncheckable catharsis. As a result it became an object of desire for me. I tried to imagine the drama of myself upon it, how I would be laid out, wan and troubled, words dropping from my lips like the fruit of a slow-grown bush, but could only think how awkward it would be to sit on its edge, mute and uncomfortable, and how the thought of lying there while someone watched me would bring panic like the fear of

drowning. Often, while Doctor K was absent from the flat, when she walked to the bakery or went on Wednesday evenings to play bridge at the house of the elderly pianist who lived on the top floor of the house opposite, I would stand in my bare feet outside the closed door of the consulting room and try to work up the courage to go inside, daring myself to approach the couch, to lower myself onto it; but if I ever did then I have no recollection of it, and nor do I know what happened to the couch after Doctor K's death. I imagine that my mother would have sold it if she could, as she sold all the books, not to turn a profit but because she was pragmatic and disliked waste; or if it couldn't be sold she would have thrown it away as she did the heavy consulting room carpet which, when we lifted a corner of it on the day after the funeral, both of us seeking a way to occupy ourselves in the solitary vacuum that comes when death's formalities are complete, we found to be so riddled with moths that, disturbed, they flew up in clouds and the carpet began to shred and fall into grainy dust in our hands.

For that half an hour in the consulting room each evening, between the end of Doctor K's working day and the start of dinner, which we cooked together, her standing over the hob while I sat at the kitchen table chopping potatoes or shredding spring onions for a salad, we sat and faced one another. Through the open window drifted the gentle roar of traffic climbing Haverstock Hill, and mixed in with it the calling voices of people turned out into the freedom of the heath's

open spaces, but we were close together and very far from them and all these outside noises came to us as though through swaddling layers of cloth. Throughout the time that we sat there my grandmother maintained a sort of listening stillness, sat upright and unmoving, her feet crossed at the ankle and her hands in her lap, her eyes focused on me as I fidgeted about and tried, without alerting her to what I was doing, to catch sight of the dial of the watch she wore on the inside of her wrist. Her face was not expressionless but nor did it convey any particular emotion and she gave the impression not of waiting, which would have implied expectation, but rather of an impartial readiness, as though she would attend to anything that might be said but would be equally content to remain as she was, sat in silence, until the seven o'clock chime from the grandfather clock in the hall set us free. On the deep windowsill which stretched between the two chairs sat two corresponding glasses, a gin for Doctor K and for me a glass of lemonade browned with angostura bitters, their outsides sweating, their ice cubes melting slowly in the cool room. These drinks, said Doctor K, were further indicators, like not using the couch and no sign pinned up outside the door, that we were not in consultation. It was, she said, no kind of analysis that we were conducting, a point which she said needed to be emphasised more for her own benefit than for mine, as it was she who had its habit and routines ingrained. Rather than analysis, she said, this was an opportunity for us to talk without any mediating activity. It was an opportunity for reflection. She told me that without reflection, without the

capacity to trace our lives backwards and pick the patterns out, we become liable to act as animals do, minus forethought and according to a set of governing laws which we have never taken the trouble to explore. Without reflection we do little more than drift upon the surface of things and self-determination is an illusion. We lay ourselves open to unbalance. Conversation, she said, helps us to reflect – and although much of what Doctor K said to me I at first failed to understand and then came to doubt, this point I have come back to; and I think that had I remembered it during those lost and lonely months after my mother's death when the contents of my mind were a formless spread that I could neither abandon nor inhabit, then perhaps things might have been easier for me.

At the time I found these evening talks with my grandmother uncomfortable, a fact that she acknowledged but which, she said, was an indication only that we were engaged in something valuable, as though my discomfort were a call sign, something to be sought and followed. Although for the most part I was little more than bored, there were times when I felt myself trapped. Reticence was no protection. Doctor K was as able to find significance in my silence as in my speech and any act of concealment would itself be considered revelatory. I felt that in the steady light of Doctor K's compassionate gaze my body, far from being the container and concealer of my mind, had become its compulsive betrayer and I wished that instead of entering the consulting room we might go

straight to the easy companionship of dinner's preparation when, stood side by side, otherwise engaged, we might talk in fragments, about what I was reading or what I had seen, about Doctor K's friends or her tangential recollections of a childhood that seemed impossibly distant to me then and more so now. Under such conditions, through such circumlocutions, I felt that what was important could be admitted, unsaid but understood; but lately I have found that some version of Doctor K's routine has returned to me. Each evening, after our daughter is asleep, surrounded by the chaos made from our once-ordered lives, Johannes and I sit together for half an hour and let our thoughts unwind in silence or in fractured sentences, this ritual proximity an attempt to touch one another across a widening space of tiredness and habit, and although we do not confess, are neither priests nor penitents, still it is a kind of undressing and we are better for it.

This was Doctor K's contention: that the formal work of psychoanalysis, the daily meeting of analyst and analysand, should not be thought of as the elucidation of a person directly but rather as the teaching by example of a skill which, once learned, might be practised internally. It is, she said, easy to see analysis as a kind of laying out, a mental correlate of that physical ordering which occurs after death: the contents of a person unpacked and spread across the patterned surface of the Persian carpet, each artefact itemised, assessed; and then, inventory made, these objects put away again, more neatly

now, their relations to one another drawn and understood; but minds repacked will tend, she said, to chaos, with more stuff shoved in lazily on top, the whole swiftly deteriorating into the same shifting mess it started as.

—It is a common mistake,

Doctor K told me, her hands lifting slightly from her lap in a gesture of emphasis that I cannot think would have been unconscious

—to think of the process in such passive terms.

These conversations – in which my part, if any, was that of unwilling interlocutor, my questions heavily prompted by my grandmother – took place not in the consulting room, where the spontaneous nature of what speech I chose to make was sacrosanct, but in any otherwise unoccupied corners of our days, on Sunday afternoons when it was hot and we would sit out on the lawn, Doctor K in a wicker chair and me on the grass in front of her, or in the evenings, after we had watched together some drama or documentary on the brown, wood-laminate television set that she kept in a small study next to her bedroom, until illness robbed her of the use both of the stairs and the evening hours. The analyst, Doctor K told me, is not a tour guide, leading their client through those vast and vaulted galleries, the cloisters of the mind, and nor is it their task to point out shadows, but rather they must provide an instruction in the mechanics of such shadows' investigation. It is only, she told me – each summer a different form of words, each summer the branches of the apple trees which grew espaliered against the garden fence a little longer, my

80

legs a little longer on the sofa – when a person has gained the skills necessary to explore the territory for themselves, to unpack their own minds and begin to understand the contents, that they might start the work necessary to make their experience, their behaviour meaningful; and then at last they might start to become transparent to themselves. This, she said, was the original significance of her name, adopted when she was young enough not to find such gestures awkward and kept to since as a way of keeping faith with herself: to mark herself as her life's subject, a case study in which she was both analyst and analysand, carried on across decades in an attempt to peel away the obscuring layers, the muddying cross-currents of desire, and to live a life which was intentional, directed not by the hidden motivations of a covered mind but by an elucidated self. Her first client, each morning, was herself, and for fifty minutes she would sit at the bureau in her consulting room and write in one of the large, leather-backed notebooks that she kept for the purpose an account of the previous day's events, her reactions to them, her dreams or reveries; and then she would read back through what she had written and annotate it with the same interpretations she would provide for any other subject. This diary keeping was, she said, not strictly necessary to the task of self-analysis but it was a methodology which she found useful, a way of holding the mind to task, like the use of a rosary in prayer. When, the summer that I was nine or ten, I tried to outgrow my childhood through mimicry, I kept for a while my own imitation of my grandmother's diary. We went

together on a Saturday afternoon to the bookshop at the bottom of the hill, and there my grandmother bought me a smaller version of the notebook that she used and a good pen to go with it, and returning to her flat we moved, between us, a small table to sit beneath the window in my bedroom and in front of it a little round-backed chair. I laid out the notebook and set the pen next to it and the next morning, after breakfast, while my grandmother sat in her consulting room, I sat at the table and tried to write. After ten minutes or so I had managed a list of everything achieved the previous day and given as much thought as I was able to the significance of it. The dormer window was open and I could hear the scratching and cooing of the pigeons who nested on the roof. At the bottom of the page I had been writing on I drew a picture of a witch. After a while I climbed onto the table and stuck my head out of the window to see if I could catch sight, from up here, of any hint of a bald spot in the downstairs tenant's hair as he stood in front of a bed of roses with a pair of secateurs held loosely in his hand.

Later, as we sat together in the kitchen over a lunch of ham sandwiches, I felt an inner swell of importance as I waited for Doctor K to ask me how I had got on. All morning, after the tedious execution of the task itself had been got out of the way, I had been imagining what I would say when asked about my diary. Concerned more with an image of myself as diary keeper than with the actual act of writing I was eager to have an opportunity to demonstrate this new facet to my personality; but Doctor K made no mention of it. Even when the next

morning, as we cleared away the breakfast things, I loudly announced my intention to go to my room and work and then, half mounting the stairs, turned back to look at her, she did nothing more than nod. It puzzles me still, this peculiar idea of privacy Doctor K had, that all my thoughts and actions, my hidden wants, the ripples of my mind across my face, my skin, should be considered little more than symptom while the act of examination itself was sacrosanct.

Despite the difficulty in its actual execution I held to the idea of diary writing for the rest of the month, keeping faith with my morning retreat to the table beneath the window, and when my holiday was over and I returned home I made my mother clear out a space for me in the box room, sorting through years of accumulated junk until I could fit a chair in there and an old writing bureau she bought at my insistence from a junk shop, and I made a sign to be pinned up on the door. I wonder now if this was some feint on my part, a testing of the waters, to see how it would feel to ally myself to Doctor K, and whether perhaps this was the year that I came to understand, if not what held my mother and my grandmother apart, then at least the presence of their separation. That my mother carried out my instructions without comment or question despite the fact that it must have irritated her was, I think, a testament to her patience, but it was sensible too, because the feeling of importance that it gave me to retreat each morning before school to the box room and hang up the sign and shut the door soon wore off, and I found other ways to entertain myself. The box room drifted back to being a repository for

odds and ends of household rubbish, for ironing boards and baskets and spare sheets, for jumpers in need of mending and chairs with broken legs or backs – those things we couldn't use but couldn't bring ourselves to throw away; and upon all this its door could be shut, granting us the illusion of a house in order. And when, years later, after my mother's death, I came to sort through it all again, to disinter object after half-discarded object from the softening dust which lay across the room, each one become through disuse little more than an imitation of itself, I found at the back of the room the bureau and, on it, the leather notebook, neatly placed, the pen set parallel beside it. The notebook I kept, saving it from the skip because it felt a part of me, vestigial but somehow still adjoining, and I expect that it is somewhere in this house now although I couldn't say precisely where, a part of that silted edifice, built in layers, which is my own paper carcass, a repository the sorting of which will be my children's task. My grandmother's notebooks she destroyed as soon as she found out that she was dying, spending an hour each afternoon between naps and medication feeding them methodically through a shredder. They had been, she said, a tool for her analysis and not its outcome, that outcome being, depending on your point of view, either the articles she had written over forty years explaining and defending her project and its method, or her life itself – what she had made of it, its worm-cast trail – but more, her own experience of it, that inner life which, so long laboured over, would soon be lost.

*

84

After my mother told me that she had ceased to dream I began to find myself lying awake, in my bedroom at home or during the summer in the room at the top of Doctor K's house, when I should have been asleep – not every night, but maybe once or twice a fortnight. Partly it was a sudden awareness of my own sleeping patterns which disrupted them – the way that, thinking about my mother and the mechanics of her dreamlessness, I would lie with my eyes shut, trying to notice the point at which dreams began – but partly also it was the preoccupying strangeness of it, those dark, imageless hours between sleeping and waking. Having learned the fact I kept it as a curiosity, taking it out during my own solitary night-lit hours to turn it this way and that, trying to make sense of it – this single artefact I had of my mother's existence apart from myself. At home in the mornings I would sit, tired, my school uniform half-buttoned, on the tall stool in the corner of the kitchen and watch my mother slot bread into the toaster, boil the kettle, reach down a pot of jam from the high shelf in the cupboard where it lived because at one time I had liked to put my fingers in it when her back was turned, and I would feel that, despite the familiarity of these gestures, despite the known quantity of her face and the predictability of her responses to me, the woman I was watching was a stranger; but surely this cannot have been the case. The truth must be that I knew my mother well because, after all, what are we if not a totality of days, a sum of interactions; and a glimpse of what is underneath the surface, the skeleton on which the outer face is hung, cannot undo the knowledge of

skin but only give it context, the way it rises and falls, its puckering, its flaws.

One particular summer, sometime between sports day and my French exam, my father left at last, his presence, always tentative, often forgotten, finally ceasing altogether. My parents sat side by side in our sitting room to tell me what I had failed to notice – that my father had gone – and I thought only how unusual it was that we should be all three in the same room. Later, when my mother came to my bedroom to ask if there was anything more that I wanted to know, I could think of nothing to say. It seemed that nothing tangible had happened and that afterwards things went on as before. Term ended. The long holiday began. My father came and went without warning so that, as I had always done, I assumed his absence, tried not to seem resentful of his presence. For a few weeks I wandered from one friend's house to another while my mother worked, and then my bags were packed and we made the journey to Doctor K's. My mother stayed for the weekend, and if Doctor K tried less hard to keep us apart than was usual, if I spent more time sat by mother's side, then I barely noticed it; and then my mother left, and I was alone with my grandmother and the flat and the heath. The weather that year was indifferent, grey and rather humid, and when I climbed to the top of Parliament Hill in the afternoons there was a pollution haze spread out across the eastward city like a caul; or perhaps this is another trick that memory plays, to point and dramatise: the

addition of an appropriate backdrop for the mood. I found myself distractible, easily bored, and I seemed to have no handle on what I felt: although I would not have said that I was unhappy small things distressed me without warning. One evening, towards the end of the first week, I sat in Doctor K's consulting room and wept because I had been unable to reach my father by phone, and although this was not unusual, although he would not have been expecting me to call and so would have had no reason to stay near a phone, although it had been nothing more than a whim which had led me to dial his number and I could think of nothing that I wanted to say to him, still I felt as though my failure to reach him was a suddenly effected, ragged wound. Doctor K poured our drinks and we sat in our usual chairs. Surrounded by the room's familiar comfort, I was surprised by my own desolation, which came as a longing not just for my own home but for my mother, or for what my mother would have done to treat my unhappiness, tending to it as though it were a fever or a graze, susceptible to the same rules of comfort as any other injury: a bath, hot milk, a kiss; those simplicities which, treating sorrow as a fact in itself, require no act of explanation on the part of one already wounded.

Doctor K:

—It is important that we talk about these things.

My mother, when she asked me how I felt about my father leaving, had offered no platitudes but left instead the complicated state of things arrayed about us like the wreckage of an ocean voyage as we sat, survivors, side by side on the edge of

my bed; and if I had any questions beyond the purely logistical I knew better than to ask them.

Doctor K:

—Would you like to tell me how you feel?

I sat in the chair opposite my grandmother, curled over on myself as though to protect an injury to my front or flank, unstopped tears running down my face to wet the knees of my summer trousers, and I shut my eyes so that I would not have to look beneath the surface of things.

Doctor K:

—Sometimes if we are angry with someone we love, it doesn't feel acceptable to us and so we find other places to put that anger.

Doctor K:

—We might think we are angry with someone else instead.

My mother, as she talked, had held my hand.

Doctor K:

—Or we might feel very sad.

Across the empty acres of the consulting room carpet, Doctor K's words reached me; but for all the promise implicit in the act of talking we did not touch and I was not comforted.

In my last year at university, sat one evening in my room eating an indifferent vegetable curry for the third night running, two pairs of socks protecting my feet from the cold, and through the window a view of the chapel lit up against the darkness in a way that never failed to make me feel mildly, half-pleasantly bereft, I read for the first time Freud's account

of the psychoanalysis of a four-year-old boy, Little Hans. Although during each of the Augusts that I had spent at my grandmother's house I had done little but read, having nowhere to go except the heath, nor any friends nearby, and although I had been given more or less free rein of the books in the house, allowed my own pick of what was on the shelves, still I had never read any psychoanalysis. Those books relating to her work my grandmother kept in her consulting room, and although not strictly forbidden them I would never have felt myself able, while she sat and watched, to run my fingers along their spines as I did with those in the rest of the house, waiting for something to catch my attention. Even now, so long afterwards, the thought of what my grandmother's response would have been, her enthusiasm, the opportunity she would have seen to teach, brings an immediate and indivisible firmness of response: the automatic certainty that I must allow my grandmother no ingress to my mind beyond what she had already granted to herself. Then, after her death, the books were gone; and with an adolescent's callousness I didn't think about my grandmother for a long time, or about the past, or anything but my own life and how I might get on with it. Now, though, reading the slightly stilted prose of a decades-old translation of Freud's case studies, I felt my childhood spread about me like a map to which I had almost learned the key, and for days afterwards I felt myself to be a little out of focus, as though I had been away somewhere and had yet to complete the process of my return. As I walked to lectures or to the library, or sat drinking weak coffee in the

college bar, I found myself haunted by the thought of Herbert Graf, anonymised by Freud as Little Hans, who at the age of four and three quarters saw a horse fall down in the street and afterwards became so frightened that he couldn't leave the house. His subsequent analysis was carried out primarily by his father, Max, with Freud offering support by letter – an extension of a process that was already in place, since Freud had for some time been encouraging those of his supporters who had young children to observe and report on their development, seeking in this way to gain confirmation of his theories of childhood sexuality. Freud himself would meet Herbert only once during the course of his analysis, on the afternoon of 30 March 1908 when the three of them – Herbert and his father and *Herr Doktor,* Freud – would sit in Freud's consulting room, awkwardly arrayed on chairs about the empty couch, Herbert's small-boy body uncomfortably still while – perhaps – from elsewhere in the apartment the sounds of freer children filtered through. Herbert was a polite, good-natured boy who tried hard to please, giving the best answers he could to questions he barely understood. Freud asked him if the horses that he was afraid of wore glasses; he said they didn't. Freud asked him if his father Max wore glasses and, confused, the boy said no to this as well although it wasn't true. Freud asked him if what he had described as the black around the mouths of the horses that frightened him might be a moustache; and Herbert, hands clasped between his knees, said he supposed it might. It was not, the eminent professor told him, horses that he was afraid of. Nor, as his

father had suggested to him, was his anxiety mere synecdoche, the whole of the dreaded animal standing in for its penis. His fear, Freud said, was of his father; and Herbert, just turned five, who had seen a horse fall down and felt the safety of his bounded world eroded, sat quietly, and tried to see how this was true. His fear, for all its power, had previously been a simple thing, susceptible to adult protection; now he was being asked to put in place of it a metastasising complexity – an enforced awareness of the unreliability of thought, the way that one thing can come to stand in for another without us noticing the difference. Even now I feel the horror of it: to be made to feel in ignorance of oneself, to be stripped of those privileges subjectivity brings – a still, sure place to stand; a premise; the right to know one's mind – and I think of them walking home together, Herbert and his father, hurrying back through busy streets towards the safety of home, the boy whose trust had been opened like a nut, split to see what mechanism it was that made it grow, falling into step beside his analyst father, who far from being the negation of fear was now its subject; and I can think only of how thin the world must have seemed to him, how fragile – what had been that morning a presumed certainty made now into something like a body of water, the taut surface on which they walked a meagre miracle stretched across its depths.

My mother lay in her bed, a barrow's shape beneath the sheets, her hair, lost on one side where surgery had stripped the skin, and on the other tufty and uneven from the effects of repeated

radiotherapy, spread about the pillow like half a greying halo. I sat across the room from her, the book I had been reading held in my lap. I said

—Do you dream, now?

She was at that stage of her illness where the weave between sleeping's warp and weft was beginning to unpick itself and I hadn't yet got used to the way that she would drift about, sliding in and out of consciousness, and when she didn't answer I thought that perhaps she had fallen asleep. Later, though, after I had put the book away and tidied the sheets, held a cup for her to drink and drawn the curtains on the fading summer night, she said

—I dream of you sometimes. Or of your father. It doesn't—

she coughed

—it doesn't mean anything,

and she shifted in her bed and turned, and she was lost again.

Herbert Graf was not alone in being the subject of an analysis by his own father. Freud himself would become his daughter Anna's analyst, albeit in adulthood, and both Jung and Karl Abraham would work analytically with their children, as would Melanie Klein, an advocate of prophylactic analysis for all children, with hers; and although when I first learned about it, my fingers like a voyeur's eyes running down the indexes of college library books to find examples, it struck me as nothing but obvious intrusion on the children, incomprehensible to me in its motivation, now at least a part of that

pity I felt for Herbert Graf is saved over for his father. Sometimes, when in the woods I watch my daughter with indefatigable hopefulness attempt to climb a tree whose first branch is five times her own height above the earth, tiny fingers thrust into crevasses or knots, red wellingtons scrabbling on curved bark for purchase, I feel myself winded by the desire to promise a protection that I cannot give; and if, then, I thought there was a way that I could make her life better than the ordinary – if I thought that I could make it smoother, softer, less fraught with the sudden, troubled revelation that hidden motivation brings, or with the half-rotted-through desire for what will come to haunt or hurt her – if I could give her clarity, self-knowledge, sight – and if, telling her the secret now to stop her searching for it later, I could leave happiness to her like a legacy – then I would; and if afterwards it turned out that she wasn't happy after all then how would it be possible to say it was my fault?

A month, perhaps, after Johannes and I had been to the V&A, we went to together to the Freud museum. We had met a few times during the intervening weeks, for a drink or for coffee, and one weekend we had walked together along the Thames from Cookham to Henley on a day when, after a week of better weather, winter had returned, bringing an icy, rain-flecked wind that tore at buds and stripped petals from crocuses and left us too cold and damp to be more than tolerably friendly. I thought about him often and in the evenings, in my flat with the sounds of other lives leeching through the

walls, I wrote him long emails which I edited down to short emails and then didn't send; and sometimes as I turned off the lights to go to bed my phone would ring and it would be him. Our conversations were awkward. Neither of us are very good on the phone even now and it was hard then to know how we stood, me half-undressed and in the middle of a darkened flat and him elsewhere, his voice emerging in bursts from a background that might have been a party or a bar or only the noise of a busy street drifting through into my empty room.

—Well, goodnight then.

—Yes, I—

—Goodnight.

The Freud museum was my idea. Cookham had been his. I had wanted to visit the museum for years; but also I think that I wanted Johannes to believe that I was something other than I felt myself to be, a person who we both might learn to like: that person who I might have become if my mother's death and my own uncertain illness which was its aftermath had not intervened to leave my life a shoreless fluidity and myself adrift inside it. I had not visited Hampstead since the day my mother and I had lifted up the Persian carpet in my grandmother's consulting room to release a cloud of moths, but still I thought of it as in some way mine, and I assumed that recognition would be reciprocal and that it would be as I had left it, waiting. Now, though, leaving the tube at Swiss Cottage, travelling up the elderly escalator with its brass fittings and elegantly fonted signs to be spat out onto the edge

of the Finchley Road, turning right towards Hampstead and leaving the churning traffic behind, I found myself wrong-footed. This was a place I hardly recognised, although it can't have been much changed. The same trees grew from the same pavements and the same houses lined them, high white stuccoed terraces with deep front steps or Edwardian mansions set back behind gardens planted with magnolia or fig, but the worlds their walls enclosed were private and I had no right of admittance to them. My grandmother and all the people that she knew were gone and I would be neither recognised nor remembered; and when, turning into Maresfield Gardens where for the last few months of his life Freud had lived in exile, cared for by his daughter, Anna, I saw in slivers eked out through windows high ceilings and broad fireplaces, bookshelves, paintings, and such gentle order, the uncrowded peace which my grandmother's flat had possessed, I felt that version of loss which is the sudden understanding of the impossibility of return, our casting out from that which memory tells us was once ours. Such an unexpected grief shook me, and by the time that Johannes arrived to find me, hands sunk deep in pockets, waiting for him in front of the museum, I had worked myself into a sullen, twitching mood I couldn't shake, my awareness that I was being unreasonable only making my sourness worse. I blamed him for my distemper. I felt that something hung between us and I resented it. I felt that perhaps I was wasting my time – here, with him – as I had wasted evenings already on unsent emails, on phone calls both imagined and real, and I wanted to take him to

95

account but knew that in truth none of it was his fault. He, too, seemed aware that we were out of step with one another. His answers to my abruptly practical questions were brief and vague and his eyes skimmed mine, sliding off to rest elsewhere; and when, as we stood side by side to study a photograph, our hands touched, it was he who pulled himself away. In Sigmund Freud's consulting room ropes held us to a narrow tunnel in the middle of the floor and we stood, staring. The furniture here, the chairs and tables, the books and the crowded cabinets of curiosities, the couch with its drapes and cushions, had been brought over from the family's apartment in Vienna, a wholesale transportation in the spring of 1938 which had required all the resources they could call upon, both financial and administrative; and when at last they arrived these things had been unpacked and arranged to mimic the lost original so that when, after her father's death a few months later, Anna had chosen to preserve the house as it was, it was already halfway to a reliquary. I looked at it all and tried to think of my grandmother but couldn't, and so I tried to think of Anna, living and working for forty years around this preserved monument to her father's memory, a static starting point, unchallenged, unexamined, but that too slipped away from me, leaving behind Johannes – my awareness of his presence and the feeling that, somewhere in the space between us, the uncertain image of our future shivered. On the landing at the top of the beautiful staircase where a small table and a chair, overhung by a rubber plant, were set beneath a long window, I wanted to say that, one day, I would

like to have such a place as this to sit; but even that felt like a presumption and so I said nothing, and neither did Johannes, and we didn't look at one another, and barely breathed; and when upstairs I found a photograph taken of one of the rooms as it had been in the late seventies, a space inhabited by Anna as an old woman, painted cabinets set against the walls and shelves of books, signifiers of an intellectual life, and between them a rather horrible armchair and, sat closely facing it, the same sort of television set that Doctor K had owned, when I remembered how towards the end of my grandmother's life the trappings of old age had intruded on her house, the television brought downstairs, electrically reclining plush armchairs placed in the rooms, and how I had felt pre-emptively bereft at the thought of what it was now too late for, the learning of that which she had been so eager to teach – the underlying, animating shape of things, the way my own cogs bit and turned – I said only

—My grandmother had a television just like that one,

and felt such inadequacy that it almost brought me to tears.

Descending the staircase again, I let Johannes go ahead of me into the shop and I stood for some minutes in front of a photograph of Sigmund and Anna, taken in 1913, at around the time that Freud began to see in his daughter for the first time the possibility of inheritor, no longer an often-worrying youngest daughter but a potential agent both for the perpetuation and the preservation of his work. In the photograph they walk on grass, the flat scrub of an imperfectly kept lawn, a flecked mass of unidentifiable bushes rising a few yards to

their backs. Sigmund wears a hat and Anna, a step behind, her hand in the crook of his elbow, a white apron over a dirndl. Squinting slightly against the sun they have the look of people caught in a moment of unguarded intimacy, and standing staring at the picture hung just too low on the wall I felt as though I were grasping for a memory just out of reach – something to do with grass and with summer, with my grandmother in her garden and my mother, the two of them standing and thinking themselves unobserved – but for all the picture seemed significant I could make no sense of it. My memory refused to resolve into anything concrete and the photograph remained impenetrable surface, glossy, chemically rendered and preserved. I followed Johannes into the shop and found him leaning against the counter talking to the assistant, a very tall woman, younger than me, with a black polo neck and bleached hair cut into a ragged coif. She was laughing at something he had said and in the moment before he turned towards me I saw him as a stranger, and I realised that he wasn't any more, but had become in some small measure a part of my own life, a knot in that complicated tangle of utterance and experience, memory, thought, which made up my extended self.

Afterwards, after we had left the museum, we walked in silence north through Belsize Park to Hampstead Village, an aimless wander which we hoped might bring us to a pub, and as we trailed up the hill towards the heath I realised very suddenly that we were standing outside Doctor K's house. I said

—My grandmother lived here,
and Johannes, moving closer, took my hand.

During the summer of 1897 Freud conducted what he described, in a series of intensely felt letters to his friend and confidant Wilhelm Fliess, as a self-analysis. 'I believe,' he wrote, 'I am in a cocoon, and heaven knows what sort of creature will emerge from it.' Since 1891 the Freud family had been living in an apartment in Vienna, at Berggasse 19, which would remain their home until 4 June 1938 when, forced to leave at last in the wake of Austria's annexation, Freud, along with Anna and his wife Martha, would take the Orient Express to Paris and, from there, to London, first to stay in a house at the bottom of Primrose Hill and then, at last, to 20 Maresfield Gardens where, after the passing of a fine summer and the difficult completion of some remaining work, he would die at the age of eighty-three. By then his followers would regard him as a kind of secular prophet and his pronouncements, handed down through Anna, as absolute; but in 1897 he had few patients and little money, five children already and a sixth, Anna, on the way. Despite an unshakeable belief in the importance of his work he had so far failed to successfully complete a psychoanalytic treatment, and nor could he articulate any sound theory of psychoanalysis. Initially, under the influence of the neurologist Jean-Martin Charcot, with whom he had studied in Paris, he had believed that the solution to those problems of mental topology which interested him might be found in hypnosis, but he had since ceased to trust it; now he

sought some alternative but seemed to get nowhere. He had been, for a while, a close collaborator with Josef Breuer but Breuer lacked Freud's faith in the idea that it was suppressed sexuality that was at the root of their patients' neurotic symptoms and, in the face of this doctrinal difference, their relationship had crumbled – a pattern which was soon to be repeated with Fliess and then, some years later, with Jung. This pattern of intense collaborative friendship followed by a difference of opinion which Freud felt as a betrayal – finding resolution at last in his relationship with Anna, whose faith in his work was absolute, a form of love, tying him to her as much as her to him – was something which Freud appeared unable either to notice or to anticipate; and I find in this a particular sadness, that a man so concerned with the possibility of understanding might remain in this case so blind. This impending separation, although still some way distant, presents itself in the letters that Freud wrote to Fleiss during the summer of 1897 as a kind of weight: the oppressive, headachy closeness of the air before thunder. Freud writes with a noisy fondness, as though the volume of his friendship will keep his doubts at bay, drowning them in the performance of affection, and he allows little space for discussion of Fleiss' own theories, commenting rarely on the other man's work.

The previous year Freud's father had died and, in the aftermath of loss, he found himself suffering through a period of depression. Jacob Freud had been an easy-going and rather shiftless man, cheerful but lacking any particular strength of character, his belief in the brilliance of his son certain but also

lazy, a general pride often standing in for specific interest, and Freud's love for him had been tinged with the wish that he might have been a stronger and more powerful man, less biddable and easier to respect; and in the wake of his father's death Freud's awareness of this edge of near-disdain which had bounded his affection left him troubled. It was as though at the moment when Freud's father had at last passed out of life, after hovering for so long at its edge that he had begun to seem, paradoxically, invincible, Sigmund had himself been shaken, and now all the settled silt was once more muddy water. Memories, long ignored, began to surface: the sight of his mother naked in the sleeper compartment of a train when Freud was two and a half; the younger brother whose birth was the cause of jealousy until his death at the age of nine months; the adult half-brother, product of his father's first marriage, who in some barely perceptible way supplanted Sigmund in the affections of his mother; and behind all these, in shadows, the figure of his father. On 12 June he wrote to Fleiss, 'I have been through some kind of a neurotic experience, with odd states of mind not intelligible to consciousness – cloudy thoughts and veiled doubts, with barely here and there a ray of light.'

Freud spent the early part of the summer travelling, first to Salzburg, where he visited his sister-in-law Minna Bernays, then to Reichenhall to see his mother, a difficult woman, dominating and egotistical, who, in contrast to his father, Freud loved uncritically. From there he returned briefly to Vienna to deal with some administrative details regarding his

father's tombstone – and all the time he felt growing in himself a manifestation of those symptoms to which he was more ordinarily an observer, reliant on second-hand experience, on imperfectly communicated half-truths, so that while still trying to construct a theory of mind he must also attempt to understand the significance of omission; and all the time he must remember that his patients were also his patrons, and he must not push them. He was listless, lacking concentration. He was unable to work even when there was occasion to do so, and he had developed a tendency to disturbingly vivid dreams; but slowly, emerging from his undeniable unhappiness, came the thought that he was also being presented with an opportunity: that in himself he might find at last that willing subject whose study would bring his disordered theories into sharper focus – and so, arriving finally at the alpine resort of Aussee, where the rest of the Freud family was holidaying, he began in earnest that formal iteration of his self-analysis which would result, at last, in his theory of the unconscious. It was, at least in part, a work of mourning: an outcome of the necessary disinterment of the past that comes in the wake of loss, the going through of attics and of drawers – the process of imposing order, understanding; and, in understanding, the jettisoning of what is unimportant. To Fleiss he wrote that 'the chief patient I am busy with is myself . . . This analysis is harder than any other.'

Beyond what can be inferred from his letters to Fleiss, Freud left little information about the methodology of his self-analysis. That he recorded his dreams in some detail is

clear from the fact that many of them, disguised in places and alongside his partially truncated interpretations, would appear as the basis of *The Interpretation of Dreams*, a work which, despite its largely unnoticed initial publication in 1899, would form the foundational text for what would become the psychoanalytic movement. In addition the struggle involved in the undertaking, which left him at times distracted and at others distraught, gave him, he claimed, a new order of sympathy for his patients—

I imagine Freud sitting all through the bright, clear summer, a middle-aged man in the mountains, grieving, the work of himself before him, and doing so I find myself fitting to the lines of him the figure of my grandmother, straight-backed at her desk each morning, hands resting on either side of her open notebook and her mind turned inwards, concentrated on those phenomena accessible only to herself. Then sympathy comes like a bloom on fruit, sudden and unlooked for, and I find that she seems softer and more human, and those morning hours no longer appear to be the execution of a grand task but only an attempt to live an ordered life. This is what we all do, after all, this striving to make sense. We bow to the drive to fit our sharp-edged pieces into a smoother shape, we clutch at agency; and perhaps my grandmother's would be the most honest way to do it, the daily effort of accounting and the acknowledgement it brings that this task can't be shirked but can only be done badly, or done well.

Despite the creative productivity of his own process of self-analysis, Freud was not convinced of its general applicability.

Analysis, he felt, required the analyst to act as a blank screen onto which the analysand's desires might be projected so that what was unconscious, unrecognised in an individual's own mind, might be made visible. To Fleiss he wrote, 'True self-analysis is impossible, else there would be no illness.' Where he saw a prohibitive impossibility though I think that my grandmother saw hope: that by applying the methodology of analysis to herself she might make her own mind clear, a thing of glass in which all desire, all motivation, want, might be seen and measured. This is the promise that with effort we might be disentangled, a straight-coiled skein, and that we might find ourselves in balance; and seeing this, as I lie resting through exhausted afternoons and choke down terror at the thought that through some act of unwitting negligence my daughter might become anything other than buoyant, whole, I think that after all it is not so strange that my grandmother should have sat down each morning at the breakfast table and, like the casting of a protective spell, asked her tiny daughter to relate her dreams.

At the opposite end of the year to my visits to Hampstead, Doctor K would come and stay with us, spending Christmas in our house, ten days during which we tried to articulate our uncooperative bodies into attitudes of familial affection. From 21 December each year until the thirtieth, when she returned home to begin preparations for her New Year's Eve bridge party, Doctor K would sit at our dining room table and continue by letter those analyses which she considered

to be at a crucial point, writing to her clients pages and pages of densely worded argument before returning to the routine of her own self-analysis. Her continual, unavoidable industriousness, her refusal to abandon even for such a brief time her attempts at understanding, made my mother and me uncomfortable. She filled the house with the almost-audible sound of pen on paper until we felt ourselves become periphery, ousted from our own comfort and routine, forced to deviate from those paths which habit trod for us across the carpet of the living room. My mother, ordinarily a lazy sort of cook with a tendency towards one-pot meals and the frequent provision of pasta, took refuge in the kitchen, baking parkin, peeling chestnuts, cutting tiny crosses into the bases of innumerable Brussels sprouts – food that the pair of us would eat for weeks afterwards, our mouths chewing stolidly until all reminders of our attempts to represent ourselves as something better than we were had been consumed. While my mother cooked I undertook enormously elaborate art projects, making out-of-scale nativity scenes from half-dried modelling clay and cards from paper and tinsel, or sewing as presents toys which ended up misshapen, bulbous, all these projects ill-planned and ill-executed, ill-conceived, and in the gaps necessitated by the drying of paint or glue I would make cups of tea, presenting them fresh to my mother and grandmother while the dregs of the last were still warm in the bottoms of their mugs; and in the evenings, when we sat around the gas fire eating spiced biscuits, carols on the radio, I felt myself compelled to enact

a version of furious good cheer I had learned from books, a dumbshow of Christmas spirit through which my mother and grandmother might be relieved of some part of the silence of their relationship, forcing them to play games of consequences until at last, exhausted, I could go to bed.

From these winter holidays I remember with unequivocal fondness only those afternoons, Christmas Day itself and Boxing Day, when the absence of any post at all let us off the hook and we would go out into the woods behind the house and walk, bare branches like the blueprints of a church above us, black lines against the winter sky, and beneath our feet a shingle of beech nuts and the soft, crumbling litter of that year's half-rotten fall of leaves. Snow, sometimes. Frozen mud. Ice in sheets across the puddles at the bottoms of the valleys where the sun barely reached during those shortest days. Without the need to face one another we became, for the duration, three independent figures amongst the trees, released from the thrall of that complicated set of forces which inside the house defined our paths. My mother and I climbed onto fallen trees and played balancing games or searched for mushrooms, vast shelves of fungi that grew like ethereal tumours from rotten places in the wood. We told jokes, horrible old saws which made us laugh, our relief at our brief release making our voices ring. I ran ahead, testing how far into the trees I could go before sudden terror at the thought of being lost overwhelmed me; but then, circling back on ourselves and climbing the shoulder of the last ridge before home we began to quieten and still, our bodies narrowing,

muscles contracting, and I felt the weight falling down on me again until we reached the front door, and, locked back into our positions, went inside.

I used to wish, during each of these Christmas holidays, that my grandmother would stop working so that we could all relax. I imagined, at the time, that this would be all it would take for our habitual selves to be returned to us, for us to meet as we did in the woods, uncompensating, not understanding then how complicated the currents are that hold us to our paths, nor how compulsive can be the tracing of them. Watching my grandmother sitting each morning at our dining table, her notebook open and expectant in front of her, I had no understanding of the drive to exhume that now turns my quiet moments into imperfect acts of reminiscence: how it is to feel that one must note each detail of one's thoughts in case that thing should pass unseen which might otherwise provide the key, laying out the shadows of the bones which rib and arch and hold the whole together. It strikes me as extraordinary, now, that we should be so hidden from ourselves, our bodies and our minds so inaccessible, in such large part uncharted; but there is a thrill to it, too: that same mixture of terror and quickening which confronts us where underneath the sea the light gives out and unnamed creatures float, eyes huge or non-existent, spines and scales unseen, or in those vast and empty tracts of space where rusting shuttles float, unmeeting. Perhaps this is what Freud felt, all through the summer of 1897, as his children played their complicated games in the shadow of the Austrian mountains and his wife,

pregnant with the daughter who would become both his work and its protector, moved around him, finding things to do elsewhere – this sense of yearning outwards into darkness, the prayer for understanding that is nothing but a silent thought in a vast and vaulted space – and Röntgen, two autumns earlier, at that moment when he saw his bones laid bare: perhaps it was some version of this same desire to marvel that moved him to place his hand upon the screen, his fingers open as if waiting for an unknown gift – but the price of sight is wonder's diminishment. This was Bertha Röntgen's fear – and perhaps, after all, her refusal to look was neither stubbornness nor failure of vision but only an intuitive grasp of what a death the loss of mystery might be.

August again, the year of my father's departure, and after the first week my grandmother abandoned her attempts to get me to talk. Instead, after days during which storms of furious tears took me by surprise, embarrassing me with the evocation of a grief I wasn't aware that I felt, we would go to her consulting room, each with our allotted drink, and sit in silence, waiting out together the time until my mother might return. Doctor K did not sit straight in her chair as usual and nor did she keep her eyes on me but sat as I did, curled slightly over on herself, looking out of the window. She seemed older, that summer, than at any other time until her death. Her face was creased. She held to the same routines but seemed to do so out of habit, her mind uncharacteristically elsewhere, and during the hour each morning that she sat alone in her consulting room I

would at times become aware, like waking to the drum of rain upon a roof, of the sound of her footsteps, pacing.

Anna Freud, a sixth and accidental child, was born into a bitter Viennese winter and a world in which all empty space had been already claimed. The apartment was not a small one but in addition to the five elder siblings it already contained there was Anna's nursemaid, and Sigmund and his work, and there was her mother, Martha, and Martha's sister Minna. Minna had joined the household a year earlier, taking over from Martha when she did so those tasks relating to travel and to Freud's work – the entertaining of his colleagues and the discussion of his theories, the journeys to visit the various psychoanalytic societies which had begun to coalesce in European cities – while Martha concentrated on the care of the children and the day-to-day running of the household until it came to seem at times that each of the sisters was half a wife, the presence of one allowing the other's partial retreat.

Later, it would be a favourite observation of Freud's that Anna shared a birthday with psychoanalysis, twins in whom his whole life's work was made manifest. By then she would be his Anna Antigone, her father's defence and his support, his better face, and her absolute loyalty both to himself and to his work would be rewarded by inheritance and by their names spoken in one breath, Sigmund-and-Anna, run together like a single salutation. Then, never one to miss a shot at mythologising, he would think of her sometimes – young and strong and faithful when all other aspirants to his seat had proved

worthless – as a Cordelia to his Lear, and his hand would creep to the beard that hid his slowly dying jaw; but at the time all that this coincidence of dates meant to either of them was that throughout Anna's early childhood Freud was absent from the second-floor flat through which the family's lives tumbled, if not physically then mentally, a fact which he would in time acknowledge, justifying his absence by remarking that such periods of inspiration will come to most of us only once in a lifetime, and even that not certain. Even when the completion of the *Interpretation of Dreams* and the end of the period of intense productivity which came in its wake left Freud with more time for his family, Anna found herself more often than not left behind, too young to accompany her father on the country walks he would take with his children or the expeditions to the boating lake. She felt herself to be overlooked and the struggle to gain that attention from her father which seemed a prerequisite for love became the defining experience of her childhood. By the time of her birth, roles had been already allotted, shared out between her brothers and her sisters so that it seemed that there was nothing left for Anna but to be pretender. It was her brother Oliver whom their father had initially marked out as his apprentice, a quick boy, bright and confident until in adolescence he began to exhibit what his father described as obsessional symptoms; to Max Eitingon, Freud would write with regret that Oliver had been 'my pride and my secret hope', failing to see the successful engineer his son had become for the analyst he wasn't. In the end, although at the urging of his father Oliver underwent

analysis, it would be distance that would bring him relief: of all the Freud children it was Oliver who broke furthest from their father, leaving Vienna as 1938 washed over them not for London with the rest but for America, where the calm of this completed journey into adulthood would be shattered by the death of his only daughter Eva in the post-war influenza epidemic, since after all the only certain thing that freedom from our parents can buy us is the right to be alone.

For Anna's own intelligence there seemed, during her early childhood, little space. It came out instead as a kind of quickness of spirit, an impish naughtiness which made her father laugh but charmed him only as a clever pet might charm, a passing diversion from more serious business. Intellect was still seen by Freud at the turn of the nineteenth century as a masculine attribute and it was not one he looked for in a daughter until all his sons, both actual and adoptive, had given him cause for disappointment; but nor did Anna feel herself physically attractive enough to aspire to a straightforward femininity. It was Anna's sister Sophie who was the pretty one, their mother's favourite and their father's pet, and her good looks seemed to bestow on her an aura too of good character of which Anna, unable to match it, was deeply envious. This envy – of Sophie's appearance and of what seemed to Anna to be her unfought-for place in their father's affections – continued throughout their childhoods until it seemed to tie them together, a falling battle that linked them more closely than any of the other Freud children. Their father watched his two unhappy daughters struggle and although it must have worried him he

couldn't keep the clinician from his gaze, nor help the small hum of satisfaction as he saw played out for him those childish desires the hypothesis of which his work was based on; and if the two girls who clawed so fiercely for their father's attention sensed this and, sensing it, clung on a little harder to one another, fought a little louder, then who could blame them?

At the end of August, during the year of my father's defection, my mother came as usual to Doctor K's house to collect me but we made no preparations for departure. She arrived in the early evening and went straight to bed, and when, after I had eaten my supper in the kitchen, I was allowed upstairs to see her she looked pale and tired. I wondered if she had been crying and then the fact that I had thought of it made me feel suddenly and unwelcomely grown up. It frightened me to see her look so unhappy. It had seemed to me until that summer that the crossing into adulthood must be a transformative process, a passage through the refiner's fire during which one would be rendered down into capability, strength; but seeing my mother blinking and shell-less, her face puffy, it occurred to me for the first time that perhaps my own fears would not be shed along with the plumpness of my face but that I would always be, essentially, what I was at this moment; and not knowing what to do I started to cry myself, and stood there in the doorway weeping until my mother, taking strength from my predictable weakness, came over to me and, carrying me like a child much younger than I was, lifted me into her bed. I lay there, my tears slowed to a comfortable trickle, nestled into

112

her side until I fell asleep; but when I woke the next morning I was in my own bed again and as I went downstairs I saw that the door to my mother's room was closed. I didn't try to visit her. All day Doctor K worked and my mother stayed upstairs and – not wanting to go out, to leave the shelter of their orbits in case they ceased somehow to have the power to draw me back – I drifted through the rest of the house, trying to feel myself tentatively backwards towards a place of ignorance or balance, until at last my grandmother finished her work and came to find me.

Although usually my mother's arrival would put an end to the time that I spent in Doctor K's consulting room, that evening, by tacit agreement, we went through the heavy door and we sat opposite one another, silence holding between us like a pact we didn't expect to break, the only sounds intruding on it those of my mother moving about: the creak of the upstairs floorboards, the running of a tap, a sigh. Later still my mother came downstairs and sat for half an hour in the living room, wrapped in an old dressing gown of Doctor K's, and I curled up at her feet with my head resting on her knee. She had begun to sneeze and complained of a headache and I tried to make myself believe that her unwonted vulnerability was the result, not of any change in her or in my perception of her, but only of a summer cold that she had caught, she said, from a woman on the Northern Line who had not used a handkerchief. At dinner time Doctor K took a tray upstairs to her and I sat alone at the kitchen table, unable to summon up much appetite for my plate of scrambled eggs; and beyond the walls of the

house, its undrawn curtains and blank windows, the evening faded into darkness, outside obliterated, and we three in our luminous bubble were cast adrift within the night.

On Wednesday evenings the Vienna Psychoanalytic Society met in the drawing room of the flat at Berggasse 19, and as soon as she was of an age to remain quiet Anna was allowed to sit on a small library ladder set in the corner and to listen, following as best as she was able the intense and voluble discussion of this earnest group of men who saw themselves, as the days lengthened and shortened through the early years of a new century, as architects of a future in which clarity was assured and all the convoluted crenellations of the mind would be unfolded; and there, perched in shadows, fighting sleep, Anna found an empty space in such a crowded house. It was uncomfortable balanced on the ladder's wooden top, hard to keep still, knees stiff and feet numbing from the effort to avoid drawing attention to herself, but still the narrow place she occupied gave her at last that closeness to her father which she had so desperately wanted. Sigmund, too, became within the confines of that room, for the duration of the Wednesday meetings, the father that she wanted him to be: not the easily distractible paterfamilias who gave the children rides on his back up and down the corridors of the flat or herded them through their Saturday-afternoon walks, but a man deferred to, forceful and assured, his words bearing the weight of strictures, a suitable object for her love.

*

August became September and the date passed that I should have returned to school, but still we remained in Doctor K's flat. It was as though we had found a way to stretch out indefinitely the moment between our injury and the onset of pain and so we stood, shock confusing us, hands clasped across the place we had been wounded, still uncertain of the damage; and I wonder now which outcome my mother dreaded most: that we should find ourselves unravelling or the opposite, that there would be no marks on us at all and, everything just as it was, the thing she had worked so hard to hold on to would slip from her grasp and become like ice in water. Each moment proceeded the next in an orderly round but I had no sense of progression, and that things were not as they ought to be unsettled me, and it unsettled me more that this difference went unmentioned. That aimless procession of days which makes holidays so pleasant when carried beyond their set limits became a kind of near-intolerable, stifled tension. I had never been in Doctor K's house beyond the end of summer before and as the evenings began to smudge earlier into darkness and the air started to chill, I became increasingly aware of my displacement. In the garden leaves drifted and rosehips hardened on the bushes that the downstairs tenant had so carefully staked. On the heath, no longer crowded with picnickers, the blackberries turned. Each afternoon I stood at the kitchen window and watched as other children walked home from school, their uniforms wearing daily from sharp newness into an accustomed shell; but still inside the house we remained stuck, and could find no way to move.

*

Anna's analysis by her father, begun when she was twenty-two years old, was the culmination both of that interest in her father's work which had started during the Wednesday evenings in the Berggasse drawing room, creeping as close to her father as she dared, and of a persistent, indeterminate ill health from which she suffered throughout her adolescence. In 1907, taken to the hospital by her mother without being warned of the reason, Anna underwent an appendectomy, and although the operation itself was successful and she seemed at first to recover well she was afterwards unable to regain the weight that she had lost. She succumbed easily to colds and to chest infections and she began to be anxious, taking on a hunched, defensive posture that she struggled to overcome, and those symptoms which had at first been physical became increasingly nervous: she tended towards a periodic retreat into meticulously worked-out fantasies which would occupy her for hours, but the playing out of these narratives left her exhausted and unable to concentrate. Learning how to weave, she found in the shuttle's run a hypnotic loss of self which at first appealed but afterwards, when for whole afternoons at a time she had sat hunched over the loom until her back and fingers ached, she would reproach herself for such time lost to unawareness. Spending regular periods in sanatoria she tried to rest, enjoying fresh air and freedom from the confines of Vienna's crowds and cold weather, but felt instead cut off, apart from her family and from her father, lonely and cast out. Freud, for his part, worried that without careful management the introspective fragility that his youngest child exhibited

could easily become hysteria. This sense he had of her as subject, his belief that her well-being depended on his good judgement, became another tie between them, until at last it would seem that her mind was half his own creation.

In the spring of 1913, finding himself once more bereft in the aftermath of his final break with Jung, his acute disappointment in the younger man's wilful apostasy and his grief at the loss of their friendship leading to a period of despondency which bordered on depression, Freud began for the first time to be aware of his growing practical reliance on Anna, and of the extent to which the idea of her eventual departure – into marriage, probably, since what other option might there be? – disturbed him. Sophie's recent engagement meant that soon Anna would be the only one of the children remaining at home and Freud began to feel that it was only her continued presence in the flat that staved off old age. Anna too was troubled by the implications of her own impending adulthood, feeling herself to be an uneasy fit with the world: what she would think of throughout her life as the masculine quality of her intellect sat uncomfortably with those desires she characterised as feminine – the desire for family, an interest in children. She didn't want to leave her father but as yet could not see a way of remaining with him as anything other than a dependent daughter; and although such arrangements were not unusual neither she nor Freud considered such an outcome particularly satisfactory. She spent the months approaching her eighteenth birthday and Sophie's marriage at a sanatorium in Merano, in northern Italy, troubled both by her jealousy of

her sister and by what she saw as her own exclusion from the preparations for the wedding, which she would in the end be judged too unwell to attend. She wrote her father fervent letters, telling him of each half pound of weight gained, each incremental advancement towards health or peace of mind; and she wrote too that 'I have read some of your books, but you should not be horrified by that, for I am already grown up and so it is no surprise that I am interested.' By the spring, although her future still felt to her both uncertain and uneasy, she had decided to start the training necessary to qualify as a teacher, successfully sitting in early summer the exam which would allow her to begin an apprenticeship in the autumn of 1914; and in the intervening weeks, by way of a rest before her training began, she travelled to England, where she hoped to develop her language skills to the point where they might be useful to her father. There she stayed with one of Freud's former patients, Loe Jones, who lived in Sussex, and together they took regular trips to London where another Jones, the unrelated Ernest, was working hard to set up and maintain an English psychoanalytic society. Ernest soon began to visit Anna, taking her on sightseeing expeditions and assuming the role of language tutor, and as a result, alerted to the relationship by Loe, Freud exercised for the first time his influence over Anna, and although he told himself that it was for her benefit, that she was both young and naïve, that she was not strong and might easily be damaged by such a relationship, he must have felt too how her marriage would have been another loss to him. To Anna he wrote, 'I have no thought of granting

you the freedom of choice that your two sisters enjoyed.' For her part she said that she had never had any intention of taking the relationship further, and she felt the pull against the cord that ran between her father and herself and found for the first time both the surety of his love which she had sought since childhood and the balance of power that there is in sacrifice.

Anna returned to Vienna with the outbreak of war and began, as well as her teaching apprenticeship, a closer collaboration with her father. The continuation of the psychoanalytic movement in the face of conflict required considerable effort, with those who had been close colleagues now split by lines of allegiance. Travel between those cities where societies had sprung up became virtually impossible and mere communication only slightly less problematic. In an attempt to keep the various journals running through which the work of Freud's followers were made available, Anna spent much of her spare time in translation work, trying to ensure that language, at least, would not be a barrier to the dissemination of psychoanalytic thought. During this process Anna began to ask her father for clarification of technical terminology or of concepts that she felt herself to imperfectly understand, and out of this discussion came both the foundations for a working relationship and the first advances in what would stand between them as a kind of preliminary analysis. In the letters Anna wrote to her father when her teaching work took her away from Vienna, she began to describe to him her dreams, his own figure winding through them, as though by doing so she might tell him also something which she otherwise had no way of saying, an

extra burden of content to the lexicon of their emerging discipline – something about her loyalty and her love, and how, apart, she missed him: the gradual incorporation of care into their shared language.

By the time the war came to its end Anna's chronic ill health, exacerbated by four years of poor diet, made the continuation of her teaching work impossible, and so at last a decision point was reached; but facing it she found that her choice had been already made. On 1 October 1918 she entered her father's consulting room for the first time as his patient and began her teaching analysis, a culmination of those twin and twisted strands – her ill health, her interest in her father's work – which had defined her life for the best part of a decade. There were practical reasons for the choice of her father as analyst – Freud's practice had been considerably reduced by the war so that while the family as a whole had little money, particularly with the loss of Anna's teaching income, he had an unusual amount of time – but it seemed also by that point already inevitable. This was what they had been slipping towards for years, the two of them working together on their first project, which was Anna's life, their progress towards it by such slight increments that by the time Anna first knocked on her father's door it seemed only the obvious thing to do. Anna's anxious loneliness, her fixation on her father's attention, and Freud's fear that in someone else's care she might be lost to him, left no option but that the two of them turn to one another; and so six times a week for the next four years Anna opened her father's door and, stepping across the threshold, lay down upon the

couch, and together they examined her until, piece by closely studied piece, they had taken her apart and built from what she had been something they could both be happy with.

In early October I sat opposite Doctor K in her consulting room and, finding in the drowsy confusion of unmarked time a sudden point of clarity, I said

—I want to go home.

Later that night, waking thirsty and going downstairs for a glass of water, I walked past the half-open door of my mother's bedroom. From around its edge light spilled, a pale wedge across the landing floorboards, and I heard the sounds of voices, my mother and my grandmother, talking softly. My grandmother said

—It would help her to talk. I could find someone.

My mother made a sound which was something like a moan, a tiny, fugitive utterance of distress, and in response to it or in defiance my grandmother said

—You could stay here. She could start school. Just for a term. She needs—

—She needs stability, that's all,

and there was silence. Moving a little I saw, framed by the doorway so that it appeared as if a picture, my grandmother sat on the edge of the bed with my mother kneeling at her feet, my mother's head bent forward and my grandmother's fingers curled into her hair; and I turned quickly, running back up the stairs, because I felt that I had intruded even by looking at an intimacy I had never known them to possess.

The next morning my mother and I packed my things into my cardboard suitcase and carried it down to sit beside my mother's bag in the front hall, my coat folded neatly on top of it. We ate lunch, all three of us, at the kitchen table, the sound of the radio filling in for conversation, and afterwards I picked up my suitcase and we said goodbye. My grandmother seemed as she always did, upright, comprehending, but as I turned at the front gate to close the latch I caught sight, for an instant, of her face as she watched us leave, and I did not understand, at the time, what her expression was, that look of long-accustomed shock, a mixture of grief and resignation, but I find myself thinking of it often, now, and wondering if it is inevitable that I, too, will in the future look that way, watching my daughter walk away from me into a complicated life that I can neither simplify nor inhabit in her stead; and I wonder what the alternative might be, and if, in fact, it might be worse.

In the end, during the last few months of my mother's life, in place of conversation or confession I read to her, picking off the shelves those same books that she had read to me in childhood, for the comfort of it and because it was a way to try and draw a link between us, so that for hours at a time we were engaged in the revisiting of worlds that we had been admitted to before, in a different configuration, when it was clearer which of the two of us led and which followed. While she drifted in and out of a sleep that grew by degrees heavier and stiller, smoothing away her features as though it were an

encroaching tide that would leave, at last, nothing but clean sand where her face had been, I allowed my voice to fill the air, keeping out the silence that might otherwise have called to be filled with what I no longer had the capacity to bear. The sentences which grew from paragraphs to chapters kept us both together and apart, creating a shared space in which we could sit, each untouching of the other, but protected and encased. We were peaceful, then. The bedroom had the stillness of a pivot's turning place; and sometimes, as the evenings bled out into darkness and I found myself still reading, unable to call a halt to the day, my body's clock unwound by night wakings and the sameness of the days, I would feel as though I were becoming, in word-long increments, disconnected from the moment I inhabited, and that I was at the same time both of us, my mother and myself, stretched out across fifteen autumns, reading: the same book and the same room, the heavy curtains and the patchwork quilt, the view across the garden to where the beech trees reached across the fence. I felt, then, how easy it would be in all this placid strangeness to lose myself, and I felt how welcome it might seem to be; and when that happened I would stop reading and, putting down the book, would step quickly across the carpet and climb into my mother's bed, and I would curl up next to her, resting my head into the hollow between her shoulder and her collarbone, folding myself inwards as though by an effort of will I could contract myself back into the outlines of my five-year-old self and, doing so, regain all that I had known then: the certainty of place and order, the safety of it, the warmth. Now

there are nights when these positions return to me, when it is my own daughter who, climbing into bed at night for comfort, curls up beside me, and I feel my body curve into the shape my mother's did; or there are the nights of illness when I sponge my child's face, smoothing damp hair back from her forehead, and I see the outline of my mother's hands beneath the skin of mine as they go through the ritual of water and cloth, the washing-up bowl on the floor with a balled-up flannel in it, and I hear her voice in mine performing the liturgy of endearments, those sibilant invitations to returning sleep – and I wonder if these things are soothing in themselves or if it is rather that through generational repetition they have become that way, a memory taught and retaught, the epigenetics of comfort; and through these nights which ebb and flow like tides I feel memory as enactment and my mother, my grandmother, in my hands and in my arms, a half-presence, no longer quite lost.

Before my daughter was born I stood once at a wedding beside one of Johannes' cousins, watching her children run across a stretch of finely mowed grass, gentle Staffordshire hills rising in the distance against a fading sky. I had met her only a handful of times, at such large family events, and we had barely spoken beyond the exchanging of courtesies, but now, separate for some reason from the main party that continued inside, the sound of it spilling out through the mullioned windows of some repurposed country house to further emphasise our remove, we were suddenly intimate.

—It is,

she said

—like having a piece of your heart outside yourself—

meaning I suppose that a child remains a part of you, vital but detached – but this is not how it feels to me. Rather I think that it is like an amputation, something that was once joined cut off, as unrecoverable now as an object fallen from the side of a boat, drifting on the current further and further out of sight. No longer coming under the auspices of proprioception, that sourceless knowledge with which the body places its own, the lost part can now be seen, it can be weighed and measured, held, but it cannot be felt and cannot be got back. When my daughter throws her arms with thoughtless grace around my neck, I respond with an agonising gratitude that I must hide from her in case, feeling the heft of it, she might become encumbered and not do what she was born for, which is to go away from me. It is a balance – to show enough love that she is sure of me but not so much that she stays close: the fact but not the size of it – and it is an effort, as I encourage her to disentangle herself from my gaze, to discard the aching want to have her back—

Some months ago I went again to Maresfield Gardens and stood in front of the photograph of Sigmund and his daughter walking across a stretch of grass, laughing. Thinking of Anna and the forty years she spent with her father's room empty at the centre of the house, a still unconsecrated monument she had the keeping of, I wondered how often, amongst the ordinary progress of her days, the comings and goings, the

journeys to the library or the shops, the letting in and out of friends, she went inside it, slipping quietly from present tense to past – and if, sitting again on the couch, leaning back against its cushions and listening to a silence which her father's voice could shape to nothing now, it was him she thought of, or herself; and after all, perhaps, instead of the sad economy of one life poured into another, what their efforts bought them was the miracle of neither having hurt the other, neither having left.

This is the crux of it: that we have no point of comparison and therefore cannot say things would have been better other-wise. I remember how it was with my daughter – how she coughed, and spat, and cried, and after being weighed was passed over to Johannes, who undid the buttons of his shirt and held her slippery, aquatic form against his freckled skin, and how from that moment on it seemed to me that the infi-nite stretch of possibilities she had started as began to collapse, falling away from our touch to leave behind the emergent outlines of her shape – curious, incautious, kind – and I remember how it terrified me, the suddenly yawning space between what is meant and what is done. Now that we wait to start it all again I find myself wondering if my mother felt as I do, or Doctor K, or if Max Graf did for little Hans or Freud for Anna; and, if so, how they managed to hide it – how we all do: the overwhelming fear of fucking up that having children brings, the awareness of the impossibility of not causing hurt like falling into endless water, and with it the attendant

agonising understanding that what success looks like is being left behind – but what is the alternative? Only the unthinkable perfection of a preserved present. Our lives are possibility reduced to rough particularity by contact, touch, and out of it the specificity of each of us comes, so that to ask if we might have been better otherwise is to wish ourselves undone.

Interlude: Florence

It is November and I am alone in a hotel room. Outside, an unfamiliar street stretches, empty. It rains a little. We have rented a villa for a fortnight somewhere to the south of here, up in the hills – a place known to us only as a green stretch on a map and a background done in mute regret: dusty slopes planted with cypress rising behind a dozen novels of the English abroad – but we have planned badly and it is the wrong time of year, damp and chilly, mist rising instead of heat above stone terraces, a constant aching mizzle and days to fill indoors. We wanted the sort of holiday that is like a slice of time extracted from the general run of things, and with it a last pass at being just the three of us, a reminder to our daughter that completion is elastic and that she was enough even as we planned her augmentation; but we had things to finish before we could come and then there is the baby to be born when we get back, sometime during the dark and empty days stuffed deep into the gap between Christmas and New Year, so that we could neither come sooner nor wait until in the

mountains there might be an outside chance of snow. We must make do with this place caught in the middle of a half-complete moult. For weeks now, oppressed at home by an ever-growing list of things that must be done before the baby comes, by clothes to be brought down from the attic and washed, nappies to be checked over, food prepared in bulk and bedding organised, bills settled, threads tied, as though at the moment of birth time will dislocate itself and these things will not be possible afterwards, I have dreamed of this room, my solitude, an empty stretch. Pregnancy has conferred on me the privileges of old age, an unquestioned pandering to my body's whims: the flight here was expected to be tiring and so Johannes has taken our daughter on ahead while I am to stay in the city resting before making the remainder of the journey tomorrow, quiet and alone on a tipped-back train seat. By the time I arrive Johannes will have organised things, mastered the geography, bought food, worked out the thermostat, and I will allow myself to be shown these things without taking the trouble to remember, my slight delay according me the status of a guest. For half of each day I will lie on a couch and the pair of them will bring me things: cups of tea, plates of biscuits, tales of their exploits. They will have adventures while I doze and I think that they have been looking forward to it, to their free immersion in those parts of themselves which exist only in my absence. Drifting in and out of sleep on the plane I heard their voices, plotting, their matched heads bent low together, and as we fell through layers of fog towards the ground they laughed.

At the airport I said goodbye to Johannes and to our daughter, and found a taxi to bring me to the hotel, and although at night, nested in pillows, I am often too uncomfortable to sleep, sat there on cracked vinyl with my legs spread to balance out the weight I do not have time to grow accustomed to, shoulders twisted, I was unconscious at once, and I stayed that way until the car reached the hotel and the driver shook me awake, tenderly in deference to my condition. Now, alone in my room, confused and chilly after the sudden rise from deep and unexpected sleep, disorientated, desolate, I sit down on the bed and start to cry. This happens to me often in pregnancy's third trimester, these sudden squalls of tears that burst from nowhere as a further reminder to me of how little my body is within my control, and there is nothing I can do but wait for it to end, this excess of emotion let out in salty water – and often it seems that waiting is all I do – for my body to complete the task it has been set, heedless of my intercession, and for the inevitable but unpredictable tract of pain beyond, for exhaustion and those first numb weeks when balance is precarious, the tumbling rush to interpret a newborn's needs. In the face of such an immediate future I find myself at a loss, those articles of rule over myself and my surroundings which I have so long taken for granted shown up as barely more substantial than a belief in prayer. I have become so accustomed to the doctrine of the mutability of pain, that suffering can be routinely eased, danger negotiated or renegotiated, that faced with its sudden failure I am terrified, as at a world remade, and I am unprepared. It seems such an unforgivable breach of promise to be reduced to flesh from

which I cannot, by thought, transcend, but blood and muscle go about their business just the same and in my side something puckers, the sharp retraction of a rock pool creature that has been disturbed—

After the tears have subsided and I have had a bath that I overfilled because I am not used to my increased body mass, after I am clean again, I go out, wearing over my jeans and sweater the old waxed raincoat of Johannes' which is the only thing that does up around me now, and which forms a further layer of skin, weather-beaten and familiar, to protect me from my unexpected and abrasive loneliness. I walk with my back arched forwards and my feet splayed out, the soles of my boots slapping against the cobbles like fat flippers. I have a vague direction in mind but I am in no hurry, and I think that this gentle amble and the soft, uninterrupted patter of my thoughts against the bricks is what it is to be alone, or as alone as I can be with a head hard in my pelvis and feet against the low ridge of my ribs, kicking, and I ought to enjoy it, the respite from requirement I have so looked forward to, but instead I feel only a panicky distress, as though I had woken to find a part of myself amputated. I miss my daughter. I have become so accustomed to her shadow falling in and out of mine, to the way she forces my attention outwards, centring my awareness of space on her small form, which is at once so sturdy and so breakable, and I am used to the sound of her voice, her constant interjections drowning out the unspooling threads of my own thoughts, her commentary filling the silence where my own has gone astray. I had thought that the temporary

removal of these things would be relief, that there would be no sense of loss and that I would not ache, nor feel my hands reach out to touch, to tuck back hair or pull up socks, and find my fingers land on empty air. It is not the first time I have been away. There have been days, nights; but last time she was still fat with babyhood and didn't have the power to withhold. Then she still hung from me, all mouth and fingers, and treated my presence as an unconsidered right, neither looked for nor enjoyed but only expected, so that to leave was respite, a moment when I could feel myself briefly to be whole. Now she has become something else, a mind inside a body, separate, and it seems to me that the extent of that separation from me is the extent to which I cannot bear to be apart from her. I had thought that I would continue to fall backwards into singularity as to a norm from which my deviation was temporary, and that without her I would be myself again, whole and undivided; but instead I am half-made, a house with one wall open to the wind—

and later still, returned to my hotel room, curled up under Johannes' coat like an abandoned pet, wanting the solidity of his presence, the way he stands about me like a wall, with a desire that is close to invocation, I will wonder if this is how it will always be, now, this longing to be elsewhere – the wish when I am with my daughter that I might step apart from her, and when I am apart this anxious echoing, the worry that the world might prove unsound, a counting down to her return; and I will be surprised that something so obvious has taken me so long to understand.

I get closer to the river. The dome of the cathedral rises, drizzle dulling it to the colour of London brick; behind it, hills which ought like the church's roof to awe and glorify are hidden by mist and when at last I cross the river it is nothing but water. My feet start to ache. I wonder what it says about me that I seem to feel love only in absence – that, present, I recognise only irritation, a list of inconveniences, the daily round of washing and child teas, the mundanity of looking after, and beyond this the recollection of what went before and how nice it was to be free; but I didn't recognise my freedom then – or wasn't free, since freedom only functions as an opposite to constraint. There were other things, then; and how can I say, now, that a different choice would have left me more content, and that I would not have felt the loss of this life as now I feel the loss of that one—

In the Giardino di Boboli I sit down on a bench to rest but the rain begins to fall more heavily so instead I go onwards to La Specola, where in a stone-floored room wax anatomical models lie, their hands turned upwards to show finely crafted ligaments, bones, in glass cases lined with white silk like the insides of transparent coffins. This is what I have come to see: the uncanny beauty of these delicate faces above flayed bodies, the fine tracery of silk-thread veins, the layers of flesh removable one by one to leave an empty cavity.

Aside from myself there is no one else in the room, and it is a relief to be unobserved. Standing beside the serene perfection of Clemente Susini's Anatomical Venus, half-closed eyes in a face framed by human hair and below it the open casing

of her thorax, her perfect lungs, her heart, and somewhere, invisible in the configuration of the museum's display, a wax-cast human child, curved and tangled and unborn. Beside her it is hard not to feel that it is I who am the imitation, mere flesh in the face of an object made, not just to educate or to instruct, but because science was once a form of worship, this stripping back of layers a way to wonder at the fierce complexity of God's work, the duty of created to creator. My own body, with its creaking joints and stretched skin, its aches and imperfections, feels by comparison to such still flesh a painful falling-short of what it ought to be. I imagine how I would look laid out like this, formed into layers, each one a shell, demountable, and at the centre of it all the indivisible nut my child makes; and how then all of it might be removed, stacked carefully up beside my open, undecaying carcass. So static I might be perfect, liable at last to a complete accounting, each piece examined, weighed and understood, disallowing surprise, mistake, decay; but amongst so much balance what would be left of me?

I return to my hotel and climb into bed, Johannes' coat on top of me, and I try to sleep so that, waking, it might be tomorrow and I might make my return to that encumbrance of minutiae, love, which anchors as much as it irks so that, tight inside its lacings, I know my shape, my place, and where my edges are.

III

Twelve weeks and four days pregnant for the first time I lay on a high metal bed, my T-shirt pulled up above the curve of my ribs and my trousers, unbuttoned, folded down to lie along my pubic bone; between them, an expanse of empty skin like tundra, unremarkable and still unrisen, a kind of fleshy middle distance. The only light in the room came from the sonographer's computer screen, its blue glow caught by her hands, the collar of her shirt, her carefully pulled-back hair. Earlier, sitting in the waiting room next to Johannes, drinking glass after glass of water and trying not to look at those who also occupied the space, the couples, the women alone, people whose lives I didn't want to give myself the right to extrapolate, the ways that they might differ from us or be the same, I had turned my face to each uniformed passer-by and anticipated in each of them a kind of jocular camaraderie, a showman's skill with patter; but the woman who had come at last to usher us through to this dim cell was so neatly professional that she seemed barely present at all, smoothed down to the perfect

confines of her role. Staring at the ceiling, the exposed skin of my abdomen filling the silence like an unacknowledged sole-cism, I wondered if this leaching of character or compassion on her part was intentional – if it were done in case, needing either later, she might find that she had squandered them on the ordinary amongst us, we whose unborn children leaped and flipped about, indistinguishable from each other; or if it were itself an act of compassion, pre-emptive and organised: a way of sparing those for whom this day would be a shattering, insulating them from her sudden change of tone, a tightening of the skin about her mouth or eyes, the lurch from friendli-ness to intercession. To my left Johannes sat, bent into a plastic chair too small for him. We ought to be holding hands, I thought, but to reach him would have meant turning my arm uncomfortably backwards at the shoulder – and my reluctance to do so seemed a subtle marker of some already prevalent inadequacy in me, indelibly wrought, that I should put my own comfort first.

At last the sonographer stood up. For a minute she fiddled with the large machine beside the bed, angling its articulated monitor, then saying

—This will feel a little cold,

squeezed gel onto my stomach, a great, chilly splurt which I would afterwards be left to wipe off with a paper towel, my furtive embarrassment at the task the first in a series of slight indignities which over the next six months would strip me, layer by layer, until at last I was nothing but flesh and would lie naked in another room and scream while strangers came

and went about me. The sonographer passed the ultrasound's transducer backwards and forwards, pressing down until I winced, staring across my shoulder at the monitor which Johannes and I were not yet permitted the sight of. I watched instead her face, the small frown of concentration that lay in the ridged skin between her eyes, and tried to force myself to some understanding of what we had to lose. The night before, Johannes and I had sat side by side on the sofa and, in half-made sentences like tendrils cautiously unfurling into dangerous territory, discussed what we might do, without either of us being able to quite articulate what it was we spoke about, and

—I don't know,

I said

—how I might feel. It would be dreadful—

meaning all the time that I knew what our decision would be but that I didn't know what degree of guilt or distress I might feel, all outcomes seeming to me so far entirely hypothetical, and I was worried I would feel nothing for this entity which was as yet more idea than child, which was in its own presumptive wellness experienced as the expectation of an unimaginably different future and as a combination of sickness and obligation, a requirement to regard my choices as circumscribed.

At last, her face relaxing into something that was almost a smile, the sonographer turned the screen around so that we could see it, her practised litany of body parts (head, legs, bladder, heart) our reward for patience. I said the things I felt

I ought to say, the exclamations of wonder or delight, and tried to make myself realise that the mass of grainy shadows on the screen was a child, and that it was ours, that it was there with us, not merely as a ghost or intimation but as something present in the room – as though the truth of it could be drummed into me by repetition.

Later, after we had paid our three pounds fifty to take home a copy of the ultrasound image that we couldn't quite bring ourselves to want and didn't know what to do with, this picture at once too intimate and too impersonal for public display, we took the bus home, the print in its cardboard sleeve tucked inside my hospital notes. The Tuesday-morning city felt strange, as when at school I would be allowed sometimes to leave at lunchtime to visit the dentist and, stepping out of the self-completeness of the classroom-bounded world, would find myself instead in one just out of whack, two degrees different from that which existed during the evenings and at weekends: a world slightly empty, industrious, quiet, its children elsewhere. Swings hung still in playgrounds. Newsagents were empty. Adults, their attention on themselves, ate sandwiches in the street. This was the same. Shadows were too sharp. There was a queue at the post office, a man sat on the steps of the library, a woman on her knees beside a crying child. The bus was half-empty but its progress was uneven, each stop a laborious rearrangement of shopping and pushchairs, and this would be my own world, soon – the buying of bananas in the afternoon, the manhandling of prams, the gratitude for open public spaces and the passing of time on benches

– a world which went about its slow business while the rest of us were elsewhere.

In the supermarket, buying bread and ham for lunch, we hovered in the dairy aisle and I asked

—Do we need milk?

and felt as though I were reading from a script. Johannes and I stood apart from one another, not touching, and although I wanted very much to be able to offer reassurance or be reassured I found that I could do neither. In the sonographer's room, both of us watching the screen, it had been as though what we looked at existed not inside my body, blood-warm, internal, but in the space between us: that what was previously a private thing, its border coextensive with myself, had been transmuted by the act of sight from subject to object. It seemed that I had, in conceiving this child, and without anticipating it, given Johannes a stake in my body; and although the extent of this was still to be negotiated, although it was a kind of temporary, partial license, like the provisional rerouting of a right of way across a private garden, still I felt this retraction of self, the shrinking back of borders to leave what had been within the perimeter now beyond the selvage. Diminished, I moved carefully, as though to protect against further incursion; but there was an obverse to it, my concession the price of purchase for my advantage. For all that it seemed to me that I had surrendered territory, still I retained the rights of ownership. The way my body interposed itself between Johannes and his child gave me an unacknowledged right to disregard him if I chose, and it gave me privilege of access, touch, an assurance of my

necessary place that Johannes lacked. It was there in the way he trailed after me through hospital corridors, his presence an afterthought, and in the subtle, unarticulated presumption made by others that he would feel love less than I, or loss; but his life too had been made strange and would be altered – and so it was hard in the end to say which of us had been put more in the other's keeping. Standing in the supermarket queue behind a man buying twenty-five bottles of bathroom cleaner I saw for the first time the unintended consequences of our actions: that in choosing to have a child we had become that we had thought ourselves to be already: inextricably involved with one another, knotted up, as though a part of our child's chimerical genetics had transferred itself to us and now we were each partially the other; and so, waiting in the checkout line, we held ourselves very carefully, just apart, to save both ourselves and each other from accidental injury.

After we had eaten our sandwiches at the kitchen table, after we had returned to our separate parts of the house to work, trying to wrest from the day some semblance of the ordinary so that we might cease to feel that we were waiting, I sat at my desk. All morning, caught up in the business of appointments, I had forgotten to feel sick, but now it returned, the constant queasy ostinato over which rose exhaustion's disharmonious cadence, a progression paused before the point of resolution, aching forwards. I had no heart to work. Instead, searching for some act of petty symbolism to cast myself off from the morning, I took from a drawer of jumbled scraps a picture

that I had clipped from a newspaper some months before and had not then known what to do with: the surface of Titan, the largest of Saturn's many moons, a sphere of ice and rock 5,000 kilometres in diameter swathed in a cloud of nitrogen. This image was taken by the Huygens probe, named after the Dutch astronomer who in the March of 1655, using a telescope that he had designed himself, observed Titan for the first time; 350 years later, after a journey which itself took six and a half years, the slow progress outwards into darkness of ticking metal in so much chilly silence, the probe landed with little more than thirty minutes expected battery life, this tiny span the culminating blink of so many years and such a journey. Lying on solid ground in the outer solar system, the Huygens probe then performed that minute central act it had been built for, its last process, sending back across so many slowly traversed miles this image of its resting place, an expanse of grainy ground, flattish to the horizon, with rocks or boulders strewn across it, smooth globules that might without context be taken for bubbles or for the cellular structure of a plant – and then at the picture's highest edge the sandy-coloured smoothness of the sky. I pinned the clipped-out piece of newsprint to the corkboard above my desk and next to it I put the photograph we had bought from the hospital, the ultrasound image of what would be my daughter. Looking at both of them, side by side or separately, I felt the same: a kind of plunging incomprehension, an absolute inability to make sense. These two things – a view of the ground in the outer solar system and a picture of the inside of

my own body, of the entity that had taken root there to build itself cell by cell towards an articulated experience of grass in sunshine or the smell of violets – existed beyond the boundaries of my constructed world, the navigable realm of named things, and into that shadowy distance which was still unmade, which had neither colour nor warmth but only spectrum and could not be spoken of except through simile (to say 'it is like this other thing' and feel the point has not been made) and I could not incorporate them: they would be neither magnified nor reduced and nor could they be imagined beyond these representations of them which were themselves little more than metaphor. Much later I saw a picture of the surface of Mars, a high-resolution image in colour, reddish-brown earth and the sharp rocks throwing shadows, and I have seen too those three-dimensional images of babies *in utero* in which each detail of their not-quite-finished faces can be picked out, their skin too smooth across the landscape of their features, their bodies foreshortened; but these did not have the same power. They were too like the images of things that are familiar: a stretch of January field, unploughed; a doll. Their strangeness has been made unrecognisable by the sharpness of their edges and although what they depict is as far from the familiar as before, they have been brought by the exactitude of these analogies within the confines of the real: I can dismiss them easily, and turn the page that they are printed on. Those two grainy pictures, though, Titan and my daughter, their figures made as if from dust or static, the ill-formed communications of ghosts, were in their strangeness

144

absolute: they were like nothing else and so they were irresolvable and faced with them, while the child I could not imagine turned its aquatic loops in a space which I contained but couldn't reach, I could do nothing but sit, silent, and try to measure against them the implausibility of things: myself, Johannes; the particular set of events that have occurred weighed against all those that might have done, but didn't, so that our lives together seemed at times nothing but an impossibly narrow pathway rising through shadows.

On a cold winter morning in 1750 three men stood in a Covent Garden basement. In front of them, spread across a table, illuminated by that grey, early light in which facts appear immutable, lay the body of a heavily pregnant woman. Her corpse, unearthed that night from one of London's mass graveyards, had just been delivered, brought round to the back door of William Hunter's recently founded anatomy school; beyond this her history was unknown – her name and place of birth, where she had lived and how or who might mourn her, what it was that had killed her and her child so close to term that the baby's head, as they would shortly find, had already settled into her pelvis, engaging itself ready for birth. Aside from William – aspiring obstetrician and social climber, lecturer in the anatomy school which was still both novelty and controversy, with the majority of medical professionals regarding a knowledge of the body's geography as tangential to their craft – and the dead woman, whose body had become possession and exemplar, an object of interest only in its generality, in the

ways that it was like all others beneath its particularising skin, those present were John Hunter, William's younger brother, and the artist Jan van Rymsdyk, who had been called quickly out of bed at the news of the woman's arrival. The body's decay, though slowed by the cold weather, necessitated haste. John had been in London barely two years and was as yet in his brother's shadow, his character and ambition not quite set, his restless curiosity still mistakable for adolescent zeal, but he had already shown himself to be a remarkable anatomist, certainly more adept than William, and so it is likely that it was he who performed the delicate operation of this unnamed woman's unpeeling: the careful parting of skin and muscle like the drawing back of heavy curtains to give sight of the horizon beyond; the injection of blood vessels with a mixture of wax and dye so that their pathways might be visible, a new-drawn map of territory claimed; and then at last the long incision in her uterus and the uncovering of that which none of them had seen before and few others had thought to look for: an unborn baby, full term, curled tightly on the pillow of its placenta. While John worked, a leather apron tied over his ordinary clothes, Jan van Rymsdyk made a series of drawings which would eventually, reproduced as engravings, form the foundation of William's greatest work, *The Anatomy of the Gravid Uterus Exhibited in Figures*, an atlas of the female body at each stage of pregnancy – and both John Hunter and Jan van Rymsdyk had cause to wonder, later, what fraction of the labour involved was William's that he should put his name so obviously to it. The idea, perhaps. The raising of subscriptions,

146

later, and the hiring of engravers, true, but neither the skill of the enterprise nor its art.

These drawings, and the others that Rymsdyk would make for William Hunter over the next two decades – not all of those in the *Anatomy* were by Rymsdyk's hand but most were – are extraordinary. In these first pictures, while the woman is reduced to meaty torso, her upper body invisible or removed, the severed ends of her thigh bones visible where her legs have been sawn off, the baby is both whole and beautiful. It might be sleeping there, this child, waiting ready for the moment of that birth which has been forever put off. Its hair, where at the nape it curls, is detailed by Rymsdyk's pencil strand by strand, the neck itself a tightly folded shrug the sight of which brings back to me with an immediacy of detail the memory of my own daughter at birth, the firmness of her skin, the unexpected solidity she had like a well-packed parcel and the way she smelt, of biscuits and sweet tea. The baby's ear is flattened slightly, misshapen by long confinement as the ears of newborns often are; the fingers of its right hand curl up about its face which is hidden from us, turned in towards its mother's body as it would have done, held in her arms, in life. The other arm, stretched out, lies along the rounded body pointing up to where, beneath the lost rafters of its mother's ribs, the baby's feet lie, folded; and I can neither bear the sight of it nor turn away because in all these things I see the way that living children lie, their unconscious assumptions of protection and their trust, the way they turn towards us, sturdy bodies lying nested into half-crooked arms, and it is easy to suppose these

things come into being with our sight of them and so to think ourselves responsible, deserving of credit – that it is our actions after birth that call faith forth, a child's reaction to the specificities of ourselves, our care and kindness – but the truth is that these things predate our meeting. Love exists regardless of ourselves and is unearned or got on credit, these gestures echoing those already made and made again, the child inside me turning over as I go about my business unaware, the only power that we are given to maintain or to destroy; and this is why it is such agony to hold a sleeping child: the certainty it brings us that trust is a gift, fragile like an egg in certain places, and so we must be careful with it, holding it in our outstretched hands and trying to make of them a shape that it will fit. All these things are present in Rymsdyk's drawing not as sentimentality or sympathy but only as a clear-eyed fidelity, an accuracy of line and tone: the reproduction of nothing more than what was seen.

Although it was William Hunter who claimed ownership of the work done in the Covent Garden dissecting room, it was John's life which fascinated me, his obsession with anatomy, the collection that he built throughout his life of specimens, as well as his reformation of the surgeon's craft which was effected through a kind of iron-willed iconoclasm: he had little interest in publishing his work, disdaining that which was taken on trust and considering what was written down secondary to what was seen, but only set about his business in the way he thought it should be done until at last the world began to follow him. Looking at the pictures from *Anatomy of the*

Gravid Uterus now, though, it is neither John nor William that I think of but the artist, Jan van Rymsdyk, standing with his chalk box at John's shoulder, his fingers stiffened by the cold, trying to keep the edges of his paper clean while in the corner of the room the discarded parts of already rotting human bodies lay in piles. Beyond his work as a medical illustrator little of the detail of Rymsdyk's life remains. He was born in the Netherlands but the place and the year are lost, as is the date of his arrival in England or what he did on reaching it, where he lived in London, or the manner of his life between the winter mornings hunched in the dissecting room. It is possible that William Hunter gave him lodging in order that he would be readily available when his skills were needed, time being critical to the examination of the body's fine structures, its vessels and membranes that start to deteriorate as soon as death occurs; certainly John would go on to make such arrangements with other artists. What is clear is that Rymsdyk was not happy with the kind of work that he was doing. He had ambitions: a portrait artist, perhaps. A recorder of the living. Anything beyond these chilly rooms, this stink. In 1758, eight years after he made his first drawing for William Hunter, Rymsdyk left London for Bristol, where he was determined to set himself up as portraitist; but he was not a success. He took lodgings for himself and his young son, Andrew, whose mother is another blank face at the periphery of the remembered or recorded, and he placed advertisements, trying to position himself as far as possible from his surgical labours, but little work came, and what did retained a tinge of

149

the mortuary: he painted the portrait of the surgeon William Barrett who had hoped, perhaps, by paying for this service to access Rymsdyk's greater talent; but on that score he was refused. Failing to find work he considered acceptable Rymsdyk was reduced to painting inn signs, funding by that means a moderate drunkenness and a life that was considered squalid even in such squalid times, relying for the rest on Barrett's petty charities – occasional meals, the passing on of cast-off clothes – until at last, in 1764, he accepted defeat and returned to London. There, resentful, he went back to the work that he had left behind, beginning again after such an ignoble hiatus on illustrations for William Hunter's *Gravid Uterus* and working in addition with John, who, himself recently returned to London from a stint as an army surgeon in Portugal and trying now to build his own reputation aside from his brother, had entered into partnership with a dentist and was spending his spare time trying to graft human teeth onto the heads of cockerels. Rymsdyk continued this work for another six years, but something must have altered in him on his return to London from Bristol – some sting, perhaps, of humiliation which he turned to determination – because he did not return to the impecuniousness of his West Country life but saved his money until he had enough to begin on what he had begun to think of as his own great work: in 1772 he applied to the British Museum for permission, with his son Andrew, to draw their exhibits, making from them an encyclopaedia of his own, *Museum Britannicum*, which was published at last in 1778. In the preface he allows himself

finally to vent a lifetime's frustration, the resentments of a man who feels his skills to be unrecognised, uncredited, taken advantage of, who considered William Hunter to have manipulated him, persuading him out of a respectable career in order that he should continue to prostitute his skills on corpses – but thinking of Rymsdyk it is this image that comes most clearly to me: the reflection of a dissection-room window, its cold clear light, striations around it as in rippled water, caught on the membrane stretched across a five-month-old foetus' bent head, the uterine home of this almost-child removed and placed upon a wooden table; and this drawn, just as it was seen, by a man whose talent lay precisely in this – the reproduction of the surface of things. This is the mean tragedy I imagine for Jan van Rymsdyk: not that of skill wasted nor diverted so much as a skill half-made, an artist incapable of artifice. Seeing, he was capable only of reproduction, eye to hand: the surface of things stretched across his paper, each fold of skin, each hair, the shadow on a cheek, a fingernail, an eyelid closed. In his drawings of William Hunter's specimens this is enough, or it is already too much – the viewer can do the rest, the very fact of the subject's existence exciting pathos; but given a living subject, one less arousing of compassionate terror, I imagine Rymsdyk's work as unresounding, the dull thud of a language spoken without understanding. His subjects would be, on canvas, no more than themselves, and perhaps not even that: Rymsdyk could add no character, could inflect his subject with neither meaning nor significance beyond that which they manifested themselves. The world, for him, was

nothing but what was, his talent in its reproduction; and from his intimation of this lack, his awareness of something missing without any conception of what it was, his bitterness rose.

Finding out that I was pregnant after months of disappointment tinged with unnameable relief, I sat down and cried and couldn't say why. Johannes sat next to me, uncertain but not unsympathetic. Expecting to feel joy or at least an end to the anxiety of small plastic strips in silent bathrooms and the hurriedly suppressed disappointment on Johannes' face I felt instead something that was closer to grief: a kind of fracture, the past lost and the future suddenly made opaque, certainty of habit or routine removed. It was not a surprise but still it felt a shock, and all evening I stayed where I was, curled up beneath a blanket on the sofa leaking tears while Johannes sat next to me, worried and quiet. I clung to him and tried to remember that I was not alone without yet understanding the full import of it: that aloneness now was in the past, and that I might come to long for it, the stillness of a body unkicked, from inside or out.

The next morning I rang the doctor's surgery but

—Can you tell me the reason for your appointment?

found myself unable to say the words. It seemed still too much of a presumption to place myself among the ranks of the pregnant with their unlearned competencies, their experiences that I lacked. Later, sitting in the surgery listening to the doctor's well-rehearsed speech, which was delivered to the empty space above my left ear while one of his hands fiddled

with his computer mouse, the dancing cursor wishing me gone, I waited for the moment that he would call me out and demand proof, but it seemed that my honesty was assumed – and after all why would I lie. He said

—Take paracetamol for your headaches.

—I don't get headaches any more.

—You might now. How are you feeling otherwise?

—A little tired—

although really I had no idea how I felt and nor did I have any gauge against which I could measure what was normal. There would be mornings, soon, when I would lie on the bathroom floor, too tired to move except when another swell of nausea came and forced me up over the toilet bowl to retch emptily; and still, then, I wouldn't know whether this was within the parameters of the ordinary and anyway what could be done about it but endure. The doctor shrugged a little and turned away.

—If you have any pain or bleeding go to A & E,

and so began the slow dividing up of time: two thirds of a year split into months, and months split into weeks and days, each one counted off as though it were a sentence to be passed and at the end of it recalibration, a return to an old life with new circumstances like a house that has been gutted and rebuilt. Walking out of the doctor's surgery, my place within the system confirmed, my status acknowledged, clutching a sheaf of leaflets on birth options, hospital choices, the risks associated with shellfish, coffee, cheese, I looked at other women sideways, wondering. I sat on the bus and felt myself

to be an imposter in both worlds: no longer singular but not yet past the point at which I could consider myself to be what other pregnant women were – and even after birth, that ten-hour lesson in topography during which I heard myself call out but couldn't understand the words, I felt that I had not quite done things properly and that my own experience lacked, in some way, that element necessary to transform it into knowledge: that it remained not the thing itself but only a picture of it, so that I was not quite yet a mother. Placental failure and my own rising blood pressure had forced us to tip our daughter early outwards and, lacking the benefit of prop-erly delivered nutrition and those last few consolidating weeks, she was at birth a half-size model of herself, her blue-ish skin stretched tight across her skull, the line of her verte-brae showing along her back like threaded pearls beneath a cotton sheet. She lay near weightless in my arms, her eyelids falling across her steady gaze, and I was almost afraid to touch her. Home from the hospital, crying again, I had to ask Johannes to pick her up and put her down, to change her clothes, to hand her to me to feed because I was too fright-ened of the feel of her; and so we began to count again, not down this time but up, back through days and weeks to months, and still that joy I had been promised didn't come. I waited, patiently, through all the dark extended hours for the instant of my own remaking when at last I would feel the things I ought: certainty, transparency, delight; but it didn't come. Instead there was only something complicated that I didn't have a name for, quite – a shifting landscape of duty

and fear, the gnawing, restless anxiety that started when I was in a different room from my daughter and the exhausted relief when she was calm and slept; the growing realisation that I would always now be pulled in two directions and that I would be filled with the compulsion to protect, which meant that even when I felt I couldn't bear another minute of it I pulled myself up in bed and reached out in darkness for the crying child; and it baffles me now that I couldn't see how all this added up to love. I can't remember quite when it was that shock subsided and I came at last to understand that what I had taken for a temporary loss of balance was only how things always would be, this tangle of broken sleep and piles of wash-ing left on chairs the sum total of motherhood's difference so that I must come to terms, and find a way to live in tiny inter-ludes – except that it had, I think, something to do with routine: this new life laid down in daily patterns, a structure ossified by repetition until I could barely remember what it had been like before and so could not compare; and even then I could not say for certain that I was happy but only that the thought of things being otherwise was unbearable—

but all this was to come. For those first few weeks of preg-nancy, as slowly sickness became coextensive with conscious-ness, and exhaustion accrued mass until it was so solid that I could make no dent in it, I felt, in place of the anticipated joy, only a tiny, private sense of loss, and, beyond that – as I went about the necessary administration, the choosing of a hospi-tal, the midwife's booking-in appointment, as I provided urine samples and had my blood drawn into vials – an overarching

disbelief that despite all evidence to the contrary I would, at the end of it, have a child.

On 21 December 1767, seventeen years after he had performed the dissection of a pregnant woman while his brother William watched and the artist Jan van Rymsdyk sketched, John Hunter again stood beside a woman's body, this one alive, albeit not for much longer, and with a name: Martha Rhodes. She was twenty-three years old, less than five feet tall and with a pelvis that was contorted to such a degree it was making the delivery of the child that she was carrying impossible. She had gone into labour the day before and the midwife, unable to provide any relief, had called for Henry Thomson, a surgeon at the London Hospital; he in turn had called for John Hunter to assist him in attempting to perform a Caesarean section. Although of the three who had been present at the Covent Garden dissection it was William who had become the obstetrician, still it was John who had the reputation for skill and for experiment; besides which, William had ascended smoothly to that strata of society he had always looked to join and was now physician to Queen Charlotte – he would not come here, to this house in Rose and Crown Court off Shoe Lane, one of those narrow alleys that lead upwards from Fleet Street, away from the river. There were others present, too, besides Henry Thompson and John: a gaggle of men, physicians and surgeons, gathered like jostling birds around the table on which Martha lay, her head resting on a pillow and her legs hanging down. None of them had performed this operation before and nor had they seen it done.

156

It was curiosity which brought them up the twisting staircase, the anticipation of something extraordinary done before them, and I imagine that there would have been amongst them a carnival atmosphere, an excitement close to joy, hands shaken firmly to greet each new arrival, shoulders clasped, as two and a half centuries later another group would gather to wait for the results of the Huygens probe, those first pictures of a strange moon, or as the crowds on the Boulevard des Capucines would wait in line all afternoon, wrapped up against the cold, to watch an infant Andrée Lumiere pat the surface of a goldfish bowl: this expectation of a line pushed back and something beyond it grasped, knowledge delivered into light and them as witnesses. Martha's terror I cannot imagine. Thomson said she consented to the operation 'cheerfully' but it seems hard to believe. Perhaps he mistook exhaustion for fortitude, the desperation to have suffering ended by any means for equanimity at the prospect of the route proposed – and I remember how, late on in labour when it seemed that everything had been this way for as long as I could remember and that there would never be an end to it, unknown people came and went about me, obstetricians, midwives, anaesthetists, and I grabbed at any hand that I could reach and begged. Martha must have known for months how things would be; hoped, perhaps, that the baby would be small so that they both might have the ordinary chances, death a risk but not a certainty, this portion of hope making the whole seem possible; and I wonder if she lay awake through long, uncomfortable nights while the baby kicked against her tangled vertebrae weighing her child's life against her own, her mind

ticking through all possible outcomes until, her body having shown no sign of offering reprieve, all that was left to her was this table, these men, the dose of opium that they gave her. There are times when pregnancy seems like the narrowing down of options to a point, and still it is impossible to make oneself believe, quite, that there is no way out of it but this: a bed somewhere, a costing up of risks and this pain that tears you from yourself, your mind disbursed by it, your body made an exit wound. Even now, when what I wait for is a path that has been mapped, its route no longer trod in darkness but seen and softened, when there are epidurals, ultrasound, the surgeon's manifold experience, my body imaged, patterned, known – even now I am terrified.

Thomson made the cut in Martha's belly. He reached in with his unwashed hands and pulled out the child, who cried; with the baby gone Martha's uterus began to contract with a suddenness that took the men by surprise so that John Hunter had to help by holding in the mass of intestines which spilled out into the resulting space. Thomson stitched the wound shut and when the needle pierced Martha's skin she cried out, and this was, Thomson said, the only sign of anguish that she gave. She died five hours later; the baby survived her by two days. Neither Thomson nor Hunter were present at her death although they attended to her again afterwards, for her autopsy, to which William Hunter also came. They could not find any immediate cause for her death, but in the notes that he appended to Thomson's account of the operation John Hunter wrote that 'an author would be more esteemed and relied

upon, if, with candour and disinterestedness, he would relate the instances wherein he has failed, that the world might judge how far the chance or hazard of the operation rendered it advisable or not' – and progress is incremental, slow, and it is cruel, but it is made. In 1793 one of John Hunter's pupils will assist at a Caesarean after which the woman will survive.

The night after the scan I lay with my belly pressed against Johannes' back, listening to his slow breathing, each round ending with a snore, my long-worn irritation at the sound a form of habitual affection. Earlier in the evening, intending to put a pile of laundry away, I had come up to our bedroom and, suddenly overwhelmed, had lain down across the bed and pulled a blanket over me and fallen asleep. Johannes had woken me when he came up, helping me to pull off my clothes, shaking out the duvet where the weight of my body had flattened it; and now, although still heavy with tiredness, disorientated and chilly, sleep would not return. I shut my eyes and felt in imagination along the plane where the two of us did not quite join, our impenetrable skins closely separating, giving warmth but withholding access, each touch an affirmation both of proximity and disjunction, and I thought of the baby, that thing which lay between us, still more mine than his. The child was, for Johannes, still largely hypothetical: his life so far remained predominantly unchanged and what I felt as a set of prohibitions and a physical incapacity, a slow-fast-slow remaking of my own biology, was for him hardly more than anticipation, like waiting for Christmas to come – the gradual, enjoyable

winding-up of affairs before the holidays. He would not feel the child's weight until he held it in his arms, an object, loved but as apart as he and I were: a thing to be learned, understood from the outside as a puzzle or a book is understood, imperfectly, wholeheartedly. Things were not, for him, so ambiguous: the harbouring of a stranger inside oneself, this the closest to another person it is possible to be but that person still unnamed, unmet. I had tried, while walking sometimes through the city in the afternoons, to reach inwards and find some connection to my unborn child, but I was not one of those who felt able to talk to it, to feel intimacy, and for me the sense of being unwell, of being incapacitated, remained immediate while my child was a distant thing, floating in a space that was a kind of void to which I had no access. This is what John Hunter found, that chilly morning in the basement of his brother's Covent Garden house as he bent over the flayed, dismembered body of a woman: that even inside the womb, intimacy is incomplete. Injecting with deft fingers the fine capillaries of the placenta, more gentle in his dealings with this already decomposing tissue than he would ever have been while it was still alive, he found two separate systems: the infant's and the mother's, coextensive but not conjoined, so that they were like the maps of two mazes interleaved, path laid on path but uncross-able, each leading back only into itself. My child and I shared breath, and we shared water, food, but we remained distinct: the line between us was a cell's breadth across but still it held us back from falling into one another and we were not the same.

160

Lying by Johannes in the darkness, envying him the unquestioned habit of sleep, the way he could remove himself, I wished that I might pause, take stock; and this is a thought that comes to me again now: that I would like to pause pregnancy like a film, to walk away, do something else, returning later when I have had time to rest or think. I would like to be unpregnant for a stretch. I had always, before my first pregnancy, regarded my body as a kind of tool, a necessary mechanism, largely self-sustaining, which, unless malfunctioning, did what I instructed of it, and so to have my agency so abruptly curtailed, revealed as little more than conceit, felt like a betrayal. I no longer listened to my own command. Inside me, while I wished that I might be able to be elsewhere, that I might leave my body in the frowsty sheets and go downstairs to sit in the dark kitchen, unswollen and cool, cells split to cells, thoughtless and ascending, forming heart and lungs, eyes, ears – a hand grew nails – this child already going about its business, its still uncomprehending mind unreachable, apart.

If Jan van Rymsdyk's talent was to see only the surface of things then John Hunter's commensurate gift, perhaps, was to see how this surface might be extended: the folds in it, the crenellations that could be laid flat. Where for others the human body had seemed a single entity, one impassive mechanism, feared more than it was understood, to Hunter it was an urn and his task its excavation, gone about in winter when the weather held its rotting back: the disinterment of our

161

long-hidden contents, the heavy organs, lungs, lymphatic system, the tree-like patterns veins make, the chambers of the heart. Seeing them, weighing them in his hands, feeling their give beneath the blade of his knife or watching pigmented wax bring ersatz life to a cadaver's bloodless tissue, he hoped to gain something – not quite fame but something close to it, renown or vindication, and with it the satisfaction of his curiosity. Since the dark ages when plague came in waves to wash whole villages clean of their inhabitants, European medicine had been largely a matter of propitiation, being more akin to faith than science: a set of habitual, heritable practices based on the untested superstition that any intervention has a better chance of success than nothing at all. What conception of the healthy function of the human body existed was based on the humour system developed by the ancient Greeks, the acknowledgement of its insusceptibility to any kind of contemporary proof buried beneath the lingering belief that humanity was in decline and what had once been obvious was now mysterious, absorbable only by rote. Treatment was a combination of quackery, alchemy, and religion, its methods unchanged for generations, passed down from master to apprentice in a training system which required neither a knowledge of anatomy nor any practical skill beyond the performing of those techniques which were considered to constitute medicine and were demanded as much by the patient as they were prescribed by the physician: bloodletting, cupping, prayer, the occasional hacking off of parts. Where elsewhere the Enlightenment had begun to prise things open at the joints, medicine lagged

behind, staid – susceptible to doctrine rather than proof, debate rather than experiment; and into this miasma John Hunter's curiosity fell like a sharp illumination.

His interest in anatomy, both human and animal, began in childhood. He was born during the second week of February 1728 at Long Calderwood, his family's farm which stood in the countryside south of Glasgow. The actual date of his birth is a matter of dispute: although he himself always celebrated it on the fourteenth it was recorded in the parish register as the thirteenth and in the family Bible as the seventh. He was the youngest of ten, and perhaps after so many the arrival of another child was routine, or, three of them having died already before he was born, perhaps his mother had learned that birth was no guarantee of life and so did not – yet – allow herself to give too much away, the lurch of affection that is betrayed by announcement, and this was why his birthday was forgotten; or perhaps it was only that he came swiftly into a world where there was work to be done, the ewes lambing out on the hillsides being more immediately important to a family with no other source of income and now another child to feed and clothe. As a boy he possessed neither an interest in nor an aptitude for schoolwork. He found reading a laborious task and one to be avoided, its rewards pale compared to those which could be got from an examination of the world outside the schoolroom, and often on his morning walk along the lane to the kirk for lessons he would allow himself to become diverted, curiosity leading him to spend long hours when he ought to have been at his books roaming about the

countryside instead. His early life became a journey of investigation through leaf mould, through the mud along the sides of streams or underneath the hedges; and during these empty, meandering childhood days John began to learn by experiment the art of dissection, poking about in the remains of dead sheep he found on the hillsides or eviscerating earthworms, skinning mice and shrews. In adulthood this dislike of academic study became a principle of sorts – he distrusted that which might be learned from books, believing that it was always better to see for oneself with truth not proved until it had been performed.

John's adolescence was marked by loss. When he was thirteen his father died, swiftly followed by two of his sisters. Shortly after he turned seventeen his eldest brother, James, whose progress through his chosen medical career had taken him to London, became unable to work due to ill health and returned to the farm, lying for days on one of the beds that pulled out from the walls of the two-roomed cottage like drawers, coughing himself to death at last while John watched or was nearby; and I find it hard to imagine, now, when death is largely hedged about with treatment plans, when it does not often come senseless out of nowhere but can be postponed, or if not that then at least explained, what grief must have been like when that boundary was a curtain you could put your hand through. It is easy to think that when death could be so quickly turned to, a matter of misstep, and all families counted lost children in their numbers, that loss must have been a blunter thing – that, having so much practice, they must have

been better at it, or inoculated, that it cannot have been for them such devastation, this laying waste – as the birth of a tenth child might be of less account in a busy week than the loss of a pair of lambs, so that the date of it was not looked for until later, when it was found to have been forgotten. It is easy to think that in an age without anaesthetics, when legs might be hacked off on kitchen tables, teeth pulled with pliers taking gobbets of jaw and gum away with them, that pain must have been somehow a less precise, less devastating thing, the alternative being unthinkable – that it was just the same but, persisting, could only be endured, too universal to allow concession; and so John Hunter watched the bodies of those he loved carried out of the tiny farmhouse one by one, making their last journey to the church, and afterwards he went about the business of his days, he went to school or to the fields, and then at last, summoned by William, the sole surviving brother he barely remembered, he went to London, and did not return.

Sometimes, walking down the street or looking outwards from the window of a bus, I saw a child run to take its mother's hand or, stretching itself upwards, be swung into a father's arms, their faces turned to one another, intimate, engrossed, and then I felt a swift pain like an upwards stab, my anticipation of this future I was in the process of laying down. Across those strangers' faces I saw our own elided, mine and Johannes', the child's who was half-turned away; but although in the other two I saw imagination's present of perfection it was my own that I bent towards, trying to trace in its lines the better version

of myself I still waited to succumb to, someone steady, solid, rooted down – and this was the first intimation I had of the complicated interplay between our children and ourselves, the ways we twine about one another, using them as mirrors to our flaws, their reflective plasticity showing us how we must first learn that which we would like to teach: honesty, patience, the capacity to put another first. It seemed, at times, an act of profound selfishness, to have a child so that I might become a parent; but selfish, too, to have a child and stay the same, or not to have one – unless the only honest choice would have been to try to become this kinder version of myself without the need to bring another into it. Once my daughter was born, of course, so much was simplified: I could not now regret any aspect of her, or wish her unmade, or do anything but try to turn myself into the thing she needed, but still I wonder sometimes if I was right to foist life, and myself, upon her; if I am right to do it again because I want her to have an ally and cannot bear the thought of never holding another sleeping baby, the agony of their eyelids, their mouths, their skin. Perhaps it is an unjustifiable act – no reason for it quite good, quite generous enough. To feel myself tired of a life which stretched out like fine sand without much weather, to be dissatisfied, wanting to become the shape a child would force me into, must stand as sufficient explanation, an ill-formulated defence; and thinking this, sat on the bus's upper deck, my forehead resting on the window's sweating glass, I would hold my hands, momentarily, across my stomach, and feel it for what it was, for me: a kind of promise I must strive to keep, the

166

commitment to make myself the best mother I could to make up for having made myself one at all.

I would like to say of John Hunter's adolescent losses that they must have been formative, bringing about through their repetition the long inculcation of a desire to save, as I would like to see in my daughter's birth a wheel rotating: the transmutation of the lives of others, lost, into a capacity for something else – kindness or happiness or an incrementally increasing volume of compassion; but I can't make myself believe it. Such events are not crucibles but are only the natural order of things, what happens and then what happens after it – the same striations of grief and its easing that all of us suffer, to some degree. Looking back, we might try to make sense – to stand in a calm spot, latterly, and examine at leisure the details of a running tumble we barely kept pace with, the cumulative outcome of decisions made blindly or not at all, and try and find significance in it, some repetition of a universal pattern played out in ourselves. This would be comfort: to believe both that things could not have been other than they were and that how they were was right, one's life a well-formed argument, each moment a logical progression from the last.

In the afternoons, home from Italy and waiting out the shortening late-autumn days, I sit upstairs while Johannes and our daughter play outside, running through the drifts of fallen leaves that skirt the garden or lifting up stones to see what lives beneath them, and I watch them through the window and feel how precarious things are. All this will soon be lost. The

solstice will be passed, and Christmas, and the new baby will be born, buds will come on the trees again and our daughter's tiny figure which seems at every moment so complete will be superseded by another version of itself. I would like to believe that what we have made of our lives is good or at least that it is inevitable, and so I try to find in all that has happened a pattern or a thread, some shape beyond the turn of past to future. I search for meaning everywhere. It is as if I believe that I might, drawing back a swathe of cloth left in an attic, find comprehension waiting for me, and with it a final understanding of the way things are, and why, and that in doing so I might feel the fragility of things less; but there is nothing there. Meaning is not found, discovered in a cold basement with an artist lurking, or as an image unexpectedly projected on a screen, but is assigned, the task of its superimposition upon what exists no more than an inelegant scramble to keep up; and underneath it nothing but events come willy-nilly into being and our need to fill the days, decisions leading to decisions, a mapless ramble, haunting and unthought-through.

The journey from Long Calderwood to Covent Garden, made in the late September of 1748, took John Hunter two weeks, at the end of which he presented himself at his brother's house, a rough young man, travel-worn, grubby, given to casual obscenity and with a stubborn refusal to temper his manners that he would maintain throughout his life, the first sign of that uncompromising streak which would manifest later as an absolute commitment to progress in the face of a largely

intractable establishment. He would work as his brother's assistant for twelve years, quickly becoming the more skilled of the two in matters of dissection so that soon he was performing almost all of the anatomical work of the school, both the routine preparation of cadavers for demonstration and the more specialised work necessary to the preservation of body parts for permanent display. At last his health began to give out, the result of overwork or of those long hours spent amongst the rot and filth of the dissection room – it would be another century before Lister introduced the idea of hand-washing to surgery and John's fingernails would have been crusted under with remnants of the tissues, living and dead, that he had been working on; or perhaps he wanted only an excuse to extricate himself from William's benevolent indenture. Lacking, despite his experience, any of those formal qualifications which would allow him to set up as a surgeon in private practice, but wanting access to the same proliferation of live subjects as he had already observed dead, he joined the army, a course of action which would have the added benefit of circumventing the need for qualification, since an army surgeon, demobbed, had an automatic right to practice on the general population; and in March 1761 he set sail on board a hospital ship to take part in the assault by the British on Belle-Île, an island off the coast of Brittany.

Battlefield medicine was a desperate affair. In an initial failed attempt upon the island, John found himself stepping across the bodies of the wounded where they had been thrown upon the decks, waiting for their limbs to be sawn through, for

lead shot or wooden splinters to be excised from the flesh of chests or flanks, the slashed skin flayed half off the heads of men to be stitched shut as best as could be managed. Deaths must have occurred from a multitude of causes: the wounds themselves and attendant blood loss but also from shock resultant upon the brutality of treatment or from infections introduced while the wounds were being enlarged, standard practice to allow foreign bodies to be removed more easily. In such conditions, men's flesh cut away without sanitation or disinfection on board a ship or in the churned mud beside a battlefield, any procedure was liable to be rendered worse than useless, and infection was so ubiquitous that suppuration was considered by surgeons of the time to be a necessary part of healing. John Hunter, watching his colleagues going about their business with the surety of those who doubt neither their purpose nor their methodology, while around them men screamed, and bled, and died, began to wonder what the point was of practices which seemed to him to save no one. Later, after April and reinforcements brought a second and success-ful assault upon the island, John would come across five French soldiers, wounded by gunfire, who had taken refuge in an empty farmhouse. Their wounds – despite no medical attention – had healed as well, if not better, than those who had experienced all the supposed benefits of the ministration of a surgeon. John began to modify his practice accordingly, treating only those injuries where treatment seemed an abso-lute necessity. He advocated too that surgery should be delayed if possible until the patient was no longer lying on the

170

battlefield but was somewhere relatively comfortable, and until their condition had to some degree stabilised, particularly in the case of amputations – and although despite these adaptations of standard practice many men still died it was not quite so many, which John Hunter, despite the opposition and at times derision of his colleagues, considered proof.

On a wet Saturday morning, Johannes and I went to see his mother to tell her that I was pregnant. She picked us up from the station in her car as she always did and drove us back to the tall and narrow house Johannes had grown up in, him in the front talking about the general progress of his work and me, trying not to be sick, in the back. The house, cleaned for our arrival, felt unoccupied, as though it were up to us to claim the space, leaving our jumpers on the backs of chairs as marks of ownership, our socks balled up in corners, our books spine-upwards on the sofa cushions, the dust motes floating in the light from the hallway window gusted by the currents that our voices and our moving bodies made. We carried our things up to the bedroom in which we would sleep and while Johannes went back down I unpacked my pyjamas and the bag with our toothbrushes and toothpaste in it, then set to untangling the coiled wire of my phone charger, stringing these tasks out for as long as I could. I hoped that Johannes might tell his mother while I was up there so that I might be spared, because I have always hated the breaking of news, the imparting of information which will affect another's life in however slight a way. I find it horrible to think that others might have such power

over me, always: that at any moment there might be someone in a room elsewhere planning the best way to break open my life. Earlier I had asked Johannes, hearing myself sound petulant

—Can't you call her first and tell her so it won't be a surprise?

but Johannes, frowning, said

—She'll prefer it this way,

and so I waited for as long as I could before going downstairs to where Johannes and his mother sat at the well-scrubbed kitchen table, the old green teapot and a silence like elastic set between them. I went to stand by Johannes' shoulder as though he might shield me and he held my hand as at last he spoke; and afterwards in the relief of having got it over with I felt a little giddy, prone to confidences, and we drank our tea and made plans and the gentle chatter of the radio turned on in the corner lent our conversation a pleasing intimacy, as though we were afraid, in this otherwise empty house, of being overheard.

Later I lay resting in the neat spare room while Johannes sat downstairs reading or watching television. There was a knock on the door and his mother came in, bringing me up a glass of warm milk with honey in it and a ginger biscuit from a batch that she had made earlier that afternoon, her hands deep in a jar of flour while I sat in a chair and watched her, wondering if such easy competence, such orderly familiarity with the making of things, was a skill that I might ever achieve. She placed the plate of biscuits and the milk on the bedside table and when I asked her she fetched me a glass of water as well

172

because I was always thirsty. This gentle solicitude felt at that moment like a slight return to childhood, like being put to bed with flu and having the doctor come, that certainty of being protected, and as she moved about me, arranging things, I realised that this was what I had been longing for: to have someone place themselves between me and adulthood, taking away for a while the necessity to make sense of things. She sat down on the bed beside me and took my hand.

—How are you feeling?

she asked and

—Okay,

I said,

—Tired.

I told her that there were days when I went to bed straight after dinner, the evening news not yet finished on the radio, and although I slept all night when I woke in the morning still I felt the same exhaustion, a chemical thing, utterly undentable. I asked

—Is this how everyone feels?

and she told me how when pregnant with Johannes, working in a theatre, she would go during every break she had to lie down in the room in the costume department where the washing machines were kept and, lulled by their constant grumbling and the rocking of their spin cycles, she would sleep. Then, she said, after Johannes was born, for weeks the only place he would reliably sleep was in front of the washing machine, and so she would set his Moses basket down on the floor in their galley kitchen and put a load of washing on and

he would sleep for the whole cycle; and not wanting to leave him alone, this her first child and his fragility unquantifiable, she would pull a duvet down from the bedroom upstairs and wrap herself in it and she would lie on the floor next to him and she would sleep, too, both of them calmed by the rattle of the spinning drum.

—In the first few weeks after a new baby is born you do things like that,

she said, telling me that it was a slight and temporary madness brought on by exhaustion – the trauma of a birth you don't have time to recover from and the need to find any pattern amongst so much endless chaos, any routine, however tenuous, and any continuity of preference which might allow you to feel that you know this tiny stranger who has ripped so much apart: your body, your home, your life. I thought of these words often in the days after my daughter was born when I suffered from an acute but transitory agoraphobia, a terror that if I took the baby outside I would become incapable, unable to protect her from some catastrophe I could neither imagine nor name. Each day I forced myself to put her in a sling, her body nestled tight against me, so that I might walk to the end of the road and back while Johannes stood at the front door and watched me as I asked him to, his expression one of kindness without understanding, and I held the thought of Johannes' mother like a talisman – this tall and capable woman, determined, calm, lying with her baby for hours each day on the kitchen floor, manufacturing washing just for the peace – and it comforted me. Now, sat in her spare

room discussing in low voices the trivia of our own experiences, I felt for the first time between the two of us the taut lines of a relationship that was not triangulated through Johannes: being each a part of this child's life we were now tied to one another and this tie was indissoluble – could be evaded, perhaps, but neither destroyed nor forgotten. This new intimacy was an unintended consequence but I recognised it too as something that I longed for, a surer place in this house, a claim over this woman's care; and I wondered if it was partly why I had been chary of coming here, because I could see how it might be an imposition, effected without her consent and not subject to her protest.

After she had gone I lay in bed, peaceful for the first time in weeks, and thought of my own mother, how what I had been feeling the lack of since the evening that I found out that I was pregnant was not the particularity of her, but rather the role she might have occupied and the fulfilment of those tasks for whose performance she would have been the obvious candidate; and this is what I miss still, now: a sense of enduring belonging, the knowledge that a place is mine regardless of the extent to which I might merit it. I would have that undemanded, undemanding love, not dependent on individuals but rather on the places that they hold – mother, daughter; except that as I no longer hold that place I cannot now imagine how it might feel to do so, since to cease to have a mother is to forget, as well, how to be a daughter. Lying in the bed at Johannes' mother's house, I could neither transpose myself backwards nor see my own mother alive, our relationship

forged into adulthood. What space she might have occupied had long ago been filled or had silted up – and this is the thing about death, that time lessens hurt but multiplies loss. I wanted to be able to say that after all it would have been better to have my own mother there than Johannes' but I couldn't, because the thought of it was an empty hypothesis; and because while my own mother had faded into imperfect memory Johannes' was here, present, a woman whose feet creaked across the floorboards of the room next door – and since I found I didn't want my mother there I found that I also missed her terribly.

Leaving the army after three years, John Hunter began the long struggle to establish himself in his profession. He worked at first as a dentist, pursuing an interest in the transplantation of human teeth, pulling them from the heads of those who needed the money and placing them instead in the mouths of those who could afford to pay. These rudimentary transplants would, he noticed, have greater success if the donor tooth was fresh, and if it was approximately the same size as that which had been lost, and although none of his transplants would have been fully successful some of them are reported to have remained in place for a period of years, which was a considerable achievement for the time. In 1764 he set up his own anatomy school, a rival establishment to William's, and he began, at last, in private practice, on top of which he pursued his own research, working late and rising early and experimenting with little in the way of ethical concern on both his patients and, almost certainly, on himself. Money was always an issue.

In addition to the ever-expanding London premises needed to house both his family and pupils, and his growing collection of surgical preparations, as soon as he could afford to he took a country house at Earl's Court where he kept a menagerie, a collection of animals of greater or lesser exoticism which he observed in life and then, dead, took to pieces. He took the temperature of hibernating hedgehogs, fed dye to pigs to prove that bone growth occurs by accumulation at the outer ends, collected fossils, crossbred dogs with jackals. To Edward Jenner, friend and ex-pupil, he wrote, 'I have but one order to send you which is send every thing you can get either animal vegetable or mineral, and the compound of the two viz either animal or vegetable mineralised.'

Jenner, who after three years as John's pupil had turned down an offer of a partnership, had left London in 1773 to return to his native Gloucestershire and a country practice; but the two maintained their relationship by correspondence, Jenner's letters lost but John's surviving, ungrammatical, enthused, a list of requests to be sent hedgehogs and cuckoos, eels, porpoise, along with instructions for experiments to be performed, treatments to be tried. The specimens sent by Jenner and those gleaned from Hunter's Earl's Court zoo along with thousands of others – skeletons hung from wires, soft tissues pickled in jars and skins dried, venous networks transcribed in wax – form Hunter's greatest monument: a vast collection, a testament to skill and curiosity which he nearly bankrupted himself to maintain and which was saved, after his death, by the dedicated ministrations of his last apprentice,

William Clift, to become at last the museum of the Royal College of Surgeons, housed now in their premises behind Holborn station. Walking through it one Saturday afternoon with Johannes, nearing the end of my first pregnancy, I felt at that vast catalogue of the interior, the mechanics of living things, an awe that bordered on bafflement, something important written too large for me to comprehend. Setting out from home we had intended to visit the John Soane museum, that other extraordinary monument to the eighteenth-century collectors' art which sits on the opposite side of Lincoln's Inn Fields from the Hunterian, its contents a map of that which is neither skin nor muscle but which seems, in the narrow corridors of Soane's house, to be as traceable. We had been there several times before and, planning with Johannes a last afternoon spent in that casual, wandering pursuit of curiosity which had made up so much of our leisure time to date but which would soon become, we supposed, less possible, I had thought immediately of the John Soane, its dim rooms and cluttered walls, its jokes, the monk's cell and the sarcophagus and the tiny gallery with its paintings fixed to shutters so that a man with a sort of boat hook has to open them for you one by one to reveal the vast and complicated skies of Turner, the satirical figures of Hogarth's modern moral subjects. It is a place that has always given me, stepping over the threshold, a rush of delight, the joy that something so extraordinary should exist; but arriving that day with Johannes we found the museum closed for a private event and so made our way instead around the dusty perimeter of Lincoln's Inn Fields, its

178

central stretch of grass browned by the summer's heat to straw, past the tall red-brick gate leading to the inn itself, to the Royal College of Surgeons on the first floor of which, in a double-height gallery of glass cases, the Hunterian museum is housed.

—Are you sure,

Johannes had said that morning as I struggled to tie my own shoelaces

—you wouldn't rather stay at home?

but I had been determined. It had always seemed to me during the long, meandering weekend days which had formed such a large part of our lives to date as though, while we were looking at these artefacts of other lives, something important was not quite being said, an utterance that existed in the spaces between our words and tied us, in our silent understanding of it, together; and we had taken it for granted, this intimate harmonic which implied concordance, until it was gone. All week, through another appointment with the midwife, the doctor, through a discussion of birth plans and a consideration of the relative merits of muslin brands, Moses baskets, this proliferation of necessary trivia which had come upon me like a curse, I had felt myself becoming increasingly unfamiliar, emptied out of all the thoughts I'd had before and refilled with these new concerns; and the stranger I became the stranger too Johannes was, different and far away, until the old presumption of ease was replaced with an algorithm of concern and debt. When we were alone together, when we sat down to eat or when we walked in the park during the long, light evenings, our pace a poor equivocation between Johannes' long stride

and my ponderous shamble, I was not peaceful but spoke at length, planning out a future that we hadn't yet the means to imagine, my speech an obsessive examination of the possible ways that we might live after the baby was born, how we might divide the labour up, and what we needed, what there was to do and what might be left till later. I harangued and argued with myself, considered out loud the possible effects of a weight of historical wrongs, the flaws in our respective characters, the way I wished things might be done, as though I might talk myself into quietness or as though, by talking, I might call into being there between the heavy summer alders the best possible version of ourselves – as though I might make myself ready; but I could not prepare myself for something so unknown nor find any way across the next months except by living them, and so my monologue was little more than benediction, the filling up of empty space with prayer. I didn't know what to do with myself otherwise. All that I had been before I had given up already and the emptiness was appalling. I twitched to be active and longed to feel Johannes close again and so I insisted that we fill our time with those things we had always done and then, embarked upon them, was angered by my inability to see them through, or exhausted by my stubborn perseverance. Through all this Johannes was patient, or he seemed that way to me; but even his patience was unsatisfactory. I wanted something more than calm capitulation to my ill-made plans, attention to my tumbled words. I wanted him to care as much as I did about those things which I wished I could not care about myself, or I wanted him to tell me how dull I had become so that in

retaliation I might break myself open against him, crack violently through this shell that separated us, and we might be ourselves again—

As we walked through the gift shop and into the museum I said

—We could go for lunch after this. We could go to the Seven Stars. Or to somewhere on the South Bank. We could have dim sum.

—Won't you be tired?

Johannes asked, and because I was already tired, because I wished that I was at home and that we had never come out, because my feet ached and the baby kicking was a constant irritation, I pulled my hand away from his and let him go on ahead.

At a meeting of the Royal Society on 27 January 1780, thirty years after William had watched and Rymsdyk had sketched while John teased apart the fabric of a nameless woman's uterus, twenty-six years after William published under his own name the discovery of the mechanism of placental blood supply, John accused William of plagiarism. This was, perhaps, the result of a long-festering complaint: that for all the work John had done for William during the twelve years he had been his assistant, John had received no credit, and nor had he been able to take ownership of any of the preparations that he had made during that time and which now formed the nexus of William's own collection, leaving John's, though its specimens were now numbered in the thousands, always incomplete. Being unable

to rectify this wrong, he niggled at that which would have seemed to him the lesser – the apportioning of published credit – although in the end there would be no satisfactory outcome to this dispute for either party. The Royal Society would refuse to publish John's paper. William, beyond a single confused and confusing response, would offer no defence but, on his death, would leave every part of his fortune including the farmhouse at Long Calderwood to his nephew Matthew Baillie, and his collection to the University of Glasgow; and, subsequently, it would turn out that priority for the discovery would after all go to neither brother but to a Dutch anatomist, Wilhelm Noortwyk, who had demonstrated the separation of maternal and foetal blood supply in 1743.

Standing in the museum, surrounded by the relics of John Hunter's quest for understanding, his attempts to enumerate what a person is, how we are made, our solid, ordinary parts assembled into something greater, a whole which can be neither contained nor comprehended – I watched Johannes walk from case to case, past the fish, the fossils, the cockerel's head with a human tooth rising from its comb like a jaunty hat, and I felt familiarity drift from him like dust until he too was nothing but parts, unidentifiable amongst so many. He paused by the skeleton of Charles Byrne, the Irish giant whose body Hunter kept against his wishes, stealing the corpse from its lead coffin as it was transported by cart to the Kent coast for burial at sea, and I saw the hunch of Johannes' shoulders, the slight tip of his head which indicated silent disapproval, and

although I knew these things as well as the feeling of my own breath rising in my lungs, for a moment I recognised him not as the complicated, sprawling pattern memory makes from faces, the words uttered and unuttered, the promises preserved, revoked, this mess of accord and arguments – that intangible nexus of thought, our own and others', which makes us who we are – but only as mechanism. There is nothing more horrible than this: a world elucidated and all that is seen, understood. Johannes turned and, catching my look, came back to where I stood and said

—Shall we go home?

and

—Yes,

I answered, and felt better at last, having found my way to this defeat.

Then there are these other moments, the ones it is so easy to forget: an evening, unremarkable. Light pooling on the ceiling from the lamps, the curtains closed. I surface from a doze to find Johannes sat beside me on the bed, reading, and half-turning towards him I reach out my hand; he takes it without looking, his fingers as they always are, dry and warm, their familiarity like the kinder obverse to desire. We do not speak but, less apart, we settle back into ourselves. I close my eyes – this moment comes again and then again, our children sleeping or unborn: the mute reiteration of the certainty that all is well, and we are as we ought to be.

*

John Hunter died on 16 October 1793 and it is hard, at times, to find quite what it was that he left us, beyond the macabre and serried rows of jars that made up his collection. So many of his experiments, taken all in all, were failures – the transplanted teeth, the Caesarean, the operations after which his patients, lacking the advantages of antiseptics, died. Perhaps, after all, it was only this: the understanding that we are objects and that we might be learned – that there is no mystery, but that we might look and see ourselves. Three years after his death, Edward Jenner, who had been his first pupil and lifelong friend, would inoculate an eight-year-old boy against smallpox. This boy would be one of twenty-three subjects on whom Jenner performed the experiment; subsequently he exposed the boy to smallpox and found that he was immune; and this was Jenner's contribution: not that he should have used cowpox as a vaccine – a practice which had been standard in Britain since the 1720s but in use elsewhere for centuries – but that he should have proved that it worked. To him, in one of the first of the letters between them, Hunter had written, 'But why do you ask me a question, by the way of solving it. I think your solution is just; but why think, why not trie the Expt.'

This another moment of clarity: sent to hospital by a midwife because, with the Doppler receiver set against the smooth dome of my rising abdomen, something hadn't sounded right. I lay on the sofa with my clothes disarranged while she went about the business of folding her things away, putting on her coat, and I tried to gauge from her movements how urgent this was.

—Do I need to go right now?

I asked, and she replied

—You might as well,

so I stood up and found a jumper, socks, and called out to Johannes, who asked

—Should I come with you?

but though I wanted him to, and though I wanted him to know it without it being said, still it seemed absurd to drag him to sit for hours in a hospital when he might be at home and comfortable. I said

—I'll be okay,

and so he contented himself with packing a bag for me, filling a bottle with water, finding my keys; and then as I put on my shoes he stood in the middle of the room, his own feet bare against the floorboards, this tiny detail of our difference prompting me to go to him and put my arms around him, to comfort him, because while in this sudden situation, which was not yet an emergency but which might turn out, later on, looking backwards, to be the start of one, we were both incapable of altering the outcome, I at least was necessary while he, no less concerned, was left behind.

Later, behind a curtain, I sat next to a foetal heartbeat monitor, its sensors attached to me by long belts whose buckles were held in place with ratty knots. A midwife had spent some time adjusting them and now I was able to move only slightly, an arm or leg shifted by millimetres, in case they slipped and the monitor could no longer get a reading. Every now and then the baby moved, turning this way or that, so that the

machine could no longer detect a heartbeat and an alarm went off, and then I would sit there, waiting, listening to its dull beeping until the midwife came back again to readjust the straps. Next to me, across an unspooling sheet of paper, a thin line traced the pattern of the baby's heart, its peaks and troughs a litany of all that was – and although at first I could think only how uncomfortable I was, how afraid, after a while it seemed that watching this line, the steady pace it kept, its spitting progress up and down, something which had long occluded fell away at last and certainty was left behind. This was fear's gift, perhaps, this sharpened vision, and in the transcription of my own child's fragile heart I could read at last not quite love, not connection nor communion, but rather the understanding that what was important was only the way we stood to one another, protected and protector, and that we had gone beyond argument and must get on with things.

A few weeks ago, looking in the bottom of a drawer for something else, I found a photo of my mother – saved, somehow, when so much else has been thrown away. In it, she is standing in front of a wall up which sunflowers grow, their circular faces higher than her head. She wears a short-sleeved Fair Isle jumper, a denim skirt, bare legs. She looks very young, and in her arms she holds her newborn child. I have pinned the picture up above my desk, between the two foetal scans and the newspaper clipping of Saturn's moon, and, looking at it, I find that when I think of my mother now it is not of that version of herself which she became when ill, nor of how she

was when, throughout my childhood, compromise forced her into unspectacular unhappiness, but rather it is of this woman whom I never knew, whose face bends down to meet her child's, whose hands enclose, who smiles. I feel such tenderness towards her. She must have known so little, then, of what it is to have a child, but had to learn it all from scratch, and did – as I have done, and all the rest of us, learning from the moment we are born how to be one single version of ourselves with all the losses that entails. I am so used to thinking of my mother as someone who is complete, her life concluded, that to imagine her at this moment, caught during those few weeks when everything was, briefly and for both of us, possibility, is to feel her startlingly close, her death unwound. She is not shut and done with but persists, and I am glad.

In the end there was nothing obviously wrong with the baby except that one of the midwives, her hand pressing hard into the flesh of my belly, suspected she was breech. A scan confirmed it, the baby's feet crossed over in my pelvis, her head tucked in beneath my ribs, turned to one side with her hands held up in front of her face, their fingers flexing, as though she were examining their tiny nails for dirt. I was sent to the waiting room until a doctor had time to see me; and it seems to me now, looking back, that from this point onwards pregnancy became for me a series of waits on uncomfortable chairs, so that very soon I became accustomed to it, to the boredom and the occasional startling kindnesses, to the

opening hours of the cafe in the hospital foyer and the smell in the corridors, the doors which opened and shut and the women behind them, crying on their knees, these just-caught glimpses of female agony, and to the way they looked afterwards, this cohort of which I was not yet a part, to their exhausted faces lit up with surprise above their freshly minted children as though at the sudden comprehension of a lesson it had taken them nine months to learn; but this first time it was new. I sat very upright and wished that Johannes was there. After a while I asked the receptionist if there would be time for me to go to the cafe and get something to eat; she said she didn't know but would see what she could do. Ten more minutes passed and she brought me an egg sandwich which was fridge cold and tasted strongly of margarine but I was grateful for it anyway and felt better afterwards. At last the doctor came and called me and, stiffly, I followed him into a tiny office. He told me his name and I forgot it instantly. I sat down. He shuffled some pieces of paper and said

—Baby's breech, I see.

I felt a kind of anxious shame, as though it were a dereliction of duty that had brought me here, my own failure to marshal my flesh and control my unborn child. I was afraid that, seeing inside me, he would find the means to judge what I hadn't even known existed and couldn't recognise although I too had seen it on the screen, that pattern of dark and light which the inside of my own body made.

—We can book you in for an ECV and try to turn the baby manually. It's a bit uncomfortable and there is a small risk of—

I tried hard to focus on what was being said but my mind wandered. I already knew that I would do what this man told me and there was a comfort in the acceptance of my surrender. It seemed that what was being talked of was not my body but only an object in the space between us, predictable and mundane, and of which he, having more experience, was the better judge – all I did was carry it about.

—These leaflets will explain—

My grandmother and I had sat like this, facing one another. It was, I thought, the same time of day, although this doctor and I were deep inside the hospital and there was no window, no sound but the footsteps of the nurses and the bleeping of machines, and in place of sweating glasses there were two plastic cups from the water fountain in the corner of the waiting room. I held mine in my hands.

—You will need to sign—

My grandmother too had tried this: to make me explicit to myself in order that I might better be able to decide how to act; and although hers was another kind of explanation it held the same promise: the resolution of a complicated pattern into one that could be understood, her voice that of the radiologist – there are the feet, the hands, there is the head. Here is want, desire, and here is fear, here anger, love. At times my grandmother's promise of transparency has seemed to me like a gift and at others like an act of violence; but always it has seemed to me that something important was left out of it, the understanding which she searched for missed, lost in that gap between an object and its name. Even

so I felt the power of it and do so still: how simple things would be if only I could know myself or others; if, stepping in between a light source and a screen, I could see the way that I was constituted, those hidden structures, the bones, the joints that give the rest its shape – and then I might know something for certain, that I was alive or that I would be dead, these two differently slanted articulations of the same fundamental understanding; but instead there is only this excavation, a digging in the dark: precarious, uncertain, impossible to complete.

All these same anxieties I feel again now. I am worried about the distance between Johannes and myself, between us both and our daughter. I am worried that the particular circumstances pregnancy forces on us will not retreat with its ending. I am worried that I will fail to be an adequate mother; that I will neither recognise nor love my child. I am worried that I have failed already, somehow; that failure has been written into my genetics or my history and will be passed on, crossing over that fragile barrier the placenta makes to infect this unknown person for whom I ought to be a shield. I am afraid of all that which, unseen, remains unknown: my own insides, the thoughts of others, the future. This baby has turned already, head downwards, waiting to be born. My daughter draws pictures of it, the three of us with our feet on a flat green line of ground and the baby floating in the air. Sometimes it is tethered to me or to Johannes by a drawn-on string and at others it only drifts, there in the empty space above us. Johannes'

mother is coming for Christmas. She will stay until after the baby is born.

I lay on another bed in another room while a consultant obstetrician pushed my unborn daughter round through the skin of my stomach, forcing her to turn by 180 degrees. I tried not to scream with the pain of it. Afterwards I sat for another hour attached to the monitor; the baby was fine but, someone else said, seemed rather small. They would do another scan. I lost track, then, of whom the people were who came and went about me, of the appointments attended, the waiting rooms inhabited. It ceased to seem important. My blood pressure was taken often; it rose a little and then came down again but each rise took it higher than the last. I was warned about vision changes, headaches, swelling of the hands or feet. At home I lay on the sofa and read or slept. Johannes tried to work. Late each afternoon we walked around the park, our steps slow, and stopped afterwards at a pub where Johannes drank cider and I a pint of lime and soda, the cordial making viscous swirls inside the glass. We said very little. It seemed that without our noticing it, without anything having been said or done, intimacy had returned, and we stood together, waiting, for what was both our end and our beginning. I had bought a Moses basket, several packs of Babygros, a swaddling blanket; there was nothing left to do. I no longer felt the need to talk. We went to Johannes' mother's for the weekend and I read detective novels in the garden. I couldn't sleep at night but no longer felt tired, only rather empty: an end might come at any moment

but while inevitable it remained out of reach, since how is it ever possible to imagine in advance how one might get from there to here. There were more scans, more machines; the baby was still small but no one seemed to know what it meant, and it seemed at times that we might stay this way forever, autumn never coming, nor the baby; and then at thirty-seven weeks I sat again in a doctor's office. Johannes was at home, his own life a thread less frayed than mine, his hours contiguous while mine drifted apart.

—Your blood pressure is very high.

I told the doctor that hospitals always made me anxious and she smiled. There was another scan, so many now that I had stopped trying to see the screen. She said

—I need to speak to the consultant,

and while she was gone I sat alone in the room and thought of nothing at all. When she came back she looked brisk, her face betraying anxiety with a slightly too-stiff brightness, and I remembered the sonographer, and how she had seemed to disappear behind efficiency.

—We'd like you to come back tomorrow to be induced.

I don't know what I had expected but it wasn't this: a bag packed ready in the hall and a bus ride to the hospital in the morning, two days spent walking round and round the hospital car park in the hope that labour might begin and then a doctor breaking my waters with a kind of pin; an oxytocin drip; the feeling that my body was turning itself inside out. I remember it only in snatches: a radio playing in the corner and Johannes' hand on my forehead, the gas which made me

feel dizzy and the throwing up of half a tuna sandwich into a paper bowl, and how I lay and begged, calling out for something to be done—

then this, the moment all else falls away from. The pain stops and someone hands my daughter to me, her tiny body beating at the air, and for an instant we are nothing but a single surface, joined, laid out beneath the light, and everything is perfect, clear: I know her absolutely and all her history is mine for I have seen it all—

then time, then growth obscures. The cord is cut; our separation starts. She is taken from me, weighed, dressed. I close my eyes in relief that it is over and a first part of her life is lost to me. Johannes holds her. She starts to cry, a newborn's wail of bleak surprise, and we do not know the reason but must try, somehow, to find it out.

Acknowledgements

That this book was written at all is due in large part to the support, encouragement and deadlines I received from both my agent, Jack Ramm, and my editor at John Murray, Mark Richards. All good bits should be considered to their credit. Bad bits are mine alone.

Thanks are also due to Ed Lake, for a certain amount of drink and conversation, and to Lyn Curthoys, whose fortnightly journeys along the Metropolitan Line gave me time.

Finally, thank you as always to Ben, who has never questioned the importance of my work to me, but who has built us a life into which it fits.

Further Reading

The following is a list of works which were particularly useful in the writing of this book. Much of my reading was done at the Wellcome Library. It is a wonderful place, and I recommend it to everyone.

Part I
Bleich, Alan Ralph, *The Story of X-rays: From Rontgen to Isotopes*, Dover Publications, 1960

Glasser, Otto, *Wilhelm Conrad Rontgen and the Early History of the Rontgen Rays*, Norman Publishing, 1989

Kevles, Bettyann, *Naked to the Bone: Medical Imaging in the Twentieth Century*, Rutgers University Press, 1997

Rontgen, Wilhelm Conrad, 'On a New Kind of Rays' (trans. Arthur Stanton from the Sitzungsberichte der Würzburger Physik-medic Gesellschaft, 1895), *Nature*, 23 January 1896

Part II
Anzieu, Didier, *Freud's Self Analysis* (trans. Peter Graham), Hogarth Press, 1986

Freud, Sigmund (ed. Marie Bonaparte, Anna Freud, Ernst Kris), *The Origins of Psycho-Analysis: Letters to Wilhelm Fleiss, Drafts and Notes, 1887–1902* (trans. Eric Mosbacher and James Strachey), Imago, 1954

Freud, Sigmund, *Case Histories, Dora and Little Hans*, Pelican, 1977

Gay, Peter, *Freud: A Life for Our Time*, Anchor Books, 1989

Symington, Neville, *The Analytic Experience: Lectures from the Tavistock*, Free Association Books, 1986

Young-Bruehl, Elisabeth, *Anna Freud*, Macmillan, 1989

Interlude

Ebenstein, Joanna, *The Anatomical Venus*, Thames & Hudson, 2016

Part III

'An Account of the Performing of the Caesarean Operation, with remarks, by Mr Henry Thomson, Surgeon to the London Hospital, Communicated by Dr Hunter', *Medical Observations and Inquiries*, 4, 1779

Hunter, John, *Letters from the Past: From John Hunter to Edward Jenner*, Royal College of Surgeons of England, 1976

Moore, Wendy, *The Knife Man: Blood, Body Snatching, and the Birth of Modern Surgery*, Bantam, 2005

Thornton, John Leonard, *Jan Van Rymsdyk: Medical Illustrator of the Eighteenth Century*, Oleander Press, 1981

From Byron, Austen and Darwin

to some of the most acclaimed and original contemporary writing, John Murray takes pride in bringing you powerful, prizewinning, absorbing and provocative books that will entertain you today and become the classics of tomorrow.

We put a lot of time and passion into what we publish and how we publish it, and we'd like to hear what you think.

Be part of John Murray – share your views with us at:

www.johnmurray.co.uk

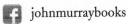 johnmurraybooks

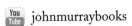 @johnmurrays

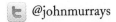 johnmurraybooks